AFRICA'S
DISCOVERY
OF EUROPE

AFRICA'S DISCOVERY OF EUROPE

1450 – 1850

David Northrup

Boston College

New York Oxford
OXFORD UNIVERSITY PRESS
2002

Oxford University Press

Oxford   New York

Auckland   Bangkok   Buenos Aires   Cape Town   Chennai

Dar es Salaam   Delhi   Hong Kong   Istanbul   Karachi   Kolkata

Kuala Lumpur   Madrid   Melbourne   Mexico City   Mumbai   Nairobi

São Paulo   Shanghai   Singapore   Taipei   Tokyo   Toronto

and an associated company in Berlin

Published by Oxford University Press, Inc.

198 Madison Avenue, New York, New York, 10016

http://www.oup-usa.org

Oxford is a registered trademark of Oxford University Press

Library of Congress Cataloging-in-Publication Data

Northrup, David, 1941–
   Africa's discovery of Europe : 1450–1850 / by David Northrup.
      p. cm
   Includes bibliographical references and index.
   ISBN 0-19-514083-4 (cloth)—ISBN 0-19-514084-2 (pbk.)
      1. Africa, Sub-Saharan—Relations—Europe. 2.   Europe—Relations—Africa, Sub-Saharan.
   3. Africans—Europe—History. 4. Africa, Sub-Saharan—History—To 1884. I. Title.

DT353.5.E9 N67 2002
303.48'6704'0903—dc21   2001038747

9 8 7 6 5 4 3 2 1

Printed in the United States of America
on acid-free paper

In loving memory of my parents

George Merring Northrup, 1909–2000
Margaret Herbst Northrup, 1908–2000

CONTENTS

MAPS AND ILLUSTRATIONS

PREFACE

This volume examines cultural and economic encounters of Africans with Europeans that took place in Africa, in Europe, and on the Atlantic during the four centuries before 1850. Its conclusions challenge many widespread misunderstandings of these encounters, but its concern is more with presenting contemporary *Africans'* perceptions of what took place than engaging in academic debates. Despite the obvious fact that all encounters have two sides, the European side has long received greater attention, not just by historians of Europe but at times even from African-studies specialists.[1] While many scholars have worked to uncover the African side of these encounters, most of this work consists of specialized case studies confined to encounters in a single part of Africa or of Europe.[2] *Africa's Discovery of Europe* draws heavily on this modern scholarship, but it also makes extensive use of first-person African narratives to introduce this scholarly understanding to nonspecialists in an engaging way.

The use of the word "discovery" does not represent a claim that Africans found things unknown to others or organized exploring expeditions comparable to those departing from Europe during these centuries. Rather, Africans were discoverers in a subjective sense—finding out things previously unknown to themselves. The word "discovery" also emphasizes that Africans played active roles in their encounters with Europeans and thus counters commonplace notions that Africans were passive victims in these encounters and incapable of shaping them. During more than four centuries of encounters before 1850 Africans observed Europeans' physical and cultural differences; adopted or rejected ideas and material goods; worked out complex commercial, political, and cultural relations; and grew increasingly sophisticated in their appreciation and estimation of Europe. Not all African encounters were voluntary, and some were brutal, but there is more complexity in Africa's discovery of Europe than Eurocentric accounts credit.

Although *Africa's Discovery of Europe* surveys a large and complex topic, it has two intentional limitations. The first is geographical. Because North Africa's proximity to Europe made its relations so different, the "Africans" in this book are the people of sub-Saharan regions, whether at home or abroad. However, its coverage does not extend to the generations born in the diaspora. The second intentional limitation is temporal. By concluding in the middle of the nineteenth century, this study omits the period of extensive and intensive interaction that began with the late-nineteenth-century European imperial conquest of Africa and continues to this day. That exclusion requires some explanation.

Robert July's pioneering survey of West Africans' cultural encounters with Europeans in the nineteenth century dismissed the importance of earlier encounters because, he believed, the Atlantic slave trade precluded meaningful cultural interaction. West African society gained "nothing of consequence from Europe's vast store of scientific and humanistic knowledge . . . but some acquaintance with guns and other war-making implements and an appetite for European products."[3] July was right to fault the slave trade, but the scholarly investigations that came later suggest that the importance of contacts with Europe during these centuries was greater than he thought. Despite its prominence and horrors, the Atlantic slave trade was not the sum total of Africa's expanding Atlantic exchanges, nor did it affect all parts of the continent. Other commercial exchanges preceded the massive sale of slaves, continued throughout its existence, and rose to new levels of intensity as the slave trade declined. It is the nature of history that early stages of an encounter contain great meaning in explaining later outcomes. Those who seek to tie modern Africa's problems to the Atlantic slave trade are applying this maxim, even if they greatly oversimplify this historical dynamic by leaving out other aspects of the commercial and cultural encounters with Europe that were even more persistent. The slave trade had lasting effects, but the patterns of cultural and commercial relations detailed in this work were equally significant and arguably of greater long-term impact. The study shows that 1800 did not constitute a watershed as July believes, but only a quickened pace of interactions that had long been underway. Similarly, the further acceleration of African-European interactions since 1850 exhibits far more continuities with the past than departures—but that fact would take an additional volume to document.

Besides these intended geographical and temporal limits (and other limitations because of unintended lapses in the author's knowledge and understanding), the historical records impose their own constraints. Because only a few Africans recorded their own impressions of Europeans before the late nineteenth century, this study makes use of many additional African perspectives that were recorded by Europeans. A seventeenth-century scholar from Ethiopia, Abba Gregoryos, was probably the first person to address the problem of error and bias that such European accounts might contain. During his long stay in Europe, he became annoyed with the distortions and inaccuracies he found in the various European accounts of Ethiopian life. He declared that Europeans "were sick of a certain itch of writing, and did both write and publish whatsoever they heard, whether true or false." Gregoryos disliked the rush to print, but recognized that it was precisely this itch to write things down that had preserved so much information (and misinformation). He was also fair minded enough to criticize his own countrymen, who wrote little themselves and gave inquisitive Europeans imprecise or misleading answers that then found their way into print. In any event, working with the German Ethiopianist Job Ludolf, Gregoryos helped produce an important new work on Ethiopia.[4] Ethiopia had a written language and other Africans were literate in Arabic, but it is revealing of the importance of their encounter with Europe that nearly all the Africans who recorded details of their lives and thoughts in this era did so in European languages. Like Gregoryos, we may complain about the sources that exist and bemoan the absence of alternative perspectives that were never written down, but we need to make the best of what does exist.

Modern scholars studying Africa have shown the value of the collaborative approach of Ludolf and Gregoryos. With care and imagination it is possible to use new information about Africa to correct inaccuracies and distortions in older European sources and thus recover much valuable information, including statements by Africans and even summaries of whole speeches. Some Africans narrated their life stories to Europeans who wrote them down. Inevitably something may have been lost, added, or misunderstood in the retelling, but few historical records are flawless. Critical scholarship has shown that even Africans who penned their own stories sometimes had faulty memories, padded their own lives with details borrowed or adapted from other Africans, or distorted their narratives in ways intended to appeal to European readers. All historical documents must be used critically, but in the many cases where no other record of an event or statement exists, one can only rely on internal consistency and plausibility. Plausibility can itself be a very difficult criterion to apply, for it references both the document and the document's critic. Too often modern cultural standards and prejudices have been used to declare unlikely what was thought quite plausible to readers closer to the time the document was written. For example, as Chapter 2 points out, modern critics have often questioned the sincerity of African interest in and adoption of Christian religious practices and beliefs. Modern secularism may find African credence implausible, but how credible would a continent so rich in spirituality have found modern secular ideas?

Given the limited number of African witnesses and the need to break down Eurocentric perspectives on African-European encounters, this study has preferred to err on the side of credulity rather than incredulity. Rather than silence an African voice because it might be distorted, let it be heard; a larger reality lies in the chorus of voices than in any soloist. Demonstrable fabrications are ignored unless they shed light on the mood of a period. Possible untruths and exaggerations are noted, but all that sounds strange to modern ears is not, for that reason, to be excluded. History is an inexact science, an approximation, hopefully close, of the truth about fellow humans, who are diverse and notoriously inconsistent. It is inevitable that some details of the past are altered when they are recounted, retold, or translated. More important than the purest authenticity is the pattern; the melody can be heard despite a few false notes.

The chapters of this volume examine different aspects of Africa's discovery of Europe in a loosely chronological order. The first two chapters deal with events beginning in the fifteenth century, the first pursuing its theme of African impressions of Europeans to the mid-nineteenth century, and Chapter 2 examining African political leaders' interest in Christianity and firearms until about 1650. The remaining chapters are largely concerned with the period from 1650 to 1850, during which the intensity of encounters grew and richer evidence makes possible a more probing analysis. Commercial relations are explored in three chapters: Chapter 3 looks at how coastal African traders and rulers participated in the Atlantic economy, Chapter 4 examines inland Africans' involvement with overseas trade and goods, and the perspectives of Africans sold into the Atlantic slave trade are the subject of Chapter 5. Taking up themes introduced in Chapters 1 and 2, Chapter 6 examines Africans' cultural encounters in Europe between 1650 and 1850.

The individual chapters contribute to three larger themes that run throughout the book. First, Africans encountered Europe with their eyes open, sometimes in amazement, usually in keen awareness of their own self-interest. Second, Africans chose to acquire much from Europe both in the form of material goods and cultural traditions, of which language, religion, and education are the most prominent. Third, in discovering Europe, Africans were discovering and redefining themselves. Those who at a young age went to Europe (or to the Americas—a subject deserving fuller treatment elsewhere) might embrace European culture completely, but their nostalgia for the motherland and their own inextinguishable physical differences from native Europeans also gave them a strong sense of themselves as Africans, an identity then rare on the continent itself. Many in Africa chose to incorporate European ways into African cultural matrixes. All three themes continued to shape relations with Europe during the period of colonial rule and are still important today.

Pulling aside the veil of assumed European superiority permits Africans to tell their own stories. However, the voices in *Africa's Discovery of Europe* challenge many prevailing stereotypes of Africans both as victims and as heroes. To be sure, African victims are abundant and African heroes not rare, but the main story lies somewhere in between. The stories that African sources tell are more about surviving than about suffering. The reasons are not hard to find. One is that those who survive and achieve are much more likely to tell their story than those who are destroyed and beaten down. Allowance must be made for voices muted by tragedy, but it is also true that Africans legitimately experienced much that they found positive and uplifting during these centuries of contact. Africans may often have been less powerful, but they were not thereby powerless, even when enslaved. Many Africans considered here steadfastly refuse to strike the heroic poses modern ideas expect, believing it in their self-interest to participate in the slave trade rather than oppose it, gladly remaking themselves in the European model rather than defending sacred cultural traditions. However unexpected the words and actions of ordinary and extraordinary Africans engaged in being themselves may be, we welcome the fascinating story they have to tell.

This study could not have been completed without the support of Boston College, which granted me periods of leave to devote to research and writing, and to the staffs of its libraries, who were tireless in helping me locate the many sources used in writing this volume. I also want to thank my assistants in my Africa's World classes who commented on earlier drafts of these chapters: John Cashman, John Russell, and Edward Rugemer. George Brooks, David Chappell, Vera Lind, and Ben Lindfors also supplied valued help and encouragement.

Notes

1. For example, Philip D. Curtin, *The Image of Africa: British Ideas and Action, 1780–1850* (Madison: University of Wisconsin, 1964), and V. Y. Mudimbe, *Invention of Africa: Gnosis, Philosophy, and the Order of Knowledge* (Bloomington: Indiana University Press, 1988).

2. The two widest ranging surveys are Hans Werner Debrunner, *Presence and Prestige: Africans in Europe: A History of Africans in Europe before 1918* (Basel: Basler Afrika Bibliographien, 1979), and John Thornton's *Africa and Africans in the Making of the Atlantic World* (New York: Cambridge University Press, 1992; 2d ed. 1998).

3. Robert W. July, *The Origins of Modern African Thought* (New York: Praeger, 1967), quote pp. 459–60. The subject was continued and extended forward in time in Philip D. Curtin, ed., *Africa and the West: Intellectual Responses to European Culture* (Madison: University of Wisconsin Press, 1972). Two anthropologists ably survey the colonial era: Melville J. Herskovits, *The Human Factor in Changing Africa* (New York: Alfred A. Knopf, 1958), and P. C. Lloyd, *Africa in Social Change* (London: Penguin Books, 1967).

4. Job Ludolf, *A New History of Ethiopia: Being a Full and Accurate Description of Abessinia*, trans. J. P. Gent (London: Samuel Smith, 1684).

AFRICA'S
DISCOVERY
OF EUROPE

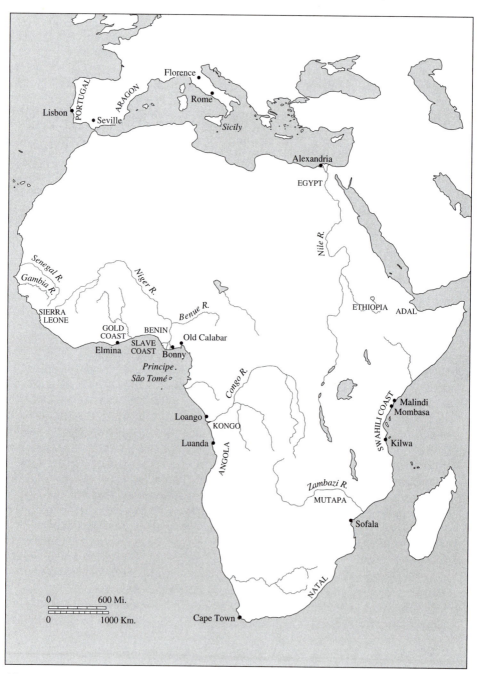

Africa, 1450–1700.

First Sights—
Lasting Impressions

In September 1895, three dignified rulers from the Tswana people of southern Africa (modern Botswana) arrived in London, the first official visitors
to Europe from that nation. Over the next three months they made an extensive tour of England, Scotland, and Wales, seeking and receiving British
support for protecting their homeland from the encroachment of European
settlement. They secured the support of the British Colonial Secretary and
received an audience with Queen Victoria. From the extensive coverage
their visit received in the press and other records a recent book is able to
recount the Tswana chiefs' impressions of this land and people so distant
from their homes. Among other reactions, they experienced trepidation at
the height of an iron suspension bridge, were delighted by the riches and
beauty of Windsor Castle, and found its royal occupant kind and charming,
although remarkably short and stout.[1]

For all the sensation the three Tswana kings created, such African visitors
in Europe were not a phenomenon that began in the era of global imperi-
alism at the end of the nineteenth century. African princes, kings, and dig-
nitaries from below the Sahara had made their way to European capitals
and courts for several centuries. A few black Africans had been present in
the Mediterranean world since antiquity, but Western Europe's knowledge
of black Africa broadened when Crusaders brought back word of kingdoms
of black Christians who dwelt beyond the boundaries of the Islamic world.
This unexpected news manifested itself in the reportrayal of Saint Maurice
as a black African knight, in the presence of Africans in the statuary of the
north porch of the thirteenth-century Chartres cathedral, and in the legend
that first appeared after 1150 of "Prester John," a powerful Christian ruler
somewhere on the Indian Ocean rim. The number of Africans in Europe
grew after 1300, as delegations traveled from African kingdoms and as
slaves brought from sub-Saharan Africa began to outnumber slaves of eastern European origins. The fifteenth-century Portuguese voyages along the
Atlantic coast of Africa greatly increased the movement of both elite and

enslaved Africans to Europe and led to a second arena of encounter between Africans and Europeans in coastal Africa. Thus the middle of the
fifteenth century marks the beginning of an era of continuous and increasing interaction between the two continents and their cultures.

As commercial and cultural interactions grew both Africans and Europeans made many adjustments in their ideas of each other. This study is
concerned with presenting the long-neglected African side of these meetings, but it is useful to begin with a few words about the changes in European perspectives about Africans. In antiquity and during most of the
Middle Ages, European images of Africans had been fairly rigid and dominated by abstract symbolism. Thus, European artists and thinkers before
1400 usually depicted Africans as the opposite of themselves; they were the
"other" in current academic usage. Some ancient drinking cups, for example, depicted a dark African face on one side and a light European one on
the other. This physical duality became overlain with an ideological one
after Islam displaced Christianity as the dominant religion of North Africa.
Although Europeans were well aware that North Africans looked little different from southern Europeans, Muslims were frequently depicted with
black faces. Verbal usage was often no clearer. Dark-skinned "Blackamoors"
from below the Sahara might be distinguished from the lighter "Moors" of
North Africa, but often the two terms were used so interchangeably that it
is difficult to sort out the meanings. The imprecision was a product of the
fact that in European minds the symbolism of the terms was more important than the reality of individual pigmentation. Africans were tokens, not
persons.

However, as Africans became more common in Europe, reality began to
triumph over imagery in Western art—or at least the reality began to temper the images. The arrival of Ethiopian delegations confirmed the long-
rumored existence of black Christians, breaking down the Islamic stereo-
type of Africans. A parade of African princes produced a striking change
in paintings of the three Magi who came to worship the Christ child.
Whereas earlier all three had been of light complexion, by the end of the
fifteenth century the convention of portraying one of them as dark skinned
became firmly established in Western art. In these and other Renaissance
paintings and drawings the generic black faces of earlier centuries were
replaced by portraits that are not only personal, but distinguishable today
as people from Ethiopia, from West Africa, or from West Central Africa.
The artists' recognition of Africans' physical diversity was accompanied by
a clear recognition of their social diversity as well, for paintings also show
both the African kings and the African servants of wealthy southern European households. Thus, even as the first Portuguese explorers contacted
the people of sub-Saharan Africa, the image of Africa in European minds
was already changing.[2]

Detail of a nativity scene painted by Hieronymous Bosch in 1500 depicting an elegantly attired African king and his attendant bringing a rich gift to the infant Jesus. Museo Nacional del Prado, Madrid.

ELITE AFRICANS IN EUROPE TO 1650

Africans were also expanding their knowledge and understanding of Europe. The first persistent effort to build ties to Europe came from the ancient kingdom of Ethiopia in the mountainous highlands of the upper Blue Nile. The kingdom's rulers had adopted Christianity in the fourth century, and the dynasty in power in the fourteenth century claimed descent from King Solomon of ancient Israel. For at least a century the Negus Nagast (king of kings or emperor) of Ethiopia had maintained a permanent listening post in the eastern Mediterranean through the Ethiopian monks who served as protectors of some of Jerusalem's Christian holy places. Perhaps prompted by the declining fortunes of the Christian communities in Egypt and Nubia, King Wedem Ar'ad of Ethiopia sent a delegation of thirty persons to Europe in 1306, seeking to forge a pan-Christian alliance against the Muslims who were worrying his neighbors. It appears that the delegation called on rulers in Spain and visited Pope Clement V at his palace in Avignon in southern

France. On the pope's recommendation they journeyed on to Rome to visit the churches of Saints Peter and Paul. Then, from Genoa, they secured passage back home via the Red Sea.[3]

No alliance emerged from this embassy, but it probably accounts for the papal letters that were sent out to the ruler of Ethiopia in 1329 and the dispatch of an Italian Dominican bishop to the kingdom the next year. From such European visitors Ethiopian rulers gathered news of the changing political geography of Mediterranean Europe. Such contacts were also at the root of Europeans' identification of the mythical Prester John, a Christian prince of the Indian Ocean region, with the Ethiopian dynasty.

Later emperors directed new embassies to Europe when the occasion warranted it. In 1402 Ethiopian ambassadors presented gifts of leopards and aromatic spices to the Doge of Venice. In 1428 Emperor Yishak (r. 1413–1430) proposed an alliance between Ethiopia and the kingdom of Aragon that was to be sealed by a double marriage of King Alfonso V's daughter to the emperor and the king's son to Yishak's daughter. This proposal was not completed, but Yishak's successor, Emperor Zera-Yakob (r. 1434–1468), the author of several works of political theology and an ardent and tyrannical promoter of ecclesiastical reform and royal centralization, in 1450 dispatched four Ethiopians to Alfonso, who by then was also ruling the kingdom of Naples. One object of this mission was to hire European artisans, whose technical skills an earlier Ethiopian appeal had enumerated: miniaturists for manuscript illumination, goldsmiths and silversmiths, architects, carpenters, organ-makers, glassmakers, trumpeters, and makers of all sorts of arms. In 1452, an Ethiopian ambassador named George went to Lisbon, while in 1459, another Ethiopian went to the Duke of Milan, who wrote the Ethiopian emperor a letter inquiring whether he possessed the magic books written "by his ancestor Solomon"—a likely reference to the remarkable *Kebra Nagast*, the Ethiopian *Book of the Glory of Kings*.[4]

Meanwhile, the Muslim armies of the Ottoman Turks were assaulting the last outposts of Byzantine Christianity in the eastern Mediterranean. When the Ottomans conquered Constantinople in 1453, leaders in the Latin West knew for themselves the fear of Muslim power that had been worrying Ethiopia's rulers for a century and a half. To meet the Muslim threat, the Patriarch of Rome (the pope) called a church council, which met at Ferrara and Florence from 1437 to 1445, in hopes of forging a united Christian front by healing the long-standing breach between Rome and the Eastern Churches. The council was attended by the exiled Byzantine emperor and Patriarch of Constantinople, by the head of the Russian church, and by delegates from the Patriarch of Alexandria (to whose jurisdiction the Ethiopian church belonged), along with two monks sent from Jerusalem to represent the Ethiopians. One of the Ethiopian monks, who bore the name of Peter, the first of the apostles and the patron of the Latin Church, made a powerful impression when he told the pope at Florence in 1441 that the Ethiopian emperor was eager "to be united with the Roman Church and to cast himself at your most holy feet." Perhaps Peter was carried away by the fervor for Christian unity, for it is very doubtful if Emperor Zera-Yakob would have endorsed such views, if he even knew of them. In any event, the Ethiopian church was not part of the short-lived Christian union that resulted from the council. Still, the Ethiopian delegates had made an impression. Their images were subsequently cast into the bronze doors made for the new Basilica of Saint Peter (1445), and an African prince also appeared in the *Journey of the Magi* painted by Bennozzo Gozzoli for Medici Palace in Florence (1459).[5]

We do not know precisely how news of the council was received and interpreted in Ethiopia, but between 1481 and 1490 three more Ethiopian delegations came to Europe to discuss Christian unity. To accommodate the first, which included a cousin of the emperor, Pope Sixtus IV repaired the church of Saint Stephen the Great and an adjoining house in the Vatican. Known thereafter as Saint Stephen of the Ethiopians, this facility functioned as a hospice for Ethiopian visitors and pilgrims during the next two centuries, as well as a center for Ethiopian studies in Europe. There between 1537 and 1552 the remarkable Ethiopian scholar Tasfa Seyon (known to Europeans as Peter the Ethiopian) edited and published a New Testament and a Missal in Ge'ez, the Ethiopian liturgical language, with the aid of two Italian Dominicans. In explanation of his presence and purpose, he wrote, "I am an Ethiopian pilgrim . . . from the land of the infidels to the land of the faithful, through sea and land. At Rome I found rest for my soul through the right faith." These were diplomatic words that did not mean Tasfa thought Ethiopian Christians were any less a part of the true Christian faith.[6]

By the late fifteenth century, other royal and diplomatic delegations from Atlantic Africa were arriving in southern Europe by means of Portuguese ships. Surviving accounts of these visits tell more of European reactions to the Africans than they do of African reactions to Europe, but African agendas are implicit in the sending of such delegations to Europe and in the subsequent course of their relations. As subsequent chapters examine in detail, these parties from Africa's Atlantic coast were often as concerned as the Ethiopians were with establishing religious ties with the Latin West, but they were likewise interested in obtaining technical assistance (largely military) and in expanding the commercial exchanges that the Portuguese voyages had opened up. Although the Portuguese ships had been bringing captives back from Atlantic Africa since the 1440s, a regular parade of official delegations from that coast reached Portugal from the 1480s on. The first, in 1484, came from the kingdom of Kongo on the lower Congo River. The king of Benin sent an embassy to Portugal in 1486. Delegations from the Jolof kingdom on the lower Senegal River came to Portugal in 1487 and 1488. A new Kongolese embassy in 1488–1490 helped make the monastery of Saint Eloy in Lisbon a second center of African studies in Europe, where Kongolese learned European religious and secular knowledge and where

Portuguese missionaries were trained in Kongolese culture. The details and larger context of these Atlantic African visits are explored in Chapters 2 and 3.

ENSLAVED AFRICANS IN EUROPE

Kings and ambassadors were not the only Africans whose numbers were rising in Renaissance Europe. From the fifteenth century European artists regularly depicted Africans in dignified but humbler roles as servants, musicians, laborers, and artisans. Padua artist Andrea Mantegne depicted an African woman servant in his portrait *Judith* in 1491, while a black gondolier glides along a Venetian canal in Vittore Carpaccio's *Miracle of the True Cross* (1494). A combo of African musicians adds contemporary detail to the Portuguese painting of *Saint Ursula and Prince Conan* of 1520. Much better known are the German artist Albrecht Dürer's striking engravings of a black man (1508) and of an African woman named Katharina.[7] This second group of Africans in Europe were the product of the African slave trades via the Sahara and the Atlantic.

In the thirteenth and fourteenth centuries, as Charles Verlinden has documented, the number of "blacks" was rising among the mostly Slavic and North African slave populations of Mediterranean Europe. In Sicily in the late thirteenth century, for example, white slaves still were more common than those identified as "black" or "olive" (a category that might include mulattoes), and female slaves were two or three times as numerous as males. In the notarial records on which Verlinden relies most blacks (and some white, brown, and olive-hued persons) were termed "Saracens," that is, Muslims, a fact that is also evident from the names of black slaves: Fatima, Said, Arrashte, Museyd. This suggests that most blacks in Europe before the fifteenth century had not been born below the Sahara, but were from the slave populations born in North Africa whose ancestors had been brought across the desert.[8]

However, as the supply of slaves coming into Mediterranean Europe from the southern Slavic regions was interrupted during the fifteenth century by Ottoman conquests, European merchants increased their purchases in the slave markets of North Africa to such a degree that dark-skinned slaves became the majority in Europe. By the end of the fifteenth century one estate in southeastern Sicily had twenty adult slaves, eight female, twelve male, all of whom were blacks except for two of the women. The African slaves were employed in agriculture. In the neighboring kingdom of Naples, which Ethiopian delegates visited in the second half of the fifteenth century, imported Africans constituted 83 percent of the slaves, who labored in sugar cane fields, vineyards, and other forms of agriculture.[9] Given the high demand, it is likely that most such slaves originated in sub-Saharan Africa and had been brought across the desert to North Africa and then sold to Italy.

By the second half of the fifteenth century Portuguese ships were also

Katharina, age 20 when Albrecht Dürer sketched her in 1521, was the servant of John Brandão, the commercial representative of the king of Portugal in Antwerp. Ufizzi, Florence. Foto Marburg/ Art Resource, NY.

bringing enslaved people directly from sub-Saharan Africa. Of the first group of various skin hues who had been captured in southern Morocco in 1444 and brought back to Portugal, four were given to churches or monasteries and one eventually become a Franciscan friar. As the Portuguese expeditions pushed further south along the African coast, the number of slaves increased steadily, reaching an average of 700 a year in the 1480s and 1490s before beginning to decline. Nearly half of the slaves brought to Portugal from Africa were sold to other lands, especially to the Spanish kingdoms. By the mid-sixteenth century Africans made up 10 percent of the population of Lisbon, Portugal's capital city, and nearly 7.5 percent of the population of Seville, the chief Spanish port. In the Iberian kingdoms most African slaves became urban servants and artisans, although some were used in agriculture in southern Portugal. To deal with the needs of the rising African population in their Spanish kingdoms King Ferdinand and Queen Isabella in 1475 appointed the "Black Count" Juan de Valladolid as *mayoral* (steward) of the blacks in Seville.[10]

Other African captives went on to the Netherlands and southern France, a few even further. In 1555 John Lok, a London merchant's son, brought to England five West Africans whom he had acquired in Portugal. The names of three are known: Binne, Anthonie, and George. A contemporary account allows a small insight into their impressions of England, noting that they were "tall and strong men [who] could well agree with our meats and drinks[, although] the cold and moist air does somewhat offend them." The latter experience was echoed 340 years later by the Tswana chiefs who "appeared to keenly feel the sudden change from the tropical heat to English autumnal weather." More and more Africans were brought to England, where it had become a desirable mark of distinction by the 1590s for elite families to have an African or two among their servants. Queen Elizabeth I, who had been entertained by black musicians and dancers two decades earlier, in 1596 issued an order to expel all blacks from her kingdom, concealing her evident prejudice under the specious complaint that the modest number of African "infidels" there were consuming food needed by the native English population. The order appears to have had little effect.[11]

Details of the lives of African servants and slaves in Europe in this period are very limited. Still, it is evident that Africans readily learned European languages and adopted Christian names and religious practices. Indeed, the enthusiasm Africans showed for Iberian Catholicism—joining lay brotherhoods and, in some cases, following religious vocations—suggests that Christianity had a positive appeal. One study of Africans in Portugal concludes, "On the whole, Christian and African moral codes were not incompatible and Catholicism offered an attractive channel for expression of the blacks' religious feelings." Even at this early date some Africans gained an exceptional mastery of European culture. To assist him in his Latin school in Évora, Portugal, in the mid-sixteenth century, for example, Flemish humanist Nicholaus Cleynaerts (known as Clenardus) trained three black slaves to drill his students in Latin oral dialogues. Clenardus later published these dialogues in a work he entitled *Grammatica Aethiopica* (*Ethiopian Grammar*) in honor of his assistants.[12] At much the same time, John Lok's five Africans were learning English so they could serve as interpreters and intermediaries in the African trade.

Along with examples of Africans' skill in acquiring European culture and their apparently harmonious assimilation into the domestic servant classes, one also finds evidence of how Africans resisted their bondage and tried to affirm their original cultures. One obvious form of resistance practiced by many was to try to escape from slave status either by flight or by legal manumission. A very early example found in the archives is of an unnamed forty-year-old black slave who fled from his Barcelona owner in 1407, only to be caught and returned. Some Iberian slaves obtained their freedom in return for years of faithful service, such as the slave of a Portuguese man who received his freedom in 1447 on the condition that he remain in his owner's service for another five years. Another slave, born in Africa and renamed Martin, obtained from his Barcelona owner a written promise of manumission in 1463 in return for twelve years of faithful service. Rather than hoping for such kindness to come their way, African slaves in Iberia commonly exercised their legal right to purchase their freedom with the portion of wages they were allowed to keep from outside employment. For example, a twenty-five-year-old black slave from Catalonia in 1441 arranged to ransom himself over a five-year period for a sum 20 percent above his original purchase price.[13] By such means, the proportion of free blacks in Iberia steadily rose.

Many Africans in Europe, free and slave, successfully incorporated elements of their original cultures into their new lives. One area of cultural retention was music. African musicians and dancers were in great demand in sixteenth-century Iberia, and enthusiasm for black musicians remained common in Europe for centuries. Most of their instruments and melodies were European, but their musicianship incorporated techniques from their homelands. The names given to African dances suggest even stronger connections to the mother continent: Guineo, Ye-Ye, Zarambeque, and Zumbé.[14] A description from 1633 of how blacks celebrated a Catholic feast in Lisbon suggests that African musical and dancing traditions also informed their religious sensibilities:

> On the day in question, the blacks donned their native dress of loincloths or skirts and tied ornamental beads around their heads, arms and chests. So attired, they marched and danced, some in African fashion, through the streets to the sound of castanets, drums, flutes and African instruments. A few of the men carried bows and arrows, while the women bore on their heads baskets full of wheat given to them by their masters.[15]

Other records give the impression that the African encounter in fifteenth- and sixteenth-century Europe was most often not distinctively European or distinctively African, but typically human. This is nowhere more apparent than in the sexual relations between Africans and Europeans, although cultural, social, and physical differences mitigated the circumstances. Since most African slaves were servants, one might imagine that they were likely to be sexually exploited by their masters and mistresses. The frequent mention of mulattoes is a clear indication of illicit or sanctioned sexual unions between blacks and whites. However, there is also some suggestion that unions between Portuguese and African-born slaves were not particularly common. Cultural differences were one impediment, and it seems that many Portuguese did not consider blacks physically attractive. Marriage resisters suggest that, while sexual relations and marriages between free persons and slaves were not rare, native Portuguese preferred lighter-skinned North Africans to the darker people from below the Sahara. Supporting evidence also comes from regulations in the episcopal constitutions of Lisbon and Évora that forbade priests from owning white women, but apparently did not consider black female slaves to be a sexual temptation.[16] It is not recorded if sub-Saharan Africans similarly preferred mates nearer to their own pigmentation.

However, as the number of blacks in Iberian states increased and adopted European cultural and religious practices, prejudices seem to have softened rather than hardened, and impediments to sexual relations between Africans and Europeans declined. The public record is silent about most of these relations, but the Portuguese Inquisition recorded the case of a free black named Bastião who in his youth had been introduced to homosexual practices by a European man and who continued such activities in later life. In 1557 he was reported to the Inquisition by a Lisbon man who, apparently ignorant of Bastião's sexual preferences, had allowed him to share his bed. This being his second offense, Bastião was whipped and sentenced to ten years in the galleys.[17]

Rather more revealing of the limits of prejudice are the records of marriages and marriage proposals between elite Africans and their Iberian counterparts. Class was a more pervasive force in fifteenth- and sixteenth-century Europe than were culture and color, so both African and European patterns of family alliances favored marriages as part of diplomatic ties. One of the earliest was the proposal cited earlier by Emperor Yishak of Ethiopia to King Alfonso V of Aragon in 1428 that an alliance be sealed by a double marriage between their families. In the mid-sixteenth century a nobleman from the kingdom of Kongo married into the royal household of Portugal. A half-century later in 1607–1608, while on a visit in Portugal, a son of the newly Christian king of Warri in the Niger Delta married a Portuguese noblewoman. Waiving aside ordinances that prohibited such marriages to new Christians, the bureau that processed his application gave its approval by declaring the West African to be an old Christian of noble blood.[18]

DISCOVERING EUROPEANS IN AFRICA

As these examples reveal, before 1650 black African visitors were becoming familiar with parts of Europe and with European culture and beliefs. As a consequence Europeans also became familiar with the appearance of Africans, so the Portuguese on the early voyages of exploration in the Atlantic coast were not surprised to encounter dark-skinned people below the Sahara. But most residents of sub-Saharan regions were clearly astounded by these first encounters. The sight of pale-skinned people in odd clothing arriving on ships of unknown design must have been as startling as extraterrestrials emerging from a flying saucer would be to people today. The Atlantic coast down which the first Portuguese sailed was the most isolated part of the continent, whose inhabitants, unlike those in other parts of sub-Saharan Africa, had not experienced prior contacts with foreigners from across the Sahara or across the Indian Ocean. The further south the Portuguese sailed, the less likely were coastal Africans to suspect that other continents, inhabited by nonblack populations, even existed. As the examples in the rest of this chapter demonstrate, it took a profound stretch of the imagination for many Africans to decide who or what their strange visitors were. Africans' struggles to understand a different branch of humanity have their naive qualities, but it took only a short time for most Africans to grasp the religious, cultural, and technological possibilities that these encounters opened up.

Africans on the Senegal River got their first sight of Europeans in 1455 when a Portuguese expedition sailed into view. Men and women crowded round to examine Cadamosto, an Italian member of the expedition, when he went on shore to visit their market. "They marveled no less at my clothing," he relates, "than at my white skin." Some Africans fingered his black damask doublet (tunic) and his grey woolen cape "with much amazement." Cadamosto further relates that "some touched my hands and limbs, and rubbed me with their spittle to discover whether my whiteness was dye or flesh." They were astounded to discover that his whiteness did not rub off.

African fishermen who ventured out to the ships anchored in their river expressed as much wonder at the Europeans' possessions as those on shore had at their persons. The ship first seemed to be some sort of monster, they told Cadamosto, the portholes in the bow looking like eyes through which it sighted its way across the water. Encouraged to come on board, the fishermen, accustomed to dugout canoes and paddles, were amazed "by the construction of the ship, and by her equipment—mast sails, rigging and anchors," as well as by the Europeans' ability to navigate when out of sight of land. Pointing out that finding one's way over long distances on land was difficult enough, they reasoned these European sailors must be truly great wizards to sail on the sea. The Senegalese fishermen also marveled at the many other material possessions of the Europeans, from musical instruments to a burning candle, and were amazed at the explanation of how they could make candles themselves from local beeswax.

Cadamosto says these practical-minded people were particularly impressed by the Portuguese weapons, both their crossbows (whose form they would have recognized from their own bows) and the unfamiliar cannon and muskets. They took fright when the Portuguese demonstrated the firing of a mortar and expressed astonishment at the assertion (which seems exaggerated) that a single shot could slay more than a hundred men. Their conclusion that "it was an invention of the devil's" echoes the opinion people in many parts of the world came to form of the deadly weapons of the gunpowder revolution.[19]

Every encounter has its own unique aspects, yet these early Senegalese reactions to their first sight of Europeans display key elements that were repeated in subsequent encounters. Two things about the Europeans caught Africans' attention immediately: their strange physical appearance and their unfamiliar material possessions. It is also characteristic of later encounters that in their effort to account for these strange persons and objects, the Senegalese drew no sharp line between natural and the supernatural or magical elements. They were not speaking metaphorically when they suggested the Portuguese might be wizards and in league with evil spirits, for neither Africans nor Europeans of this era lacked credence in the power of supernatural forces to control their lives.

It did not take long before these first impressions led Africans to two more profound but somewhat contradictory conclusions. One was that these creatures, so different in appearance from normal (i.e., African) humans, might be dangerous sorcerers or evil spirits whose marvelous possessions came through the use of evil magic. Since such powers could only be obtained by malevolent actions that went against normal ethical values—such as murder, cannibalism, and other horrific rites—such wizards ought to be avoided. The second African conclusion went in the opposite direction: It would be good to befriend these visitors from across the ocean in order to acquire some of their marvelous goods and gain access to the spiritual power or practical knowledge that lay behind them. Tracing how these several responses played out over the next four centuries is the central task of this book.

Word of strange visitors spread rapidly. Africans along the Gambia River had already formed a very negative impression of Europeans during the few weeks it took the first Portuguese expedition to work its way south from the Senegal. As Cadamosto tells it, a fleet of large canoes surrounded the expedition as it mounted the Gambia in 1455, and poisoned arrows rained down upon the ships. When the Portuguese returned the fire with crossbows and cannon, the resulting consternation and bloodshed persuaded the Gambians to agree to a cease fire. Through interpreters the Portuguese asked for an explanation for the attack, insisting that the expedition members "were men of peace, and traders in merchandize," who wished only to have "peaceful and friendly relations . . . with them, if they were willing." The Europeans asserted that they "had come from a distant land to offer fitting gifts to their king and lord on behalf of our king of Portugal." The Gambians replied that they already knew of the trade the Portuguese were engaged in along the Senegal River and were certain that if the Senegalese had sought Portuguese friendship, it could only be to gain access to their evil powers. For, the Gambians were sure, "Christians ate human flesh, and . . . only bought blacks to eat them," a belief that would endure for the next four centuries. Finally, the Gambians asserted, they would rather slaughter the Portuguese and plunder all their goods than be on friendly terms with such monsters.[20]

On reflection, the Gambians must have realized that their chances of success in a violent confrontation with the well-armed Portuguese were remote. Cooler African heads soon decided there was more to be gained from trading peacefully with the Europeans than from fighting to destroy them. After negotiations with the local ruler on the Gambia, both sides agreed to open trading relations. Within weeks the Gambia River was on its way to becoming an important center of trade between Africans and Europeans.

Over the centuries Africans at dozens of additional sites along the Atlantic coast of Africa decided to open commercial relations with the merchants of many European nations. Yet the tug-of-war between material gain and moral repugnance grew stronger as the purchase of human beings grew in importance in the trade. Coastal Africans grew accustomed to the Europeans' appearance, but captives brought from inland regions for sale into the Atlantic slave trade were as struck with terror by the Europeans' strange looks and stranger intentions as those on the Senegal River had been in 1455. One eighteenth-century African echoed the Senegalese reactions three centuries earlier when he wrote that his belief that European seamen were monsters or spirits was reinforced by the seemingly magical way they could make a ship move across the water by means of "cloths put upon the masts by the help of . . . ropes" and stop by dropping the anchor, as well as by their use of navigational devices such as the quadrant.[21]

Over time, Europeans and their ships grew to be familiar sights along the coast, but a white man could still excite great interest (and fear) in isolated parts of inland Africa centuries after Europeans first reached sub-Saharan Africa. At the end of the eighteenth century, Scottish explorer Mungo Park generated a range of reactions from the inland West Africans who encountered him as he trekked along the southern rim of the Sahara in search of the Niger River. Some individuals displayed a relatively sophisticated understanding, such as the ruler of the Fulani imamate of Bundu in December 1795, who spoke favorably of Europeans, "extolling their immense wealth, and good dispositions," although these compliments seem to have been part of a ploy—successful in the end—to relieve Park of his best blue coat. The king's wives' reactions were more direct:

> They rallied me with a good deal of gaiety on different subjects; particularly on the whiteness of my skin, and the prominence of my nose. They insisted that both were artificial. The first, they said, was produced when I was an infant, by dipping me in milk; and they insisted that my nose had been pinched every day, till it had acquired its present unsightly and unnatural conformation.

Invited to the encampment of a Moorish people (the Oulad Mbarek) in March 1796 to satisfy the curiosity of the ruler's wife, Fatima, Park was received with great interest and a considerable lack of decorum:

> My arrival was no sooner observed, than the people who drew water at the wells threw down their buckets; those in tents mounted their horses, and men,

women, and children, came running or galloping towards me. I soon found
myself surrounded by such a crowd, that I could scarcely move; one pulled
my clothes, another took off my hat, a third stopped to examine my waistcoat
buttons . . .

There again the women restrained their curiosity least: "[T]hey asked a
thousand questions; inspected every part of my apparel, searched my pock-
ets, and obliged me to unbutton my waistcoat and display the whiteness
of my skin: they even counted my toes and fingers, as if they doubted
whether I was in truth a human being." A few days later a delegation of
women visited Park on a brazen mission: "to ascertain, by actual inspection,
whether the rite of circumcision extended to the Nazarenes (Christians), as
well as to the followers of Mahomet." Park is discrete about the outcome
of that particular mission, but notes that the women "were very inquisitive,
and examined my hair and skin with great attention; but affected to consider me a sort of inferior being to themselves, and would knot their brows,
and seem to shudder, when they looked at the whiteness of my skin."[22]

Other inland Africans expressed their surprise or horror at such a sight
in more demonstrative ways. For example, the first European to enter the
Hurutse capital of the Tswana people of modern Botswana in about 1820
recorded, "The sight of the white men threw [the crowds of adults] into fits
of convulsive laughter." The children "screamed, and in the utmost horror
fled to the first place of concealment they could find." At about the same
time a neighboring Tswana people began to describe Europeans as "white
lice" of the sort that occupied the hind quarters of domestic animals. It was
not meant to be flattering metaphor.[23]

Africans of greater sophistication might conceal their distaste at what
they saw, but their reactions were not notably different. In 1824, Shaka, the
great founder of the Zulu nation, disclosed his impressions of the handful
of Europeans he had permitted to enter his southern African kingdom to
his English friend Henry Fynn. Shaka conceded that the Europeans had
inherited many valuable skills and manufactured goods from their ancestors, but he opined that such forefathers had held back "the greatest of all
gifts, . . . a good black skin, for this does not necessitate the wearing of
clothes to hide the white skin, which was not pleasant to the eye." To be
sure, as Africans became more accustomed to the sight of "whitemen," their
views moderated. The Zulu composer of "The Praises of Mbuyazi," a poem
in Henry Fynn's honor, found a way of casting his skin in a somewhat
more flattering light. Fynn was said to be:

Beautiful as the mouse-birds of the Bay,
Which are yellowish on the wings.
Our whiteman, through whose ears the sun shines.[24]

As these examples suggest, the age, sex, sophistication, and knowledge
of African observers affected their responses. So too did the circumstances
of the Europeans. The observations of a ruler on the Gold Coast in 1482,
whose name the Portuguese rendered as "Caramansa" (perhaps a corrup-

tion of Kwamin Ansa, i.e., King Ansa), are instructive. An official delegation from the king of Portugal had arrived in the realm to negotiate the construction of a trading fortress. Caramansa graciously welcomed the delegation led by Diogo de Azambuja. Having bedecked himself from head to foot in golden jewelry in preparation for the meeting, the African ruler praised the appearance of the Portuguese delegates, who for their part had put on their finest silk and brocade garments, along with abundant jewels and gold. He noted the contrast between this official delegation and the occasional "ill-dressed and ragged" Portuguese who had visited his shores earlier, men whom he judged "foul and vile."[25] In the era of the slave trade, Africans would continue to see a mix of Europeans "foul and vile" as well as richly clothed in silk and brocade, but, as in Caramansa's case, the goods Europeans brought to trade determined their welcome more than the finery of their appearance.

Europeans' reputation for valuable trade goods was evidently an important reason for the enthusiastic reception one group of Africans gave to the English explorer William B. Baikie and his party four centuries later. On a voyage of exploration in 1854 motivated both by an interest in geographical knowledge and commercial opportunities, Baikie's ship stopped for the night outside the walled town of Gandiko far up the Benue tributary of the Niger River. As Baikie tells it, most local Africans fled when they realized the visitors intended to come ashore:

> the only person left to receive us, was a solitary individual, who between fear and excitement could hardly utter a single word. I walked up to him, extending my hand, which he surveyed most suspiciously, and at length touched it with as much reluctance as he would a piece of red-hot iron, but finding that it did not burn him, and that we were quite friendly, he threw down his spear, and danced and shouted for joy, . . . shouting all the time [as he led us to the town] at the top of his voice in Hausa, "White men, white men! the Nazarenes [Christians] have come; white men good, white men rich, white men kings; white men, white men!"

Assured by this message that the visitors were friendly, townspeople crowded around them, some shaking their hands, others evidently showing their own absence of malice by pointing at the visitors with the butt ends of their spears and drawing empty bow-strings. Many, Baikie relates, "threw themselves on the ground and went through an extemporaneous course of gymnastics" in an apparent "ecstasy of delight." More sedately, the ruler of Gandiko "thanked God that the white men had come to his country."[26]

A careful analysis of Baikie's account also reveals other elements. The very first African reaction to the sight of the Europeans was fear and suspicion of their intentions; most hid themselves. This was true even though the inhabitants of this relatively sophisticated community clearly were not ignorant of the existence of such "Nazarenes," as they termed them in Muslim fashion. Gandiko was an unusual town. Settled by Fulani people in the midst of a Jukun area, its inhabitants were able to speak the Hausa language widely used in the region by the Hausa trading people. Baikie's party may have been the first Europeans the inhabitants of the town had seen, but some had probably seen light-skinned North Africans who sometimes crossed the desert to the Hausa cities to the north. As improbably exuberant as the reactions of some Gandiko residents appear, Africans had a tradition of lavish hospitality that was well documented over the centuries.

Hospitality was indeed a virtue commented upon by nearly all European visitors to sub-Saharan Africa. Cadamosto, although characterizing Africans as ill-mannered at table (because they ate with their hands), as well as liars and cheats, praised them for being generally "charitable, receiving strangers willingly, and providing a night's lodging and one or two meals without any charge."[27] Such hospitality had also been commented upon by early Muslim visitors to sub-Saharan Africa, such as North African traveler Ibn Battuta in the fourteenth century and Leo Africanus in the 1510s, as well as many later nineteenth-century European explorers. For various reasons such hospitality might be withheld as well. After escaping from Africans who had mistreated him, denied him food and water, and robbed him, Mungo Park reached the Fulani state of Segu, only to be refused shelter. Finally, an old woman took pity on him and offered him food and shelter for the night. While she and other women of the household stayed up spinning cotton, they improvised a song about their visitor:

> The winds roared, and the rains fell.
> The poor white man, faint and weary, came and sat under our tree.
> He has no mother to bring him milk, no wife to grind his corn.
> Let us pity the white man; no mother has he, etc.[28]

As these examples suggest, West African reactions to unfamiliar European visitors showed many variations but also suggest that fear and curiosity, repugnance and attraction persisted over many centuries. Two early cases from below the equator permit these reactions to be explored in greater depth.

SOUTHEAST AFRICA, 1589–1635

Another rich trove of African reactions to first encounters with Europeans comes from the several accounts of Europeans shipwrecked along the coasts of Natal and southern Mozambique in the late fifteenth and early sixteenth centuries. Chronicles of treks over several months to reach a port from where the refugees might get passage home tell of how rural African villagers reacted to the European refugees who passed their way. The most common response was the characteristic offer of hospitality, although, given the size of the parties, it is not surprising that Africans on this impoverished coast often sought payment in metal or cloth. But the accounts also reveal a deeper range of human interactions.

Compassion at the sight of unfortunate fellow humans—however strange in appearance—was often in evidence. The Africans in southern Mozambique who encountered survivors of the *São Thomé* wreck in 1589, for example, made the refugees welcome, offered them shelter, and came to stare. The "women of the village gathered to see the white women, as something marvelous, and all night they gave them many entertainments and dances." At another village a few days later, the African women also marveled at the unfamiliar sight of their European sisters trudging toward their village and, "seeing them so weary and distressed, made signs of compassion, and drawing near caressed and fondled them, offering them their huts and desiring even to take them there at once."[29]

Thirty-five years later, Africans further south along the same coast expressed their heartfelt compassion in other forms for a different group of European castaways. Having learned in response to their questions the misfortune that had forced this strange group of men, women, and children to trek through their land, the villagers "twisted their fingers as if invoking curses upon whoever had caused our shipwreck." The women and children in a village two days further on made even more dramatic gestures of their sympathy. They went down to the seashore and threw stones into the water, while apparently uttering curses on the sea that had caused such anguish: "[T]hen turning their backs upon it they lifted up the skins which covered their backsides and exhibited their arses to the ocean. This is the worst form of insult which they have, and they did it because they had been told that the sea was the cause of our suffering so many hardships and of our wandering for five months through strange lands."[30]

In other cases, Africans were initially less welcoming, withholding their hospitality and expressions of empathy until they were sure that the visitors were really humans. One group of Africans meeting the castaways of 1623 became suspicious that people who claimed they came from the sea might actually be some sort of sea creatures. They first asked the Portuguese to prove their humanity by showing their navels, and, after some did, the Africans asked them to demonstrate that they breathed like human beings. Although on this occasion the villagers seemed satisfied by these demonstrations, concluding, "These are human beings like us," two centuries later Henry Fynn could report that the Zulu of much the same area were convinced that all Europeans had "sprung out of the sea."[31]

In 1635 a group of Natal Africans approached with caution yet another party of a few dozen Europeans stranded on their beach. Whether this caution sprang from fear of the strangers' military or supernatural power is not clear. Each side approached the other warily, until, "being a stone's throw apart" and apparently satisfied of the strange Europeans' humanity and absence of ill intentions, the Africans "all rose and, clapping their hands and dancing in time with the sound and singing . . . , came toward us [Europeans] with great celebration and signs of joy."[32] A dozen years earlier, other African villagers in Natal met castaways with weapons drawn, convinced that they were cannibals, perhaps on good evidence in this case. By their own account, some of the refugees, after consuming their dogs, had satisfied their hunger by eating the bodies of dead members of their party, including some who were executed for such trivial offenses that one is led to wonder if they had not been killed in order to supply food.[33]

But if some Africans were inclined to suspect the worst of the castaways, others assigned lofty origins to them. In Natal in 1589 and again in 1593, other Africans decided, on the basis of the Europeans' light coloring, that they had come from the sky, rather than from the sea. One old man joyfully shouted to his village, "Come, come and see these men who are children of the sun." Believing these "children of the sun" to possess supernatural powers, sick and crippled Africans in one place asked the Portuguese leader for a spell to make them well. In another place people offered food to Europeans who would touch parts of the Africans' bodies that were in pain, and they went off singing when this was done. Another village refused burial to a deceased "child of the sun" lest his remains contaminate their land.[34]

Aware of Africans' inclination to believe they possessed preternatural powers, Europeans sometimes actively promoted the notion to suit their own ends, especially by discharging their firearms. When fearful of being robbed or attacked, all three of the castaway groups of Portuguese mounted demonstrations of this unfamiliar technology. Sometimes the sound and fire of the guns reinforced African suspicions that the whites possessed powerful magic, and some sought to get these white wizards to cure their ills. In one case, an African attack on the castaways quickly came to a halt when three of their men were struck dead by a single shot. The Portuguese's fears that this deed would provoke retaliation proved false. Indeed, the dead men were blamed for their own deaths and punished by being left unburied, while the "king" of the area made a formal visit the next day and presented the Portuguese with an exceptionally fine ox as a gift. However much the firearms' underlying technology eluded them, Africans quickly grasped the practical implications of the weapons when the Portuguese shot an animal such as a cow. After one such demonstration, one clan chief examined the harquebus thoroughly and commented thoughtfully that since the gun could kill cows, it could also kill men. He soon withdrew to his villages.[35]

KONGO COSMOLOGY

Like people everywhere, Africans sought to understand new experiences within existing cultural frameworks. We saw that Africans devised various tests to determine whether or not Europeans were humans like themselves: seeing if their skin color would wash off, checking for gills, counting fingers and toes, and so on. Placing Europeans geographically was much more of a problem for most Africans, who had no more idea of the existence of a continent of Europe in these early times than Europeans had of the existence of the American continents before 1492. Even though the large ships on which Europeans arrived made it generally clear that the pale visitors came from across the seas, it was not easy to decide if their home was a place like Africa or something of a quite different order. Just as some Europeans found it difficult to place Amerindians in the family of humanity descended from Adam and Eve, some Africans persisted in the belief that, despite a superficial resemblance to ordinary humans, Europeans were actually something else. Their odd appearance, strange ships, and unusual possessions suggested otherworldly origins. There are hints of this misperception in many early accounts, but the richest African cosmology of Europeans comes from the Kongo people, whose kingdom lay along the lower Congo River.

The Portuguese explorer Diogo Cão reached the mouth of the Congo River in 1483, where he left four missionaries to seek contact with the inland capital of the manikongo (the king of Kongo). Because the missionaries were still at the capital when he returned to fetch them, Cão sailed away with four Kongolese hostages, who were treated rather more as ambassadors by the time they reached Lisbon and were taught Portuguese so that they might serve as interpreters. The return of the four in 1485 was a key event in the formation of Kongolese perceptions of the Portuguese. The manikongo welcomed the four "as though they had seen them resuscitated from under the earth," a phrase, as anthropologist Wyatt MacGaffey points out, that resonated with significance in the context of Kongolese cosmological beliefs about the world of the living and the world of the dead.[36]

Drawing on the Europeans' arrival by ship, their appearance, and other aspects of their culture, many Kongolese regarded their visitors as voyagers from the world of the dead, a world that in their cosmology lay across the ocean. The unfamiliar language spoken by the whites and the rich and unusual presents they brought also served to mark them as not of this world. To the Kongolese, as to many other Africans, Europeans looked like people whose skin had been painted with white pigment, the color of the underworld. Analogously, their pale skins resembled those of albino Africans, whom the Kongolese believed were water spirits. Moreover, the claims of the king of Portugal to great authority were interpreted by the king of Kongo as a claim to superior *spiritual* powers. Finally, as will be examined in detail in the next chapter, the efforts of the Portuguese to introduce their religion, accompanied by claims of Christians' access to mystical powers, reinforced these impressions of the Europeans' otherworldliness.

Thus the welcome given to the repatriated hostages was one accorded to persons returning not from a distant land otherwise like their own, but from a place incomparably different: the underworld of the dead. In keeping with that perception, the manikongo dispatched Mani Vunda, the priest of the fertility cult addressed to the local spirits, as his first ambassador to Portugal. For the next five centuries Kongo relations with Europe were filtered through such cosmological presuppositions, each new encounter and understanding being interpreted in terms of such fundamental beliefs.

As in other parts of Africa, greater familiarity with Europeans soon eroded the supernatural mystique the first comers acquired. This certainly occurred in the kingdom of Kongo too. A number of Kongolese gained firsthand experience of life in Europe, while many others came to know the Europeans who took up residence in their kingdom. Yet in the minds of many Kongolese these later experiences did little to alter the first impressions of Europeans as being from the land of the dead. MacGaffey found that, even after decades of Belgian colonial rule in the twentieth century, most Kongolese still interpreted Europeans in terms of a cosmology that posited the existence of two parallel worlds inhabited by the living and the dead and divided by water. The living were black in color, prone to disease and death, while the dead turned white and acquired magical powers and immortality.

As MacGaffey argues, although Kongolese perceptions may seem "mistaken, if not downright irrational" to those outside the cosmological system, such misperceptions were no stranger or more removed from empirical reality than were the racist images of Africans that took hold of European minds in modern times.[37] The development and persistence of Kongolese images of Europe are especially richly documented, but very largely from the European side. Unfortunately none of the Kongolese who traveled to Europe wrote an account of their impressions and experiences there. Yet there is good reason to believe that the Kongolese cosmological conception of the encounter with Europe was not unique. Although documentation is thinner, other African societies must have interpreted their encounter in an analogous manner.

Africans' first reactions to Europeans tell much of the rediscovery of humankind underway around the world in this era. Yet they also seem more naive than Europeans' reactions to their encounters with Africans. The educated Europeans who recorded these reactions may have exaggerated African responses somewhat, while presenting their own in a more sophisticated light, but there is good reason to expect that the differences were quite real. Europeans were intruding in various parts of Africa that had virtually no contact with the outside world, whereas Africans had become familiar sights in southern Europe much earlier. European seafarers were not encountering Africans for the first time, and most early ships carried African interpreters. For Africans who had had no previous inkling of the existence of Europe's inhabitants and their material possessions, first sights could be traumatic. The more sophisticated concealed their wonder and disgust, but others exclaimed their amazement or tested the Europeans' humanity in elementary ways. Some aspects of Europeans' strangeness persisted, while others moderated with longer acquaintance. Perceptions of Europeans as fundamentally similar to Africans and as fundamentally different seem often to have coexisted. Revulsion and attraction also went hand in hand. For reasons that are both realistic and deeply ingrained in African patterns of thinking, the Europeans' culture, technology, and material goods proved to be highly attractive to Africans. The opening of trade also opened doors of understanding. In discovering Europeans, Africans would discover their own relative position in the larger world. In entering into Atlantic exchanges, they would test the strengths and expose the weaknesses of their own societies. These subjects are examined in the chapters that follow.

Notes

1. Neil Parsons, *King Khama, Emperor Joe, and the Great White Queen: Victorian Britain through African Eyes* (Chicago: University of Chicago Press, 1998).

2. See F. M. Snowden, *Blacks in Antiquity: Ethiopians in the Greco-Roman Experience* (Cambridge: Harvard University Press, 1970); Jean Devisse, *The Image of the Black in Western Art*, vol. 2, *From the Early Christian Era to the "Age of Discovery,"* part 1, *From the Demonic Threat to the Incarnation of Sainthood* (Cambridge: Harvard University Press, 1979).

3. O. G. S. Crawford, ed., *Ethiopian Itineraries, circa 1400–1524* (London: Cambridge University Press for the Hakluyt Society, 1858), pp. 212–15; Adrian Hastings, *The Church in Africa, 1450–1950* (Oxford: Clarendon Press, 1994), pp. 65–70.

4. Charles G. de la Roncière, *La découverte de l'Afrique au moyen âge* (Cairo: Institut Français d'Archéologie Orientale pour la Société Royale de Géographie d'Egypte, 1924–27), I:67–68, II:112–20, III:79; Hastings, *Church in Africa*, pp. 34–42.

5. Hastings, *Church in Africa*, p. 43; Jean Devisse, *The Image of the Black in Western Art*, vol. 2, *From the Early Christian Era to the "Age of Discovery,"* part 2, *Africans in the Christian Ordinance of the World* (New York: William Morrow, 1979), p. 119.

6. Hans Werner Debrunner, *Presence and Prestige: Africans in Europe: A History of Africans in Europe before 1918* (Basel: Basler Afrika Bibliographien, 1979), pp. 48–51; Hastings, *Church in Africa*, pp. 140, 147.

7. Devisse, *Image of the Black*, II.2: 78–120.

8. Charles Verlinden, *L'esclavage dans l'Europe médiévale* (Ghent: Rijksuniversiteit te Gent, 1977), II:141–55.

9. Verlinden, *Esclavage*, II:217, 353–54.

10. A. C. de C. M. Saunders, *A Social History of Black Slaves and Freedmen in Portugal, 1441–1555* (Cambridge: Cambridge University Press, 1982), pp. 29–30, 59–60, 87, 149; Ivana Elbl, "The Volume of the Early Atlantic Slave Trade, 1450–1521," *Journal of African History* 38 (1997), tables 5 and 7; Ruth Pike, "Sevillan Society in the Sixteenth Century: Slaves and Freedmen," *Hispanic American Historical Review* 47 (1967): 345–46.

11. Peter Fryer, *Staying Power: The History of Black People in Britain* (London: Pluto Press, 1984), pp. 9–12, quote p. 5 (spelling modernized); Parsons, *King Khama*, p. 154. Eighty-nine Africans were subsequently exchanged for English prisoners in Spain, but many others remained even after a second banishment decree was issued in 1601.

12. Saunders, *Social History*, pp. 101–2, 149.

13. Verlinden, *Esclavage*, I:498, 524–26, 631.

14. Pike, "Sevillan Society," pp. 348–49.

15. In Saunders, *Social History*, p. 150.

16. Ibid., pp. 102–4.

17. Ibid., p. 160. Saunders found another example in 1565 of a free black man sentenced to the galleys by the Inquisition for sodomy.

18. John Thornton, "Early Kongo-Portuguese Relations," *History in Africa* 8 (1981): 191; A. F. C. Ryder, "Missionary Activity in the Kingdom of Warri to the Early Nineteenth Century," *Journal of the Historical Society of Nigeria* II.1 (1960): 5–10.

19. G. R. Crone, ed. and trans., *The Voyages of Cadamosto and Other Documents on Western Africa in the Second Half of the Fifteenth Century* (London: Hakluyt Society, 1937). pp. 49–51.

20. Crone, *Cadamosto*, pp. 57–60.

21. Olaudah Equiano, *The Interesting Narrative and Other Writings*, ed. Vincent Carretta (New York: Penguin Books, 1995), pp. 57, 59.

22. Mungo Park, *Travels in the Interior Districts of Africa: Performed in the Years 1795, 1796, and 1797* (London: John Murray, 1816), I:52–54, 119–20, 130–31.

23. John Campbell, *Travels in South Africa . . . : Being a Narrative of a Second Journey into the Interior of That Country* (London: Francis Westley, 1822), I:222; John Burchell, *Travels in the Interior of Southern Africa* (London: Longman, Hurst, Rees, Orme, Brown & Green, 1822), 2:559, cited by Jean Comaroff and John Comaroff, *Of Revelation and Revolution: Christianity, Colonialism, and Consciousness in South Africa* (Chicago: University of Chicago Press, 1991), 1:189–90.

24. Henry Francis Fynn, *The Diary of Henry Francis Fynn*, ed. James Stuart and D. McK. Malcolm (Pietermaritzburg: Shuter and Shooter, 1969), pp. v, 81.

25. There are two detailed accounts of this encounter. That by Ruy da Pina has been translated by John William Blake in *Europeans in West Africa, 1450–1560* (London: Hakluyt Society, 1942), I:70–78; a translation of the account by João de Barros is in Crone, *Cadamosto*, pp. 114–23.

26. William Balfour Baikie, *Narrative of an Exploring Voyage up the Rivers Kwóra and Bínue (Commonly Known as the Niger and Tsádda) in 1854* (London: John Murray, 1856), p. 123.

27. Crone, *Cadamosto*, pp. 32–33.

28. Park, *Travels*, I:193–94.

29. Diogo do Couto, "Narrative of the Shipwreck of the Great Ship São Thomé in the Land of the Fumos, in the Year 1589 and the Toil and Tribulation Undergone by Dom Paulo de Lima in the Regions of Kaffraria until His Death," in C. R. Boxer, ed., *The Tragic History of the Sea, 1589–1622* (Cambridge: Hakluyt Society, 1959), pp. 79, 81.

30. Francisco Vaz d'Almada, "Treatise of the Misfortune that Befell the Great Ship *São João Baptista*, 1622," in Boxer, ed., *Tragic History*, p. 241.

31. D'Almada, "Treatise," pp. 245–46; Fynn, *Diary*, p. 129.

32. Jerónimo Lobo, *The Itinerio of Jerónimo Lobo*, trans. Donald M. Lockhart, ed. M. G. da Costa (London: Hakluyt Society, 1984), pp. 323–24.

33. D'Almada, "Treatise," p. 230.

34. Couto, "Narrative," and João Baptista Lavanha, "Shipwreck of the Great Ship *Santo Alberto* and the Itinerary of the People Who Were Saved from It," in Boxer,

ed., *Tragic History*, pp. 92–95, 120–21, 158, 167. Cf. Andrew Batell, *The Strange Adventures of Andrew Batell of Leigh, in Angola and the Adjoining Regions*, ed. E. G. Ravenstein (Nendeln/Lichtenstein: Kraus Reprint, 1967), p. 51.

35. Boxer, ed., *Tragic History*, pp. 79, 161–62, 208–10, 216, 227, 243–44.

36. Wyatt MacGaffey, "Dialogues of the Deaf: Europeans on the Atlantic Coast of Africa," in *Implicit Understandings: Observing, Reporting, and Reflecting on the Encounters between Europeans and Other Peoples in the Early Modern Era*, ed. Stuart B. Schwartz (New York: Cambridge University Press, 1994), p. 257. The following interpretation also depends on Anne Hilton, *The Kingdom of Kongo* (Oxford: Clarendon Press, 1985), pp. 50–52.

37. MacGaffey, "Dialogues of the Deaf," p. 267.

Suggested Readings

Blake, John William. Translator and editor. *Europeans in West Africa, 1450–1560: Documents to Illustrate the Nature and Scope of Portuguese Enterprise in West Africa, the Abortive Attempt of Castilians to Create an Empire There, and the Early English Voyages to Barbary and Guinea*. London: Hakluyt Society, 1942

Boxer, C. R. Editor. *The Tragic History of the Sea, 1589–1622: Narratives of the Portuguese East Indiamen São Thomé (1589), Santo Alberto (1593), São João Baptista (1622), and the Journeys of the Survivors in South East Africa*. Cambridge: Hakluyt Society, 1959.

Devisse, Jean. *The Image of the Black in Western Art*, volume 2, *From the Early Christian Era to the "Age of Discovery,"* part 2, *Africans in the Christian Ordinance of the World*. New York: William Morrow, 1979.

Saunders, A. C. de C. M. *A Social History of Black Slaves and Freedmen in Portugal, 1441–1555*. Cambridge: Cambridge University Press, 1982.

Schwartz, Stuart B. Editor. *Implicit Understandings: Observing, Reporting, and Reflecting on the Encounters between Europeans and Other People in the Early Modern Era*. New York: Cambridge University Press, 1994.

POLITICS AND RELIGION

Bumi Jeleen had taken over the administration of the Senegalese kingdom of Jolof at the request of his maternal half-brother, who was the rightful heir to the throne but preferred to devote his life to the pursuit of pleasure. Regarded by his subjects as their de facto ruler, Jeleen ruled according to Muslim principles, but his encounters with the Portuguese in 1487–1488 pulled him in a different direction. Jeleen enjoyed a mutually beneficial trade with the Portuguese, from whom he obtained horses "and other needful goods," treated the Portuguese traders well to encourage their return, and sent presents by them to King João II (1481–1495) of Portugal. King João sent rich gifts in return, along with agents charged with persuading Bumi Jeleen (whom the Portuguese called "Bemoy") to join the Christian faith.

At first Jeleen did no more than listen respectfully to these religious messages, but events in his kingdom soon made him seek a closer alliance with Portugal. In 1487, sons of the former king by another mother killed Jeleen's half-brother (the nominal ruler) and then made war on Jeleen in an effort to seize the Jolof throne. Jeleen dispatched his nephew to King João to plead for the horses, arms, and men he needed to hold on to his kingdom. King João, who had only recently (1484) foiled a plot by his own brother-in-law to usurp his throne, was sympathetic. He sent some horses but also sent priests, specifying that additional aid would be conditional on Jeleen's conversion. While pondering these conditions, Jeleen succeeded in getting some additional military assistance from Portuguese merchants in his kingdom, whom he promised to repay from the booty his soldiers might capture from the rebels.

When King João ordered the merchants to halt their military aid, Jeleen sent his nephew back to King João in 1487, with a rich present of a hundred young male slaves and a thick golden bracelet. Before further negotiations could take place, Jeleen's enemies succeeded in seizing control of the kingdom, forcing Jeleen to seek refuge on a Portuguese trading caravel on its way back to Lisbon. Jeleen and his retinue of retainers received a gracious welcome, were shown to a place to stay, and were provided with "silver and attendants and every other civility." Then, wearing fine clothes João also provided, the African delegation was received by the vacationing king and queen at a court improvised in the house of the royal exchequer in the picturesque mountainside village of Palmela.

The accounts make clear that, even without his new European finery, King Jeleen had a commanding presence. A tall, dark-skinned man of about forty years of age, he was well proportioned and sported a long beard. As was befitting such desperate supplicants, Jeleen and his men threw themselves at João's feet to kiss them and went through the motions of the ancient West African ritual of throwing sand over their prostate forms as a sign of submission and respect. The courtesies completed, Jeleen rose at João's bidding and, "with great ease, majesty, and considerable gravity," delivered a long speech, not at all in the manner the Portuguese expected of an African but "with all the eloquence of a Greek prince of [ancient] Athens." After recounting the painful circumstances of his deposition, Jeleen repeated his plea for arms and men. Recalling that his earlier request for aid had been refused because of the long-standing Portuguese prohibition against giving arms to non-Christians, he now pronounced himself ready to accept the new faith along with all of his royal retinue. He expressed profound regret that his unfortunate present circumstances cast his religious sincerity in doubt but insisted his desire for conversion was genuine, offering "many sound reasons" in defense of its sincerity.

The Portuguese monarch received his words with great pleasure at this and subsequent private meetings at which Jeleen displayed "shrewd judgment and very natural dignity." The chronicler tells us, "In his honor the king ordered bull-fights and tournaments, and he held fancy-dress balls and dances." Between these festivities, Jeleen received detailed instruction in the Christian faith. Then, the chronicle relates, during the elevation of the host at a special mass, Jeleen had a profoundly moving religious experience that left him fully convinced of Christianity's truth.

On November 3, 1488, Jeleen and six of his chief followers were baptized as Christians, with the Portuguese king, queen, other members of the royal family, a papal commissioner, and the bishop of Tangier serving as their godparents. Jeleen was knighted and renamed Dom João in his patron's honor. In due course he was furnished with twenty caravels, well armed and carrying priests and religious articles in preparation for the conversion of the entire kingdom that was expected to follow Jeleen's restoration to the throne. The vessels were also loaded with materials for building a Portuguese trading fort at the mouth of the Senegal River, for, in aiding Jeleen, King João of Portugal was also strongly motivated by the desire to establish contact with the fabled inland city of Timbuktu, "where are the richest trades and markets of gold in the world." None of these plans succeeded. Soon after arriving in Senegal, the captain of the fleet, fearful of dying of a tropical disease, killed King Jeleen and sailed straight back to Portugal without completing the building of the fortress or making contact with

Timbuktu. The kingdom remained in the hands of the rebels and the plans for its conversion to Christianity were abandoned. King João was deeply saddened by Jeleen's death, but he left its perpetrator unpunished.[1]

Despite an outcome that precludes further testing of the motivations on both sides, Jeleen's complex saga raises difficult but important issues that are central to exploring how African rulers reacted to early encounters with European visitors. It shows how intertwined African (and European) political, religious, and commercial motives could be. No one has ever doubted that the commercial motives that are subjects of the next two chapters are genuine. The eagerness with which Jeleen and other Africans sought military alliances and arms from Europe is also beyond doubt. Yet modern historians often express great skepticism about the sincerity of Jeleen's and other Africans' interest in Christianity as well as of the Portuguese crown's commitment to evangelization. One English authority on Portuguese expansion goes so far as to charge that the tale of Jeleen illustrates "the way in which the Portuguese tried to hide policy behind a show of missionary zeal."[2] However, as many other examples will demonstrate, Portuguese zeal to spread their Christian tradition was not a false facade for something else, even though that zeal was usually mixed with other policies. But what are we to make of the equally mixed motives of Jeleen and other African rulers during the first two centuries of direct European contact?

Does the political expediency of Jeleen's adoption of Christianity preclude his sincerity? In his address to the royal court Jeleen himself pointed out the problem, yet he so convinced the Portuguese rulers that his conversion was genuine that they provided him with the military aid that they had earlier refused him. There was nothing new in Portugal's commercial motives that could explain their change of policy. In short, although the evidence does not suggest that Jeleen's motives for conversion were purely religious, it suggests that contemporaries judged his religious conversion to be sincere. Jeleen's circumstances are especially difficult, but if there is a possibility of accepting his conversion as genuine, other cases will be easier to judge.

THE MEANINGS OF RELIGIOUS CONVERSION

In the modern West, religious beliefs are commonly viewed as personal matters that ought not to intrude into public life. In the fifteenth and sixteenth centuries, Africans as well as Europeans saw religion and public policy as intimately linked. Religion was expected to serve political ends, and public policy to promote the established religion. African rulers shared with early modern European monarchs the belief that political authority had a divine base. Many African kings were thought to be so charged with spiritual powers that they could not live like ordinary mortals: They appeared in public rarely or from behind a curtain, spoke through "interpreters," might not touch the bare ground, and received special treatment at death. A Portuguese account from about 1540, anonymous but not by a missionary, attested to the spiritual nature of rulers throughout western Africa, but specifically in the two kingdoms of Benin and Kongo to be examined in this chapter: "The kings are worshipped by their subjects, who believe that they come from heaven, and speak of them with great reverence, at a distance and on bended knees. Great ceremony surrounds them, and many of these kings never allow themselves to be seen eating, so as not to destroy the belief of their subjects that they can live without food." Other African rulers were less restricted in their movements, but all shared with their European counterparts the belief that spiritual power was essential to winning wars, ensuring successful hunts and harvests, and protecting their realms from evil.[3]

Given the close ties of African rulers to a state religion, it might seem improbable for them to adopt a new religion. Doing so was admittedly a big step, and it could be a dangerous one, but it was not unknown. Because Africans did not see their traditional religious understanding as complete and unerring, they were open to practices and beliefs from elsewhere and to new revelations that might come to individuals from the spirit world. Thus, at times, a ruler might adopt sufficiently attractive new beliefs and practices to enhance his own powers. What happened next could vary. In some cases, the changes might meet with resistance and provoke rebellion. Often the new religious practices became part of a special cult practiced only by the elite and inaccessible to the masses. Occasionally a ruler might succeed in making a new faith the official practice of his kingdom mandatory for all his subjects. Even in the last case, however, many older religious traditions might either continue as unauthorized practices or be reconfigured into the new religion.[4]

Some perspective on conversion to Christianity comes from considering that African rulers in the Western Sudan for some time had been adopting Islam under circumstances in which it also suited their economic and political interests in dealing with trans-Saharan traders, but without suggesting to North African Muslims that their conversions were fraudulent. An eleventh-century Arab of Cordoba tells of a Malinke ruler's conversion to Islam in which faith and practical self-interest are openly mixed. The kingdom of Malal was suffering from one of the prolonged droughts that periodically afflict the Western Sudan. After priests of the local religion failed to call down rain, a visiting Muslim proposed that the ruler turn to Islam for help. When the king agreed, the Muslim "taught him to recite some easy passages from the Koran and instructed him in [the religion's] basic obligations and practices." Then on the next Friday, the Muslim holy day, the two went to a nearby hilltop where the Muslim led the king in a night of prayers. According to the account: "The dawn had just begun to break, when God brought down abundant rain. The king ordered the idols [of the old religion] be broken and the sorcerers [priests] expelled from the country. He together with his sons and the nobility, sincerely embraced Islam, but the common people of his kingdom remained pagans."[5] One cannot authenticate these events from any other source and it is likely that the details of so edifying a story have been simplified, but it is worth noting that this account finds no conflict between such a pragmatic test of divine power and the sincerity of the Malinke leaders. The account of Jeleen's conversion to Christianity four centuries later is in a similar literary tradition and appears to describe similar circumstances.

Just how Africans viewed what they were doing can be difficult to get out of texts written by the would-be converters, but modern studies offer some important insights into how to view such events. Besides the skeptics, those who have attempted to make sense of the religious encounter between Portugal and Africa approach the issue from two seemingly opposite perspectives that are in fact compatible. One approach emphasizes the great differences between European Christianity and traditional African religious beliefs and practices. This view was heartily endorsed by most contemporary European missionaries, who, convinced of the unique validity of their own faith, insisted that Africans burn their shrines and abandon all their old ways. Africans sometimes saw things in terms of incompatible contrasts, too. We have already seen the idol burning ordered by the king of Malal in the story of his conversion to Islam. A more fully historical example comes from southern Africa in the early nineteenth century, where the Xhosa leader Ngqika repulsed a European missionary's efforts to convert him (and thus his people) with this explanation: "You have your manner to wash and decorate yourself for the Lord's Day and I have mine, the same in which I was born and that I shall follow. . . . If I adopt your law, I must entirely overturn all my own and that I shall not do."[6] The approach is also taken by modern scholars seeking to explain why both Europeans and Africans, incapable of thinking outside the paradigms of their own cultures, frequently misunderstood each other's religion. From this perspective, Africans were capable of syncretism but not of conversion.

The second approach stresses that a large measure of mutual understanding was facilitated by the fact that European and African cosmologies had so much in common. Thus in his magisterial history of African Christianity Adrian Hastings argues, "the Catholicism of fifteenth- or sixteenth-century Portugal or Spain had far more in common with African religion than might be imagined."[7] Iberian Christians fully accepted the existence of lesser spirits such as angels and devils, of spiritually powerful intercessors such as saints, and of the malevolent power of witchcraft, all of which had ready counterparts in African beliefs. Moreover, at the popular level European Christianity was infused with folk beliefs in nature spirits that featured prominently in African beliefs. Finally, most European Christians accepted that their monarchs should play major roles as the arbitrators and enforcers of religious orthodoxy. Since the Roman Emperor Constantine adopted Christianity in the fourth century and made it the official religion of his empire, the spread of Christianity had occurred through the conversion of rulers, the last of which were the rulers of Poland-Lithuania in 1386. Although Protestant reformers emphasized individual "conversion," to end the German Wars of Religion even Lutherans accepted the principle that rulers could impose religious orthodoxy in their realms, codified in the famous formula *cuius regio, eius religio* (whoever's region, his religion).

From this second perspective, it was quite easy for Africans to grasp the essentials of Western Christianity and to adopt it as their own without abandoning everything of the old ways. Instead of being discarded, much of the old religion could readily be "converted" to the new ways. Thus conversion consisted in conserving what remained valid of the old, adapting what needed to be redefined, and adding new elements. Disagreement might be common about exactly what needed to be dropped or altered, but in time a successful formula might be worked out—or the conversion process might pause at some intermediate point or be abandoned entirely. In all likelihood the more informed and elite would change at a faster pace and in a more substantial way than less sophisticated rural people. Such transformations had been underway for many centuries in Europe, whose Christian leaders were forever struggling to suppress "superstitious" beliefs and practices that dated from older folk religions. Viewed from an African perspective, such transformations in Africa were both important and inevitable. Christianity or Islam needed to be Africanized to be accessible to Africans every bit as much as African beliefs and practices had to become Christianized or Islamicized.[8]

As Robin Horton has argued, these two approaches are not in practice incompatible—an argument the growing body of African Christians dating from this period would second. An eighteenth-century African, Olaudah Equiano, who had become a Christian in Britain in 1759, was surprised, when trying to read the Bible for the first time a few years later, by the great similarities between what he found there and the religion of his childhood in Igboland. He wrote in his famous autobiography, "I was wonderfully surprised to see the laws and rules of my own country written almost exactly here; a circumstance which I believe tended to impress our manners and customs more deeply on my memory."[9] Equiano's comment also draws attention to the important point that, however compelling the moment of ecstatic religious feeling that sparked a conversion, the intellectual process extended over a much longer period.

It will be clear from some of the better documented cases that follow that in Africa in this period (and later) becoming Christian involved adapting Christian beliefs and practices to existing African beliefs and practices. As Horton points out, it is now generally agreed by scholars who study religious conversion in various disciplines "that the phenomenon of 'conversion' can only be understood if we put the initial emphasis, not on the incoming religious messages, but rather on the indigenous religious frameworks and challenges they face from massive flows of novel experience."[10]

BENIN AND WARRI

An embassy from the powerful and expanding kingdom of Benin had arrived in Lisbon two years before Jeleen and his party. After the first official

Portuguese explorers had reached this important coastal kingdom west of the Niger Delta in 1486, Benin's ruler, the oba, sent the chief of his port city back with them to learn more about the lands from which these stranger visitors came. The Benin ambassador, "a man of good speech and natural wisdom," was received with the same hospitality that would greet the Jolof delegation two years later: "Great feasts were held in his honour, and he was shown many of the good things of these kingdoms" and given presents of "rich clothes for himself and his wife" at his departure. He also brought back gifts for the oba of Benin, missionaries to persuade him to adopt Christianity, and traders to buy additional quantities of pepper and other goods from Benin that had already begun to reach Portugal.[11]

Because the oba's interest in the Christian religion rose and fell with the Portuguese trade, one may assume some link between them. But the power of Christianity proclaimed by the missionaries would surely have attracted the interest of a monarch whose authority was intimately linked to the supernatural. According to Benin traditions, the previous ruler, Oba Ewuare, known for his military expansion of the kingdom and the growth of its capital, Benin City, also "made powerful charms, and had them buried at each of the nine gateways to the City, to nullify any evil charms which might be brought by people of other countries to injure his subjects," activities that "earned for him the title Ewuare Ogidigan (Ewuare the Great)."[12]

It is not recorded how the new oba and his advisors responded to the rival charms brought by the missionaries who had returned with the Benin ambassador in 1486, nor do we know for sure the fate of the missionaries, who may well have died of tropical diseases, but in 1514 Oba Ozolua sent another embassy to Lisbon to discuss trade, conversion to Christianity, and the sale of firearms. By a Portuguese account, when the new missionaries "arrived in Benin, the delight of the king of Benin was so great that I do not know how to describe it, and likewise that of all his people." This report might be exaggerated, but a close reading of it reveals circumstances that might indeed have delighted the ruler. At the time the missionaries arrived, Oba Ozolua was at war, so he summoned the priests to his war camp and kept them there for a year. Then, when the ruler returned to his capital, he studied this "deep mystery" of the missionaries for a month. His conclusion was evident in the decision at the end of August 1516 to give "his son and some of his noblemen—the greatest in his kingdom—so that they might become Christians" and in his order for a church to be built in the capital.[13]

Why did the oba of Benin take such an interest in Christianity? The decision of so powerful a political leader is unlikely to be free of political considerations. The mid-sixteenth-century Portuguese chronicler João de Barros knew of Benin's subsequent rejection of Christianity when he offered the explanation that Oba Ozolua remained "very much under the influence of his idolatries, and sought the priests rather to make himself powerful against his neighbours with our favour than from a desire for baptism."[14] Historian Alan Ryder, who has written the most detailed study of these

Brass casting of a Portuguese soldier with a flint-lock musket crafted by an African artist at the royal court of the kingdom of Benin in the sixteenth century. British Museum, London 1944Af.4.7.

events, is inclined to agree that the "power" the oba sought was not spiritual but firepower, the muskets the Portuguese would not sell to a non-Christian. That interpretation is certainly possible, but would an African ruler of this era (or, indeed, a European one) have divorced religion so sharply from statecraft? It seems more likely that the oba sought the combined power of the firearms and the spiritual force behind them. If the oba had summoned the missionaries to the battlefront not just to hear their teachings more conveniently but to test their spiritual power to influence events, his sudden interest in Christianity following his success in battle becomes clear.

In the end, Christianity in Benin endured little longer than it did in Jolof. No definitive explanation is possible, and the role of individual personali-

ties may have been quite significant. However, it seems likely that the opposition of palace officials and the rituals of kingship played a determinant
role. In Benin royal succession was an orderly process, in which court officials designated the rightful heir at the death of the oba. The anonymous
Portuguese description of 1540 recounts that after death the oba's body was
cast down a well, where a favored number of close associates voluntarily
joined it. A large stone sealing the opening was removed daily to see if
anyone was still alive. When all had died, a great feast was held at which
the new oba was proclaimed. Ryder believes that the burial described may
well be that of Oba Ozolua "the Conqueror," who died in a battle in
late 1516 or early 1517, shortly after he expressed interest in Christianity.
What happened next is obscured by the loss of most Portuguese records of
this period in the Lisbon earthquake of 1755. New Portuguese missionaries,
who are known to have set off from the island of Principe at the end of
August 1517, would have met an oba whose commitment to Benin's traditional religion had just been reinforced by the burial and coronation
rituals.

By 1538, when three new Portuguese missionaries went to Benin, it was
clear that the effort to introduce Christianity in Benin had failed. Although
Oba Orhogbua, who received them, had been among those baptized in 1516
and had learned to speak Portuguese as a child, he was not receptive to
their religious mission and declined further meetings. One cannot be sure
how much he was influenced by the new missionaries' lack of diplomacy,
by the decline of Portuguese trade, and by his commitment to the old ways,
but, for whatever reasons, the moment had passed.

A few Benin Christians remained in 1538. The missionaries reported that
the oba was holding a number of Christians captive, including some of high
birth. One of them, Gregorio Lourenço, who had learned Portuguese and
become a Christian while a servant in nearby the Portuguese colony on the
island of São Tomé, served as interpreter for the new missionaries, just as
he had done in 1516. He asked the missionaries to baptize his children and
wives, but the oba would not allow it. English traders who came to Benin
in 1553 found the same Oba Orhogbua very eager for trade, but on that
occasion neither side brought up the subject of religion.[15]

The experiment with Christianity was not forgotten in the royal palace
of Benin. An oba who met with new Spanish missionaries in 1651 showed
interest in Christianity and even talked of building a church, but the encounter ended in rancor. Italian missionaries to Benin in 1695 and again in
1709–1710 also had no success in breaking through the opposition of royal
officials who surrounded the oba, although there are hints that the oba
himself was interested in the religion or at least curious about it.

Yet a Christian presence in the smaller neighboring Itsekiri kingdom of
Warri persisted through difficult circumstances for many centuries. The interest in Christianity in Warri dates from the second half of the sixteenth
century. In 1600 the ruler sent his eldest son (christened Domingos) to Lisbon to be educated in European ways, as an accompanying letter directed.

Following studies lasting some eight years at various schools and a pilgrimage to the shrine of Saint James at Compostela, Domingos returned to Warri, with his wife (a Portuguese noblewoman), a chaplain, ten servants, and a commitment to promote Christianity. After he succeeded his father as ruler, Domingos built a church, instructed those around him in Christian doctrines, and, according to the Portuguese bishop on São Tomé, held religious processions, although the influence of Christianity does not appear to have gone beyond the royal court. In a letter of 1652, the ruler of Warri, describing himself as "a faithful Christian," pledged his devotion to the pope and begged for a regular supply of priests. Pleas for priests feature prominently in letters from later rulers: from Dom Domingos II, who built a new church in his capital, and from Dom Agostinho in the early 1730s. Thereafter the fervor for Christianity seems to have cooled, although there were Christian rulers of the kingdom into the early nineteenth century.[16] The records are too fragmentary to explain precisely why the rulers of Warri persisted in their devotion to Christianity and why the faith did not spread beyond the royal court, but it seems apparent that the reasons are due to the meaning rulers found in the religion rather than to the only occasional presence of foreign missionaries.

THE KINGDOM OF KONGO

South of the equator in the powerful kingdom of Kongo on the lower Congo River there developed a much larger community of Christians than in Warri—and a more complex political situation. The people of Kongo first learned of the Portuguese when a small fleet of ships led by Diogo Cão arrived at the mouth of the river in 1484. Not wanting to delay his mission, which was to explore the coast and find an all-water route to India, Cão sent four Franciscan monks to meet with the manikongo (the Kongo ruler) at his distant capital while the fleet continued its exploration south of the river. The missionaries were still at the royal court when the fleet returned, so Cão took four Kongolese noblemen, including Prince Kasuta, back to Portugal with him, promising to bring them back on his next expedition. Although the four were apparently hostages for the missing monks, the Kongolese were welcomed as lavishly as the embassies from Benin and Jolof when they reached Lisbon. For fifteen months Kasuta and his companions studied the Portuguese language and received religious instruction.

When they returned to Kongo in 1487, Manikongo Nzinga a Nkuwu joyfully received them and the presents they brought from King João, as we saw in Chapter 1. The ruler sent back his own royal gifts of colorful palm-cloth and carved ivory, along with a delegation to seek people skilled in spiritual and material arts for his kingdom. In response Kongo received three Portuguese ships in 1491 bringing priests and religious objects, along with carpenters, masons, and their tools. The manikongo welcomed the delegation warmly in the capital in May and a month later, when a rebellion broke out in a northern province of the kingdom, invited the missionaries to accompany his forces to the war front. Marching under a banner embroidered with a cross, Portuguese auxiliaries were instrumental in defeating the rebels. Beginning on Christmas Day 1491 a series of highly placed Kongolese accepted baptism, including the royal family, who took the baptismal names of their royal Portuguese patrons: King João, Queen Eleanor, and Prince Afonso.

Just as in Benin a quarter century later, the Kongolese initial acceptance of Christianity may have been strongly influenced by the military success the Portuguese had helped to achieve. The manikongo would have appreciated the fighting skill of the Portuguese but, like the oba of Benin, he would also have seen a providential hand in the outcome. No African army went to war without specially prepared amulets to protect them from harm, any more than the Portuguese would begin a battle without assisting at a Mass for their success and marching under a religious banner. Whatever the reasons why the Kongo elite took this momentous leap of faith, Christianity collapsed nearly as quickly in Kongo as it did in Benin. Like other African rulers, the manikongo had to deal with the fact that his subjects still followed the old religion, of which he remained the center. Many Kongolese were offended by the arrogance of Portuguese who unceremoniously threw the "idols and fetishes" of the old religion onto bonfires. Even the Christian elite were alienated by missionary attacks on the plural marriages that underpinned aristocratic Kongolese society (and also persisted among African Christians in Benin, Warri, and Ethiopia). Not surprisingly, Manikongo Nzinga a Nkuwu objected to any interference in his role as head of the religious and political life of his kingdom. Whether he turned against Christianity or simply against the excesses of its propagators is open to question, but, in contrast to events in Benin, the new faith survived and prospered in Kongo.[17]

Why did Christianity succeed in Kongo when it failed in Benin? The personal character of the African rulers seems to be a key factor, but differences in how the two kingdoms chose their rulers also seem to have been important. In contrast to Benin's orderly, palace-directed process, royal succession in the kingdom of Kongo was less formal and gave popular opinion a greater role. Any of a manikongo's sons by his many wives could be his successor and, as age took its toll on a reigning monarch, competition among them grew. After a king's death the struggle intensified, with each claimant vying for support of powerful interest groups in the kingdom. Such rivalry might last for months or even years and frequently was tested by fighting among the various competing groups—producing what anthropologists have called an "anarchic interregnum." In the succession struggle in Kongo the Catholic party became an influential interest group. African Catholics and their Portuguese allies actively supported the candidate most committed to their cause. Naturally the anti-Christian "traditionalists" supported another candidate. In the first such confrontation at the death of King João (Nzinga a Nkuwu) in 1506, the Catholic party was successful in pushing the candidacy of Afonso, who could also claim João's deathbed nomination, against a brother supported by the traditionalist great chiefs (who was executed after his defeat). Afonso's success at this critical stage and his long rule from 1506 to 1543 sealed the commitment of Kongo royals to a religious, commercial, and cultural partnership with the Portuguese. There is no reason to think that Afonso's own formidable faith in Christianity needed strengthening, but his success in gaining the throne gave him a mandate to promote Christianity, formal education, and new technologies. He had no wish to alter Kongo's political or legal systems, nor, it seems, to replace all traditional Kongolese religious and social customs with those imported from Europe. Rather, he pursued a dual policy of promoting selective borrowing from Europe while Africanizing the new religion.

As part of the first policy, in 1508 Afonso sent his young son Henry (Henrique), who had been a student in missionary schools in Kongo, to study with the order of Saint John the Evangelist in Lisbon. Their monastery of Saint Eloy in Lisbon had become a center of African studies, where Kongolese students studied European religious and secular subjects and where Portuguese missionaries were trained for work in Kongo. During his studies there, Prince Henry led a Kongolese embassy to Rome in 1513 or 1514, which some scholars believe may have been part of the lavish Portuguese delegation that created a huge sensation by bringing the new Pope Leo X a trained Indian elephant.[18] Upon completing his studies in 1518, Henry was ordained a priest, benefiting from Pope Leo X's new encyclical waiving, in the case of non-Europeans, of the requirement that candidates for the priesthood be children from a lawful Christian marriage. In December 1520, Henry was consecrated a bishop, Pope Leo X again smoothing the way by dispensing him from the rule that a bishop be at least thirty years of age and by persuading some less favorably inclined cardinals to agree to the appointment. Henry was the first sub-Saharan African to become a Catholic bishop—and the last for over 250 years. In 1521 Bishop Henry and four other new African priests returned to Kongo to take up their duties under the watchful eye of King Afonso.[19]

The father and son undertook a series of steps to Christianize Kongo— and to Africanize Christianity to a degree that would not be seen again until after the Second Vatican Council (1962–1965). For example, the traditional Earth Priest (Mani Vunda) became the official Holy Water bearer, not a trivial assignment given the powerful symbolism of water in African religion. Their approach was from the top down, or geographically, from the capital outward. The mission station and its schools produced a steady stream of literate youths to serve in the government and to carry the Christian message to the provinces. Despite an acute shortage of priests and religious objects for the churches, schools and Christians multiplied.

There is ample evidence that King Afonso sincerely believed in Christianity and the practical utility of the changes being made. A Portuguese priest may have exaggerated when he wrote in 1516 that Afonso's "Christian life is such that he appears to me not as a man but an angel," but he testified realistically that Afonso was a diligent student of the Hebrew prophets, the gospels, and the martyrologies and a moving preacher to his people. Like Equiano, Afonso may have found much in the Bible that confirmed the validity of traditional African beliefs and practices. At the same time his personal devotion to Christianity made him a zealous reformer of the old ways.[20]

However, this interesting experiment in cultural change and exchange quickly developed a destructive side. The craftsmen, teachers, arms specialists, and missionaries whom Afonso invited from Portugal had to be paid. Kongo's raffia cloth, although said to be "as soft as velvet [and] as beautiful as any made in Italy,"[21] did not find the export market that Benin's cotton textiles would, and the kingdom lacked the gold or spices sold from West African states north of the equator. From an early date Kongo's balance of overseas payments were sustained by the sale of slaves, for whom there was a considerable market in the rapidly expanding Portuguese sugar plantations on the island of São Tomé to the north. Initially a royal monopoly that depended upon prisoners taken in wars, the slave trade soon attracted other Kongolese. By the mid-1520s a poignant series of letters from Afonso to his royal brother, the king of Portugal, and to the pope were testifying to the expanding slave trade's destructive effects. One letter of 1526 points to the root of the problem: "[O]ur people, keenly desirous as they are of the wares and things of your Kingdoms, which are brought here by your people, and in order to satisfy their voracious appetite, seize many of our people, freed and exempt men; and very often it happens that they kidnap even noblemen and the sons of noblemen, and our [royal] relatives, and take them to be sold to the white men who are in our Kingdoms." The letter is not less poignant for the king's concern being with the fate of Kongo's elite, not its commoners. Another letter that same year contained an equally revealing proposal for stopping, or at least limiting, the slave trade—the king of Portugal should command his agents to send no more merchants or wares to the kingdom of Kongo: "[W]e need . . . no more than some priests and a few people to teach in the schools, and no other goods except wine and flour for the holy sacrament." This pious wish was not to be. Later in the year (with Henry's failing health perhaps in mind), Afonso wrote again to "Dom João, King our Brother," bemoaning the prevalence of sickness in general and among his own children and relatives, as well as among the Christian youth. He asked the king to send a surgeon, two physicians, and two apothecaries with their stores of drugs to treat his people so as to provide a Christian alternative to the herbal medicines and pagan ceremonies of his people.[22]

Afonso's death in about 1543 set off a prolonged power struggle with inevitable religious undercurrents. Despite a growing breach between the government of Portugal and the Portuguese residents of Kongo and São Tomé, the Catholic party retained its dominance. The throne was claimed by Afonso's grandson Diogo, who rallied strong popular support in the Kongo capital and in Lisbon. During his long reign from 1545 to 1561,

Diogo cracked down on the rebellious Portuguese settlers and sought to follow a middle road between the Traditionalist and Catholic parties.

One issue that he needed to address was polygamy. In Kongo, as in most African states, multiple wives were the norm for rich and powerful men and an important mechanism for binding the different parts of their kingdom together. In Afonso's time the ideal of a single Christian wife had been accepted, but elite Kongolese Christian men also had multiple extramarital "concubines" (as did not a few Portuguese nobles). Seeing no reason why the new religion should impede this political practice, Manikongo Diogo entered into multiple marriages, including some to close relatives, as a means of cementing ties to his provincial governors. This led to a well-documented dispute with the manikongo's confessor and namesake, Father Diogo Gomes, a Kongo-born Portuguese who had become the ruler's trusted advisor. In 1554 Father Gomes won the king's agreement to dismiss his "concubines," but the agreement was never put in practice. Indeed, Manikongo Diogo shortly concluded a new marriage with a prohibited relative. It is instructive that the other priests of the capital accepted this, but Gomes would not and left the kingdom in discouragement the next year. It is instructive that monogamy is not mentioned in fundamental Christian creeds but had become the norm among Europeans. Kongo Christianity needed a pragmatic approach if it was to find lasting success.[23]

For a time, Kongo's political and religious autonomy was secure, but African invaders forced Diogo's successor into a closer alliance with the Portuguese that had worrisome consequences. In the 1560s Imbangala forces (known to the Portuguese as "Jaga") invading from the east disrupted a wide area of Kongo, first defeating Manikongo Álvaro I (1566–1587), then driving him and his court into refuge on an island in 1569. His appeals for help to the Portuguese crown brought a force of six hundred soldiers in March 1571, whose firearms frightened and helped drive the "Jaga" away over the next eighteen months. However, in the aftermath Kongo became increasingly dependent on its Europeans ties.

Most of the Portuguese soldiers stayed on in the kingdom of Kongo, and they were soon joined by new Portuguese settlers in the ocean port of Luanda, founded in 1575, which became the center of the slave trade. This growing European community and their Afro-European descendants and African dependants became important in supplying guns directly to the Kongo monarchy. Although few in number and far from accurate, such weapons provided Kongo and other African states with an acoustic and psychological edge in battle. But the complex political, cultural, and commercial mission of the Portuguese in West Central Africa narrowed to obtaining an ever-increasing supply of slaves for export to Brazil that left Kongo in a weakened state. Adrian Hastings concludes that by the late 1500s what Portugal delivered "was little more than a few half-ruined church buildings, the absurd importation of titles [and] Western finery . . . , and, principally, a host of unruly slave-traders."[24]

Was Kongo's experience with a European alliance a failure? Kongo's rulers didn't think so. Instead, as Portugal proved an unreliable ally, they turned to other Europeans for religious and political support. One thrust of their diplomacy was to establish direct relations with the pope. Henry's visit to Rome in 1514 had made no permanent impression on the papacy, and Afonso's embassies to Rome after the death of Henry in 1535 failed to secure the appointment of a new bishop who would shield his Christians from the control of the Portuguese bishop on São Tomé. In 1583 Manikongo Álvaro I dispatched a Portuguese named Duarte Lopes to Rome, who, after many misadventures, made it to Rome. There he told the astonishing story of this new Christian kingdom to Filippo Pigafetta, whose book about the unknown Christians of Kongo, published in 1591, galvanized Rome and other religious leaders to action.

Another Kongo embassy was sent to Rome in 1606, led by a Kongolese nobleman named Antonio Manuel Marchio, who was the Mani Vunda, the most powerful religious official after the manikongo both in the old religion and in Christian Kongo. After arduous voyages that took him first to Brazil and then back across the Atlantic to Lisbon, the Mani Vunda reached Madrid and, gravely ill, finally made it to Rome on January 5, 1608. One may well imagine the impression created by the arrival of this African prince on the eve of the Epiphany, a feast that for more than a century in the Latin West had commemorated the visit of a black king to the Christ child. Perhaps this dramatic coincidence and the fact that the Mani Vunda died immediately after receiving a visit from Pope Paul V served to magnify this extraordinary visit, which was commemorated in the frescos of the Vatican Library. Catholic missions over the next two centuries were sporadic, but Christianity survived at the Kongo court. The early nineteenth century even opened with another Christian manikongo sending a son named Afonso to Portugal to be trained for the priesthood, echoing events of three hundred years earlier. Christianity survived, as it did in Warri, even if it did not prosper.[25]

Paralleling this religious diplomacy was a search for political allies to help defend the Kongo from the growing Portuguese presence in the region. Throughout the early seventeenth century Kongo kings courted the Dutch, whom Manikongo Pedro II promised gold, copper, and ivory for their aid. His successor, Garcia II, had to deal with a Dutch occupying force in Luanda that pressured him to convert to Calvinism. Garcia then allied himself with the remarkable Queen Nzinga of the neighboring state of Ndongo against the Dutch and the Portuguese. When the Portuguese regained the upper hand over the Dutch and reoccupied parts of his kingdom, Garcia sought to strengthen his religious position by closely associating himself with the members of a new Capuchin mission that arrived in 1645. These Italian and Spanish monks depended directly on the pope, unlike the Jesuits, who were under the arm of the Portuguese monarch. Garcia even sent two Capuchins to Europe as ambassadors in hopes of countering some Portuguese efforts to unseat him.[26]

Unfortunately for Kongo, Portuguese success in dispelling the Dutch from Angola in 1648 was followed by a rapid deterioration in the kingdom's autonomy. By the 1650s parts of the kingdom were again suffering from the depredations of the overseas slave trade. After Queen Nzinga signed a mutual aid treaty with Luanda in 1656, Garcia had to withstand a Portuguese attack in 1657 alone, and his son and successor, António I, had to go to war in 1665 to halt attempts of local Portuguese to seize the kingdom's copper mines. In the battle King António fielded a Kongo army of 100,000, including 219 mulatto and Portuguese musketeers. Even so, Portuguese forces and their African allies gained the day. The death of António in the war, along with many of the kingdom's nobles, was a severe blow to the kingdom's integrity.[27]

It is too easy to conclude that Kongo was a victim of its European connections. Such a perspective demeans African intelligence and exaggerates European strength. Kongo's rulers had entered into its political, commercial, and cultural relations with Europeans with their eyes open and in pursuit of their own ends. Neither side could have predicted how these relations would work out over time. The Kongolese had immense control over the pace and direction of their transformation, but they could not escape the consequences of their choices or the devastation caused by the Imbangala attacks. Portuguese forces helped save the kingdom and then exploited its weakness. The kings of Portugal became unworthy allies, too focused on a new global empire to continue the mission they had begun and too willing to permit private interests to dominate in West Central Africa. Both sides bear responsibility for their actions, but neither had control of the larger forces at work in these centuries.

SWAHILI AND MUTAPA

On the eastern side of Africa religion and politics moved at a different pace and to different ends. The rulers of the city-states on the Swahili coast who observed the progress of Vasco da Gama's fleet up the coast in 1498 were Muslims, long tied into the rich Muslim-dominated trading system encompassing the Indian Ocean and its many tributary routes. Because this trading area had generally been free of sectarian strife, open to Hindus and Jews as well as Muslims, it is likely that the coastal rulers would not have been hostile to Christian Europeans simply on religious grounds. However, the intrusion of a well-armed Portuguese fleet, on whose sails were emblazoned Crusaders' crosses, certainly suggested that caution would be the wisest course of action. Only the ruler of Malindi, sensing that an alliance with the Portuguese could give him an advantage over the larger rival city of Mombasa, was willing to provide da Gama with a guide to find his way across the sea to India.[28]

Caution turned to apprehension, however, as larger and more aggressive Portuguese expeditions sailed up the Swahili Coast. In July 1505, for example, the ruler of Kilwa, an rich and elegant trading town, witnessed the arrival in his port of a well-armed fleet led by Dom Francisco d'Almeida that announced its presence by discharging "many volleys of artillery." To be sure, these were only blank charges, discharged as a form of greeting but also intended as a display of European power. The next day, Admiral d'Almeida's boat set out from the mother ship, under "a canopy of scarlet silk, with numerous flags bearing his device," and accompanied by "the sounding of trumpets and the booming of artillery, which was discharged from all the ships at the moment of his departure."[29]

When Swahili rulers refused to accede to all their demands, the Portuguese moved from displays of power to acts of conquest. Kilwa was attacked with live ammunition and sacked. Two weeks later, d'Almeida's fleet reached the important city of Mombasa, whose defenders, forewarned of Kilwa's sack, fired their own guns on the Portuguese from a strongpoint overlooking the harbor. But their guns were no match for the Portuguese cannon that, according to an eyewitness, returned the fire "with such intensity that the gunpowder in their strongpoint caught fire." As Mombasa's inhabitants began to flee, the Portuguese force sailed close enough to bombard the town itself and then set it on fire.[30] For the next two hundred years the Portuguese used force to maintain a presence on the Swahili coast as part of their effort to dominate the Indian Ocean trade, but made no move to penetrate the thinly populated hinterland. Their efforts to spread Christianity were minimal and had no lasting effects.

To the south of the Swahili Coast African contacts moved at a slower and less violent pace, as political and religious encounters followed a course similar to those on Atlantic coast. Much of the prosperity of the southern Swahili cities depended on the gold trade from mines south of the Zambezi River. The gold trade naturally attracted Portuguese interest to the Zambezi Valley and, in this region of shifting political power, the non-Muslim African rulers great and small showed interest in the trade, firearms, and the religion brought by the Portuguese. Of all the Portuguese brought, firearms aroused the greatest immediate interest. Early in the sixteenth century, Inhamunda, a chief who was the subject (slave) of the powerful inland ruler known as the mutapa, sought an alliance with Portuguese who were based at the coastal port of Sofala. By this means, he gained their support for his claims to territorial jurisdiction over Sofala's hinterland and was also the first African in the region to secure some firearms of his own. At least partly as the result of his possession of these weapons, Inhamunda was able to increase his political power over the area and loosen his dependence on his overlord, while restricting the power of his erstwhile Portuguese allies.[31]

Aware of Inhamunda's success in using firearms to build an independent base of power, the mutapa remained cool to the Portuguese traders and missionaries who were establishing contact along the Zambezi. So it was not until 1561 that the ruler (and his mother) were persuaded by a Jesuit missionary to accept Christianity. The Portuguese plan of converting the kingdom from the top down quickly came to nothing. Less than two months after his baptism, the mutapa had the Jesuit strangled, apparently on the advice of rival Muslim traders.[32] The Portuguese used his death as a pretext for invading the Mutapa kingdom and attempting to seize the gold mines, but in 1571–1572 the mutapa's armies were able to defeat the Portuguese.

Although the Portuguese could be troublesome meddlers, their firepower made them attractive allies, much as in the kingdom of Kongo. Faced with a rebellion within the royal family, Mutapa Gatsi Rusere (r. 1589–1623) approached the Portuguese traders at fairs on the Zambezi in 1597. A renewed appeal for aid in 1606 brought a response from the Portuguese adventurer Diogo Simões Madeira, who was trading at the Portuguese outpost of Tete on the Zambezi. Madeira offered to provide the mutapa with an army on the condition that the ruler cede his kingdom's gold and silver mines to Madeira (who claimed to be acting on behalf of his "brother-in-arms," the king of Portugal) and agreed to send four of his sons to be educated as Christians. Madeira's Portuguese-led force (with many African soldiers and firearms) was successful in defending the mutapa, while gaining additional power and wealth for Madeira. Fortunately for the mutapa, Madeira's rising power was curtailed by the jealousy of Portuguese rivals in the Zambezi region.

The struggle left the Mutapa state weakened and vulnerable to enemies without and rivalry within. A new ruler, Mutapa Mavura (r. 1629–1652), soon sought additional Portuguese military aid to blunt the claims of rivals for his throne. In return for their aid, Mavura agreed in 1629 to make himself a vassal of the king of Portugal, to give Portuguese traders free movement throughout his state while expelling Muslim traders, and to permit Christian missionaries to preach to his people. Little came of this sweeping proposal, however, as Portugal's Indian Ocean empire by that date was in rapid decline. By 1700, the expansion from the south of the Changamire empire drove the Portuguese from the plateau and ended the existence of the Mutapa state, too. All that remained of Portugal's venture was small community of African and Afro-Portuguese Christians in the Zambezi Valley, whose loyalties to Lisbon were weaker than those of earlier Portuguese adventurers.[33]

ETHIOPIA

In striking contrast to these events was the remarkable success in northeast Africa of the kingdom of Ethiopia's military alliance with Portugal and the prolonged efforts at a reconciliation of Africa's largest community of Christians with European Christianity. As Chapter 1 recounted, the Christian rulers of Ethiopia had been seeking a European ally off and on since the fourteenth century to aid them against sporadic threats from their Muslim neighbors. Contacts with Europe increased significantly during the latter half of the fifteenth century, and in 1508 Empress Eleni, regent for her young grandson, received two new envoys from the king of Portugal seeking Ethiopian help in his struggle with Egypt for control of the Red Sea. In about 1510 Empress Eleni wrote to her "very dear and well-loved brother" suggesting that the two Christian states form an alliance against the Ottoman Empire, whose rising power was threatening Ethiopia. She was particularly interested in Portugal's naval capacity, since Ethiopia had no warships to counter the Turkish and Egyptian fleets. Her messenger Mathew brought as tokens of esteem two tiny crosses said to be made from wood of the cross on which Christ had died, perhaps brought from Jerusalem, where many of the Christian shrines were tended by Ethiopian monks.

By the time Mathew returned with a new Portuguese embassy in 1520, interest in a military alliance had cooled on both sides. The Muslim threat seemed diminished as a result of a successful Ethiopian campaign against the neighboring Muslim state of Adal in 1517 that had led to Ethiopia's occupation of several Red Sea ports. Ethiopian Emperor Lebna Dengel (r. 1508–1540) showed greater interest in modernizing his own weaponry than in importing Portuguese soldiers. He quizzed the Portuguese repeatedly about the arms Portugal had promised to send him, had them put on a show of firepower and swordsmanship, asked about the techniques and resources needed for making gunpowder, mused about his need for artillery, and examined their armor and swords. After years of delays and missed connections, the Portuguese delegates and Ethiopian ambassadors left Ethiopia carrying rich gifts of gold and silver for the king of Portugal. Part of Emperor Lebna Dengel's letter contained a request for a different sort of craftsmen—not gunsmiths, but printers, goldsmiths, and silversmiths to further the kingdom's production of liturgical books. Another section of the letter was critical of Western Europeans' fratricidal wars: "Brother," he wrote to King João III, "I disapprove of the kings of Europe, because though they are Christian they are not of one mind, but make war upon each other all the time. Had I a Christian king for neighbor, I should never quarrel with him."[34]

By the 1530s the emperor again had great need of Christian Europe's weapons and the military skills honed in the Latin West's fratricidal wars. A new Muslim aggressor, the Somali upstart Ahmed ibn Ibrahim, known as Granye ("Lefty"), had reversed Ethiopia's military successes with the aid of Turkish musketeers. By the end of the decade, many churches and monasteries, the repositories of Ethiopia's art and culture, lay in ruins and Emperor Lebna Dengel had been forced to seek refuge in a mountain-top monastery accessible only by a basket-elevator hauled up by ropes. When he died there in 1540, direction of the kingdom's defense passed to his widow, Empress Sabla Wangel.

A few months later, the empress was able to welcome a Portuguese rescue mission of two hundred armed men led by the young Christopher da Gama, the son of the famous explorer. After reaching the Red Sea coast from their Indian enclave of Goa, the Portuguese knights had impetuously set off on a crusade against Granye, only to suffer a devastating defeat that reduced their numbers by half. However much the Ethiopian armies were strengthened by the Portuguese survivors and their artillery, the empress must have wondered if her new allies could be equal to the task. Perhaps Granye's relentless advance might be slowed, but there seemed little chance of defeating his much larger forces, which included Turkish musketeers and artillery. After many narrow escapes, Christopher da Gama and many of his men were indeed taken prisoner in 1542 and tortured to death. Yet by a stroke of extraordinary luck in the final battle in 1543, a lucky shot from a Portuguese musket mortally wounded Granye. Deprived of their brave leader, most of his dispirited force, in the words of the Ethiopian chronicle, "dispersed like smoke and like the cinders of an oven." The Christian allies displayed that curious mixture of religion and military might in the Easter celebrations that followed, as the Portuguese made a merry din with their muskets, captured Turkish artillery, and other specially made gunpowder devices.[35]

The young new Emperor Galawdewos (or Claudius) (r. 1540–1559), to whom it fell to pick up the pieces of shattered Ethiopian empire, proved equal to the task of restoring its political institutions, rebuilding the churches and monasteries, and reconciling with those who had gone over to the Muslim side. But Galawdewos knew he badly needed whatever aid he could get from the Portuguese alliance that had saved his ancient kingdom from extinction. The Portuguese were willing to help, but the price of closer ties was healing the rift between Ethiopian and Latin Christians that dated back to the sixth century. The prevailing good will on both sides made it possible to hope that a formula might be found to resolve the fine points of theology that been the occasion of the split. Because the small Egyptian Christian church to which the Ethiopians had been tied historically was now under the control of the Ottoman Turks, it was consistent with Ethiopia's interests to seek ties to the powerful Latin church, as the Europeans wanted. Yet for these changes to be acceptable to Ethiopia's people, Galawdewos knew that the beloved rituals and thousand-year-old traditions of Ethiopian Christians could not be altered in any hasty or radical way. Like the new Christians in Kongo, he had to find a way to reconcile African and European traditions. He wrote a *Confession of Faith* that eloquently argued that Ethiopian practices such as male circumcision and the avoidance of pork that seemed so strange to the Europeans were simply social customs that should be left to individual choice and not be considered as doctrinal matters.

Would the emperor's unpolemical and tolerant plea find acceptance on the other side? For a time the Latin church also seemed favorable to a conciliatory approach. Catholic scholars had become quite well informed about the Ethiopian church from Ethiopian scholars in residence at the chapel of Saint Stephen in Rome since the 1480s and especially, as Chapter 1 recounted, through important publications under the Ethiopian scholar Tasfa Seyon between 1537 and 1552. The pope placed the delicate task of negotiating the reconciliation in the hands of the talented and well-educated men of a new missionary order, the Society of Jesus (the Jesuits). Shortly before his death in 1556, their founder, Ignatius of Loyola, drew up instructions for the mission in Ethiopia to be undertaken with gentleness and sensitivity. However, this was also the age of the Protestant Reformation in Europe, a conflict that split the Latin church, turned fine points of belief and practice into litmus tests of orthodoxy, and imbued the Roman curia and the Jesuits with the militancy and doctrinal rigidity of the Catholic Counter-Reformation church. Hastings comments, "Strange as it may seem, Galawdewos wrote far more like a modern man than did his Jesuit opponents, gripped as they were by the intransigence characteristic of the Counter-Reformation."[36]

Under Galawdewos negotiations and discussion continued, but Ethiopian Christian leaders held themselves apart from the small Latin church they tolerated in their midst, to which the missionaries, a few Ethiopian converts, and the European soldiers, their Ethiopian wives, and their children adhered. Some of these Latin Christians insisted that for reconciliation to be achieved the Ethiopian church must move closer to Rome, but it is noteworthy that by 1600 many among the Latin Christians were adopting Ethiopian practices such as male circumcision (then forbidden among Latin Christians).

The second Ethiopian ruler who attempted to keep the European connection open was Emperor Susenyos, who reigned from 1607 to 1632. Like his predecessors, Susenyos struggled to find a way to strengthen ties with European Christians so as to gain access to their weaponry and knowledge without forsaking the religious traditions and social practices revered by Ethiopia's large clerical population, the powerful noble landlords, and the common people. It was a delicate task and perhaps an impossible one. Susenyos was vividly aware of the fate of his immediate predecessor, who, having sought to clinch an alliance with Europe by declaring himself a Roman Catholic and imposing Catholic customs on his people, had been quickly overthrown and killed by the opposition he aroused in the Ethiopian clergy and nobility. Susenyos devoted the first part of his reign to war against his fragile kingdom's African and Turkish enemies. His successes gave him the great personal prestige and the strengthened political power he needed to make a second try at securing the European connection. In 1622 he put aside his extra wives and was received into the Catholic church. Was it a sincere conversion? So it seems, yet, like the other African conversions already considered, it was a political decision as well. Susenyos was a practical and determined man *and* was sincere in his beliefs, but it is fair to say that he was led to embrace the Catholic church more to save his kingdom and people than to save his soul. His decision had been influenced by the arguments of his scholarly half-brother Cela Krestos, the more deeply religious of the two, who had already become a Catholic, and by those of the extraordinarily sensitive and skillful Spanish Jesuit, Pedro Paez. Strong popular opposition was predictable, although within the emperor's power to contain. After the head of the Ethiopian church rejected the move, he was replaced by a Catholic patriarch chosen by the king of Spain. The new patriarch's rash decrees that cast all of Ethiopian Christianity in doubt provoked ever more people to rebel. Susenyos canceled some of the more extreme religious decrees and defeated the last of the rebels by 1629. But, worn out by endless opposition, he resigned his throne, issuing a last decree abandoning union with Rome, although he himself remained a faithful Catholic.

Ethiopians danced and rejoiced, chanting that "the sheep of Ethiopia [are] freed from the bad lions of the West [and the] follies of the Church of Rome." Susenyos's son and successor, Fasiladas, soon ordered the Jesuits expelled, and Ethiopian Catholics who refused to accept the old ways were banished or killed. When the Catholic patriarch called for Portuguese military intervention, the breach became impossible to heal, as two Capuchins sent in 1638 found when they were executed along with the last of the Jesuits. For a time the intellectual ties to Europe remained open, as the extraordinary career of the Ethiopian scholar Abba Gregoryos detailed in Chapter 5 exemplifies. But a larger and more secular opening to the West had to wait until after 1850.[37]

CONCLUSION

This chapter has argued that religion and politics were inseparable within African states and in the complex relations between Africans and Europeans to 1650. Some rulers (especially Muslims) had little interest in Christianity, some (such as the oba of Benin and the mutapa) turned quickly away after embracing the faith, and still others (as in Kongo and Warri) clung to the Christian faith under the most trying of circumstances. While it is theoretically possible that a ruler might feign interest in European Christianity merely to gain a political advantage or might embrace the faith with no thought of its political consequences, the cases this chapter have considered suggest that in practice African rulers were more likely to be acting from a mixture of personal beliefs and political motives.

Because of its special circumstances the Ethiopian case is the clearest. There can be no doubt of the rulers' sincere belief in Christianity since their monarchs had been Christians for over a millennium. Nor can one doubt their need of European military aid in the face of their kingdom's impending extinction. Nor do commercial profits add a confusing additional issue. Even so, religious and political motives were intertwined in Ethiopian rulers' embraces of union with Rome and in their decisions to withdraw from that union. If ultimately Ethiopians found a change of jurisdiction and ritual within Christendom impossible, how could other Africans have made the seemingly greater leap from traditional religions (or Islam) to Western Christianity? From their perspective perhaps the simplest answer is that the leap was not so large. African beliefs and religious practices were close enough to those of Iberian Christians to permit mutual understanding and accommodation, syncretism and synthesis, as long as Africans retained control of the transition. Had not Christianity gradually supplanted the practices of older religions in Europe centuries earlier? Misunderstandings were inevitable, as were conflicts over social customs, but this was not a sign of insincerity. Where outside interference was low, as in Kongo and Warri, the experiment with Christianity endured the longest. Yet the "network of Catholic rulers spread all across Africa" in 1600 faded, so that, as Hastings notes, by 1700 the "likelihood of any Catholic presence in black Africa of more than minuscule size had become extremely slight."[38] In the nineteenth century, as Chapter 6 recounts, many Africans were again becoming Christians. The ups and downs do not make the process less interesting.

The political strand of this arrangement is also clear. European military power, especially the new firearms, was everywhere appreciated. The destruction of the Swahili cities showed the power of ship-mounted cannon, but the unilateral use of firearms by Europeans on the Swahili coast was exceptional. Elsewhere, African rulers drew Europeans and their armed forces into local disputes. Away from the shore, European forces lacked the strength to operate independently, while Africans, lacking the ability to acquire many firearms as well as the necessary skills to deploy them, welcomed military alliances with Europeans. The most notable alliances—those that rescued Ethiopia and Kongo—took the form of diplomatic pacts between royal brothers bound by a common Christian faith.

In other cases, Africans hired European-led and European-trained mercenary forces as auxiliaries under circumstances that owed nothing to religion. In January 1568, for example, a Sierra Leone chief made a compact with the English adventurer John Hawkins. The chief welcomed the aid of Hawkins and his force of 120 men in attacking his African neighbors' well-stockaded town of eight thousand inhabitants. In return, he promised Hawkins he might take all the prisoners away as slaves. Besieged by African and European troops on land and bombarded by the English ships from the sea, the town was captured and burned. Presumably well satisfied to be relieved of his enemies, the Sierra Leone chief decamped in the night, taking with him six hundred prisoners that he had promised to Hawkins and leaving Hawkins to contemplate the folly of forty men wounded and six killed in return for the 250 men, women, and children his men had managed to capture themselves during the assault.[39] The Dutch and English who became increasingly dominant in the trade from the mid-seventeenth century showed little or no interest in missionary enterprises, but as Chapter 4 relates, became major arms dealers.

If politics and religion were not inseparable, in most cases it is difficult if not impossible to consider one without taking up the other. Nor can one understand these encounters without paying attention the motives of both Africans and Europeans. The Portuguese refused to sell arms to non-Christians and promoted Catholicism to form political alliances. Africans saw political power tied to both spiritual and military resources and many rulers sought to strengthen their position by spiritual and material means. However, as the next two chapters recount, Africa's commercial relations with Europe would be far more substantial and enduring than the religious and military alliances of these centuries.

Notes

1. Bemoy's activities in Portugal are told in Rui de Pina, *Chronica d'El Rey Dom João II* (c. 1500) in John William Blake, trans and ed., *Europeans in West Africa, 1450–1560* (London: Hakluyt Society, 1942), pp. 80–86; the translation has been corrected at one point. The African circumstances of Bemoy's life are in João da Barros, *Da Asia . . . Primeira decada* (1539) in G. R. Crone, ed. and trans., *The Voyages of Cadamosto and Other Documents on Western Africa in the Second Half of the Fifteenth Century,* (London: Hakluyt Society, 1937), pp. 128–41. Names have been modernized. For a larger discussion of the Portuguese texts and context, see A. Taxeira da Mota, *D. João Bemoim e a Expedição Portuguesa ao Senegal em 1489* (Agrupamento de Estudias de Cartagrafia Antiga, Série Separatas, No. 63; Lisbon: Junta de Investigações do Ultramar, 1971). For Bumi Jeleen and the larger African context, see George E. Brooks, *Landlords and Strangers: Ecology, Society, and Trade in Western Africa, 1000–1630* (Boulder, CO: Westview Press, 1993), p. 134 and passim.

2. Blake, "Introduction," *Europeans in West Africa,* p. 32.

3. In Blake, ed., *Europeans in West Africa,* p. 150. The classic statement of European divine kingship is from Ernst H. Kantorowicz, *The King's Two Bodies: A Study in Medieval Political Theology* (Princeton, NJ: Princeton University Press, 1957).

4. An insightful discussion of African religious change in quite different contexts may be found in John Thornton's *Africa and Africans in the Making of the Atlantic World,* 2d ed. (New York: Cambridge University Press, 1998), pp. 235–71.

5. Al-Bakri, summarized and quoted by Nehemia Levtzion, "The Western Maghrib and Sudan," in *The Cambridge History of Africa,* vol. 3, *from c. 1050 to c. 1600,* ed. Roland Oliver (Cambridge: Cambridge University Press, 1977), p. 389.

6. Adrian Hastings, *The Church in Africa 1450–1950* (Oxford: Clarendon Press, 1994), p. 308.

7. Ibid., p. 74. See also Richard Gray, *Black Christians and White Missionaries* (New Haven, CT: Yale University Press, 1990), pp. 1–10.

8. Robin Horton, *Patterns of Thought in Africa and the West: Essays on Magic, Religion and Science* (Cambridge: Cambridge University Press, 1993), pp. 155ff. In too many places to acknowledge conveniently, Horton's thoughtful and elegant essays have shaped this analysis, but he cannot be held responsible for efforts to apply his insights to an earlier historical period.

9. Olaudah Equiano, *The Interesting Narrative and Other Writings,* ed. Vincent Carretta (New York: Penguin, 1995), p. 92. He does not say what part of the Bible he was reading, but if it were a part of the Old Testament, he would not be the only African to find much there in common with customary African beliefs and practices.

10. Horton, *Patterns of Thought,* p. 315.

11. Pina in Blake, ed., *Europeans in West Africa,* pp. 78–79.

12. Egharevba in Thomas Hodgkin, ed., *Nigerian Perspectives,* 2d ed. (London: Oxford University Press, 1975) p. 111.

13. Duarte Pires to King Manuel, Benin, 20 October 1516, in Blake, ed., *Europeans in West Africa,* pp. 123–24. Throughout I have relied on Alan F. C. Ryder, *Benin and the Europeans, 1485–1897* (London: Longmans, 1969), pp. 24–75.

14. "Extracts from the Asia of João de Barros," in *The Voyages of Cadamosto and*

Other Documents on Western Africa in the Second Half of the Fifteenth Century, ed. and trans. G. R. Crone (Hakluyt Society, 1937), pp. 124–25.

15. Ryder, *Benin and the Europeans*, pp. 46–72; the account of the royal burial is in Blake, *Europeans in West Africa*, I:150–51. The identification of the ruling obas is problematic; see R. E. Bradbury, "Chronological Problems in the Study of Benin History," *Journal of the Historical Society of Nigeria* I.4 (1959): 263–87.

16. Ryder, *Benin and the Europeans*, pp. 99–123; A. F. C. Ryder, "Missionary Activity in the Kingdom of Warri to the Early Nineteenth Century," *Journal of the Historical Society of Nigeria* II.1 (1960): 1–26. For other West African Catholic rulers, see Robin Law, "Religion, Trade and Politics on the 'Slave Coast': Roman Catholic Missions in Allada and Whydah in the Seventeenth Century," *Journal of Religion in Africa* 21 (1991): 42–77.

17. John K. Thornton, "The Development of an African Catholic Church in the Kingdom of Kongo, 1491–1750," *Journal of African History* 25 (1984): 148.

18. François Bontinck, "La première 'ambassade' congolaise à Rome (1514)," *Études d'histoire africaine* I (1970): 37–73; Silvio A. Bedini, *The Pope's Elephant* (Nashville, TN: J. S. Sanders & Company, 1998).

19. Hans Werner Debrunner, *Presence and Prestige: Africans in Europe: A History of Africans in Europe before 1918* (Basel: Basler Afrika Bibliographien, 1979), pp. 41–45; A. C. de C. M. Saunders, *A Social History of Black Slaves and Freedmen in Portugal, 1441–1555* (Cambridge: Cambridge University Press, 1982), p. 157.

20. Hastings, *Church in Africa*, pp. 83–84; for a broader discussion, see Thornton, "Development of an African Catholic Church," pp. 147–67.

21. Duarte Pacheco Pereira, *Esmeraldo de Situ Orbus*, trans. and ed. George H. T. Kimble (London: Hakluyt Society, 1937), p. 144.

22. Quotes from Davidson, ed., *African Civilization Revisited* (Trenton, NJ: Africa World Press, 1991), pp. 223–24. This section depends on David Birmingham, *Trade and Conflict in Angola* (Oxford: Clarendon Press, 1966), pp. 21–25.

23. Jan Vansina, *Kingdoms of the Savanna* (Madison: University of Wisconsin Press, 1966), pp. 61–63; Thornton, "Development of an African Catholic Church," pp. 158–59; Anne Hilton, *The Kingdom of Kongo* (Oxford: Clarendon Press, 1985), pp. 61ff.

24. Hastings, *Church in Africa*, p. 86.

25. Hilton, *Kingdom of Kongo*, pp. 69–74; Debrunner, *Presence and Prestige*, pp. 46–47; Hastings, *Church in Africa*, pp. 126–27, 94–102, 194–96.

26. Hilton, *Kingdom of Kongo*, pp. 142–61.

27. Ibid., pp. 162–79.

28. David Northrup, "Vasco da Gama and Africa," *Journal of World History* 9 (1998): 194–95.

29. From d'Almeda's account in G. S. P. Freeman-Grenville, ed., *The East African Coast: Select Documents from the First to the Earlier Nineteenth Century* (Oxford: Clarendon Press, 1962), pp. 80–82.

30. Account of Hans Mayr in Freeman-Grenville, *East African Coast*, pp. 108–110.

31. M. D. D. Newitt, *Portuguese Settlement on the Zambezi: Exploration, Land Tenure and Colonial Rule in East Africa* (London: Longman, 1973), pp. 33, 36.

32. Hastings, *Church in Africa*, pp. 78–79.

33. Newitt, *Portuguese Settlement*, pp. 41–59, 119–20; cf. Allen Isaacman, *Mozambique: The Africanization of a European Institution, the Zambezi Prazos, 1750–1902* (Madison: University of Wisconsin Press, 1972), pp. 3–16; Shula Marks and Richard Gray "Southern Africa and Madagascar," in *The Cambridge History of Africa*, vol. 4: *from c. 1600 to c. 1790*, ed. Richard Gray (Cambridge: Cambridge University Press, 1975), pp. 385–93.

34. Elaine Sanceau, *The Land of Prester John: A Chronicle of Portuguese Exploration* (New York: Alfred A. Knopf, 1944), pp. 20–102; Francisco Alvares, *The Prester John of the Indies: A True Relation of the Lands of Prester John, Being a Narrative of the Portuguese Embassy to Ethiopia in 1520*, trans. Lord Stanley of Alderley (1881), ed. C. F. Beckingham and G. W. B. Huntingford (London: Hakluyt Society, 1961), pp. 288–89.

35. Sanceau, *Land of Prester John*, pp. 105–62; Tadesse Tamrat, "Ethiopia, the Red Sea and the Horn," in *The Cambridge History of Africa*, vol. 3, *from c. 1050 to c. 1600*, ed. Roland Oliver (Cambridge: Cambridge University Press, 1977), pp. 177–82.

36. Hastings, *Church in Africa*, pp. 139–143, quote 144.

37. Ibid., pp. 148–161.

38. Ibid., pp. 127.

39. John Hawkins, "The Third Troublesome Voyage . . . to the Parts of Guinea, and the West Indies, in the Yeers 1567 and 1568," in *The Principal Navigations, Voyages, Traffiques and Discoveries of the English Nation*, ed. Richard Hakluyt (New York: Hakluyt Society, 1928), pp. 53–55.

Suggested Readings

Hastings, Adrian. *The Church in Africa 1450–1950*. Oxford: Clarendon Press, 1994.

Hilton, Anne. *The Kingdom of Kongo*. Oxford: Clarendon Press, 1985.

Horton, Robin. *Patterns of Thought in Africa and the West: Essays on Magic, Religion and Science*. Cambridge: Cambridge University Press, 1993.

Newitt, M. D. D. *Portuguese Settlement on the Zambezi: Exploration, Land Tenure and Colonial Rule in East Africa*. London: Longman, 1973.

Ryder, Alan F. C. *Benin and the Europeans, 1485–1897*. London: Longmans, 1969.

Thornton, John K. "The Development of an African Catholic Church in the Kingdom of Kongo, 1491–1750." *Journal of African History* 25 (1984): 147–67.

THREE

COMMERCE AND CULTURE

In February 1730, an African Muslim cleric dispatched his son, Ayuba Suleiman, to an English ship that had come 110 miles up the Gambia River to trade. The father instructed him "to buy paper, and some other necessities" and sent along two slaves to be exchanged for the purchases. Ayuba Suleiman did not reach an agreement with Captain Pike over the price of the slaves, but instead sold them to Africans south of the river in exchange for some cows. On his way back home, Ayuba Suleiman and his interpreter had the misfortune to be seized by Mandingo brigands and sold into slavery to the very same Captain Pike. The Englishman agreed to release Ayuba if his father would refund his purchase price, but the ship sailed before the ransom arrived. At the end of the voyage, Pike sold Ayuba to a Maryland tobacco cultivator for £45. Ayuba Suleiman's story is remarkable in that he was not only redeemed from a life of slavery but also received with gracious hospitality in England (including a reception by the reigning monarchs) and loaded with rich presents before being returned to his homeland in 1735—all through the aid of some English sympathizers in the Royal African Company who believed his literacy in Arabic and his intelligence might be of use to their commercial ventures.[1]

Despite the exceptional aspects of Ayuba's case, it illustrates some common themes in Africans' commercial and cultural relations with Europeans during the centuries before 1850. First, his life shows how the Atlantic trade was partly driven by African demand for specific goods that European traders made available. Second, it links the external trade in slaves to an existing internal slave trade and to acts of violence used in enslaving people. Third, the twists of Ayuba's fate illustrate how varied Africans' personal relations with Europeans might be: Ayuba was first welcomed as a valued trading partner, then cruelly treated as a commodity, then later feted as an honored guest. Finally, the fate of Ayuba's interpreter, who died in slavery in Maryland despite Ayuba's efforts to free him, suggests the essential importance of cultural and linguistic intermediaries in these contacts and exchanges. To recognize that the Atlantic trade was a partnership—as complex on its African side as on the European—is not, of course, to prejudge the moral debate about which side bore greater responsibility for the slave trade and its terrible consequences. However, paying due attention to both sides of these relations prevents seeing them in stereotyped black/white terms and forces one to look at "gray" areas where interests and even identities blended.

AFRICAN TRADING STRATEGIES

Popular accounts of the Atlantic slave trade most commonly present Africans as victims—and little else. Even African slave traders are usually cast in the role of victims, not eager participants: persons easily duped and deceived by European slavers, naive persons caught up in the vicious machinery of a larger economy they could not begin to comprehend. From this perspective, only Ayuba's tragic enslavement is worthy of regard, not his role as a slave trader. The theme of Africans' deception is even emphasized by as sophisticated a historian of Africa as the late Walter Rodney, who could not resist the cheap shot of insisting that "the majority of the imports were of the worst quality as consumer goods—cheap gin, cheap gunpowder, pots and kettles full of holes, beads, and other assorted rubbish."[2] The widely used textbook by the Ghanaian historian Adu Boahen presents a rather more accurate tally of the goods Africans received—"guns, gunpowder, calico, rum, beads, and iron and copper bars," but still declares categorically, "The slave trade did not confer benefits of any kind on West Africa."[3] Such facile images of African weakness, gullibility, and victimization go hand-in-hand with exaggerated images of European dominance and control. As one modern historian has pointed out, "In the popular impression of the Atlantic slave trade few notions are more fixed than that the trade was immensely profitable [for Europeans]."[4] He might have gone on to explain that the exaggerated image of European profits is so popular precisely because it is the logical complement of the image of African victimization.

As Chapter 5 will recount, African victims in the Atlantic economy were abundant—as were European victims.[5] Nevertheless, most modern historians who have examined the mechanics of Africa's Atlantic exchanges agree that African traders and rulers expected to benefit from these transactions and worked hard to ensure they did.[6] Deceit and trickery were rife on both sides, but Africans who sold slaves were no less successful than their European counterparts in getting exactly what they wanted at an acceptable price. Experienced European traders harbored no doubts about trading skills of the Africans with whom they dealt. Indeed, they regularly complained about the prices they had to pay for each slave or other item, prices that rose more rapidly in Africa than they did in the Americas. It is possible to argue that Europeans got the better of these exchanges—but only in the long time frames used by historians.[7] It is much harder to make a convincing case that either Africans or Europeans believed they had the upper hand in these exchanges in the shorter time frame of individual lives.

Short-term relations, of course, were not static, and there is much value in examining how trading relations evolved over the centuries in different parts of the continent. For example, the Africans on the Gambia River who, we saw in Chapter 1, initially refused to deal with the first Portuguese visitors in the mid-fifteenth century within a year became eager traders with those they at first accused of being man-eating demons. The Gambians offered the Portuguese local weavers' finely made cotton cloths, both plain white and striped in red and blue, along with little gold rings fashioned by their smiths, animals skins prepared by hunters, and a variety of locally grown fruits. Given that Gambians had long experience in regional trading networks that were linked to long-distance routes across the Sahara, it is surprising that the Portuguese reported they were willing to accept "objects of little worth" in return. Perhaps the Gambians deliberately sold their goods cheaply just to get a good look at the curious strangers or expected that a first-time bargain would ensure many return visits. One can't be sure of their secondary motives, but the Africans' willingness to sell attractive merchandise for low prices can also be understood in terms familiar to any economist: Each side placed a higher value on the rare items they were receiving than on the familiar goods they were selling. For example, the Portuguese were delighted to buy an ounce of a musky fluid from scent glands of the civet cat for only forty to fifty small coins, since civet was highly valuable in Europe, where it was used as a fixative in perfume, but it was neither rare nor so highly valued in this corner of Africa. How subjective commercial values could be is also revealed by the contradictory statement of an early European concerning another people on the Gambia in 1456: "Gold is much prized among them, in my opinion, more than by us, for they regard it as very precious: nevertheless they traded it cheaply, taking in exchange articles of little value in our eyes."[8] Regular participation in the Atlantic economy would do much to bring African valuations into line with those in global markets, but the difference in values from one place to another was the engine drove overseas trade.

One hundred eighty years later and 4,000 miles to the southwest, another body of Africans traded valued goods for what a superficial observer might reasonably consider trinkets. In June 1635 some Portuguese were shipwrecked along an isolated stretch of Natal, whose coastal inhabitants, they believed, lived "in extreme poverty and wretchedness" compared to the more affluent Africans further inland. After gazing in wonder at the jumble of items these strangers had salvaged from their wrecked vessel, the Africans bartered sour milk and grain for some old nails, which on this iron-poor coast were seen as valuable. When the shipwrecked Portuguese ran out of nails, they offered large ornate keys in exchange, objects that brought forth whistles of appreciation from the African women, who saw the keys' decorative possibilities as body ornaments. The next day, some Africans acquired more substantial items, "a knife, a copper pot, and a pewter vessel," when they waylaid and killed a Portuguese youth sent to fetch water from their brook. A fleet-footed African man was even able to snatch a large iron cauldron, which the Portuguese had placed in the stream as bait, before those waiting in ambush could get off a shot. Later, some Africans scavenged other treasures that the departing Portuguese had to leave behind: a portable writing desk, a keg of musket-balls and powder, and a ship's anchor that the Portuguese had buried in hopes of being able to retrieve it later.[9]

Both of these examples demonstrate that Africans had considerable interest in acquiring all sorts of goods in their early contacts with Europeans, by trade or other means, even though their appreciation of the value of such goods in the world market was still limited. However, naive and impulsive bartering declined once trade with Europe became regular. Instead, as the volume of the Atlantic trade grew, sophisticated professionals on both sides calculated market exchanges closely. On the European side, large trading companies with shareholders and annual dividends replaced passing expeditions or bands of castaways. Coastal Africans became equally adept both in discerning the quality and value of the goods Europeans offered for sale and in developing their own sophisticated techniques for maintaining their bargaining strength. Europeans dominated the long sea routes that tied the continents into a new global economy, but Africans remained dominant over the land and resources of their continent.

From an early date, African rulers played a central role in regulating trade and determining fair prices. The great kingdoms of Benin and Kongo, whose cultural and political relations with Europeans were examined in earlier chapters, illustrate the first phase of these relations in the last quarter of the fifteenth century. Rulers in both kingdoms actively encouraged trade and tried to monopolize the profits from it. The oba of Benin established special markets for overseas visitors, which they had to open and close with costly presents. At first most of Benin's exports consisted of pepper, ivory, cloth, and beads, but Portuguese demand for slaves for sugar plantations on the island of São Tomé led the oba in 1516 to create separate markets for male and for females slaves (each requiring separate presents to open and close). The Benin rulers adopted similar controls when they established trade with other Europeans later in the century.[10]

While the oba of Benin remained in control of the monopoly and effectively used his power to regulate the trade's volume and content, this was not true of the king of Kongo, whose kingdom produced little that Europeans wanted besides slaves and whose control was less absolute. As we saw in Chapter 2, King Afonso was soon lamenting the destructiveness of the slave trade as it slipped from his control. His letters to his royal brother, the king of Portugal, in 1526 seeking aid in ending the slave trade are poignant, but that was not his final position. Although Afonso's pleas failed to change of Portuguese policy, the destructive effects of the slave trade within his kingdom soon abated for other reasons. First, Afonso's wars with the neighboring kingdom of Tio generated a ready supply of *foreign* captives to be sold abroad. Then Tio itself began to sell slaves it obtained from still further inland at such low prices that the kidnapping of slaves within Kongo that Afonso had complained about largely ceased. No longer suffering the loss of his own citizens, Afonso came to regard the trade that passed through his capital as beneficial, since it employed Kongo middlemen and required purchases of the nzimbu shells that were Kongo's currency. In these changed circumstances Afonso wrote again to the king of Portugal in 1540 expressing a very positive view of their mutual trade: "[N]o king in all [of coastal western Africa] esteems the Portuguese goods so much or treats the Portuguese so well as we do. We favour their trade, sustain it, open markets, roads and Mpumbu [an area where many slaves were traded]."[11] As this letter's quite different sentiments suggest, the ruling and commercial elites of Africa saw advantages of the trade with Europe that, when properly managed, far outweighed the disadvantages.

In other places, rulers were also quick to use their strengths to promote the overseas trade on terms favorable to themselves. On the Zambezi, for example, at the end of the sixteenth century the Portuguese paid the Mutapa ruler a substantial annual tribute (*curva*) for the privilege of trading, in addition to a 50 percent tax on all imported cloth. The dependant position of the Portuguese there has been called "subordinate symbiosis," since the Portuguese came as suppliants, even prostrating themselves on the ground before the mutapa in order for the mutually beneficial trade to take place.[12] The term effectively describes many other African-European commercial relationships. Each side needed the other to prosper, but for all their superior economic, maritime, military, and organizational resources, Europeans still had to acknowledge and submit to African customs and rulers.

Although the Zambezi continued to be an important source of gold for the Portuguese, the main focus of gold trading was in West Africa. It is there that the evolution of trading relations may most readily be documented. In 1482 the Portuguese crown had obtained the permission of local Africans to establish the trading post it called São Jorge da Mina (Saint George of the Mine) in the center of what was soon known as the Gold Coast. So eager were Africans to buy the goods Europeans brought from Europe, Asia, and other parts of Africa that by the end of the century gold exports from Mina were averaging 20,000 ounces a year.[13]

When he agreed to let the Portuguese erect this trading post, the ruler of this section of the coast had warned that at the first sign of any treachery or deceit he would withdraw his people, depriving the Europeans of the gold they so desired. Because it was important to both sides, most trade on this coast was conducted peacefully, but sometimes trade disputes led not just to boycotts but to violence. The Portuguese had stirred up a bit of trouble in 1482 when they inadvertently trespassed on a sacred site, and in 1598 the Dutch provoked similar reaction by cutting branches in a sacred grove for their May Day celebration. These disputes were readily resolved, but others were more serious. In 1570, when the Portuguese tried to settle a dispute by force, local Africans captured and killed three hundred of their number. Eight years later, a small Portuguese outpost up the coast at Accra was captured and destroyed by local Ga warriors. The more serious conflicts, however, were between European rivals. The Dutch finally unseated the Portuguese from their Gold Coast headquarters in 1637 and took over the fortress whose name in the meantime had been transmuted to Elmina.[14]

During the seventeenth century, trade on the Gold Coast grew larger and more complex. The many autonomous African states along the coast entered into trading relations with one or another of the growing number of European trading companies that flocked to these shores. According to a Dutch source, these small states were "indescribably envious of each other" and competed vigorously to establish a favorable and profitable relationship with the Dutch. The equally fractious European trading companies negotiated with different coastal authorities to erect a series of trading posts or "factories," some grandly styled "castles." By 1700 some twenty-five major factories and a similar number of smaller trading posts belonging to Portuguese, Dutch, English, Danish, Swedish, and German trading companies lined the 250-mile coast.[15]

The coastal Africans who welcomed the trade had little reason to fear European conquest and dominance. As has often been pointed out, the cannon on the walls of these forts pointed outward to the sea to defend against attacks by European rivals, not inward against the African partners. In reality, the European factories were more joint African-European ventures than outposts of European power, since the Europeans owed rents to the local rulers and employed scores of individual Africans as brokers, interpreters, porters, and (on occasion) priests to carry out the trade.

As the trade grew, African merchants became even more skillful in defending their interests. Whereas it had once been possible to pass off imperfect goods, seventeenth-century European accounts lamented, African buyers now scrutinized linens for flaws, basins for holes, and knives for rust and counted every bead. A German observer later in the century reported that coastal traders were "careful and crafty" in their dealings, having become so familiar with trade goods that they could readily tell the difference between good quality Dutch or Indian textiles and the cheaper imitations made in England and Germany. Not only were the "cautious and wary" Africans now adept at catching any "Christians" who tried to cheat them, he reported, but these "heathen" traders had also found ingenious ways to adulterate their gold so as to cheat the European buyers. He noted with regret how much the Europeans' bargaining position had weakened since earlier in the century: Africans no longer permitted adulterated gold to be seized and the cheaters punished, and European agreements to fix their prices had been undercut by the growing competition for African business among different European companies and private traders, each wooing the African traders with "sweet words and presents."[16]

Many talented Africans from outside the ruling class found opportunities to enrich themselves from the growing trade with Europe. One example from the seventeenth-century Gold Coast is Quacounoe Abracon (as the English spelled his name), who from 1681 to about 1683 functioned as the Royal African Company's chief broker at their Little Komenda "factory" and represented the company in its dealings with the ruling officials of

Little Komenda. Styled a "captain" (headman), he may have come from a chiefly (*ofahene*) family, but his success was the result of hard work and talent. In addition to his personal trading profits, he received an annual stipend of three ounces in gold, plus commissions on sales for the company that may have earned him forty ounces of gold a year—enough to make him a wealthy man. Abracon was not alone. Other Africans skillfully played the different European companies against each other. Another Komenda trader, John Kabes, used the Dutch-English rivalry to his advantage from about 1688 until his death in 1722. During much of that time he ruled his own settlement. A measure of his importance is that three different English agents were removed by the company for failing to stay on good terms with him. Up the coast at Cape Coast Castle, a Eurafrican, Edward Barter, was doing much the same.[17]

THE EIGHTEENTH CENTURY

By 1700, Africa's commercial relations with Europe were undergoing major changes. Most notable was the rapid increase in the volume and value of the Atlantic trade, which rose almost sixfold between the 1680s and the 1780s. The growth came primarily from the slave trade, which for the first time surpassed gold, ivory, and all other African commodity exports combined in value.[18] Not surprisingly, the expanded scale of trade was accompanied by changes in its structure. On the European side, the chartered national monopoly companies slid into bankruptcy, saddled with high fixed costs and inefficient practices. England's Royal African Company (RAC), for example, lost its official monopoly in 1698. Although the RAC and the chartered companies of other nations continued to function well into the eighteenth century, private traders and partnerships dominated maritime commerce with Africa. In this increasingly competitive environment the British were able to expand their already strong trading position because of two advantageous sources of trade goods for Africa. One was a strong overseas connection with India for cotton textiles, and the other was Britain's highly productive domestic smelters and armorers, who could supply Africans with great quantities of low cost iron, guns, and gunpowder.[19] In contrast to the increasing competitiveness among Europeans, the most notable change on the African side was growing centralization of the trade. Powerful new kingdoms of Asante behind the Gold Coast and of Dahomey on the western Slave Coast effectively manipulated the operation and the terms of the trade, while other expanding African kingdoms exerted growing influence over the Atlantic trade of the Angolan hinterland. States were not the only source of greater African strength. In the densely populated hinterland of the Bight of Biafra east of the Niger, the Aro trading community dominated a more centralized market network that managed the rising volume of external trade.

The sharply increased demand for African slaves, the rising competition among Europeans, and the growing centralization of African ties to the Atlantic trade all served to strengthen African trading positions.[20] As the terms of trade shifted steadily in their favor, African traders received goods for each slave worth three or four times as much in 1800 as a century earlier. In addition, African rulers who were best able to satisfy the demand for slaves were also able to increase the port charges, customary gifts, and other fees they demanded from each ship. These developments were evident on all of the main eighteenth-century trading coasts.

The shore between the Gold Coast and the Niger Delta became known as Slave Coast, for it was the premier source of slaves in West Africa in the early eighteenth century. According to a Dutch agent in 1700, Whydah's then independent ruler was powerful enough to exact from each European slaver a customs duty (or *comey*) of "about 100 pounds in Guinea value" (the value of about ten slaves) to open the market and required them to purchase his own slaves at a premium price before he would let them begin general trading with his subjects.[21] Two decades later, when Whydah had become the greatest trading port along the West African coast, visited by forty to fifty ships a year, the *comey* had been refined to give the king the value of twenty slaves per ship, first refusal on all goods, and the right to sell his own slaves at a premium.[22] A great many of the slaves that were marketed through the important port of Whydah and its rival Allada were the products of wars associated with the rise of the inland kingdom of Dahomey, which then turned its attention to controlling the coastal ports. However, the conquest of Whydah and Allada by Dahomey's King Agaja (ca. 1716–1740) was challenged by punishing annual cavalry invasions by the much larger inland kingdom of Oyo, Whydah's protector. As the next chapter recounts, the power struggle ended with Dahomey independent but tributary to Oyo and serving as the conduit to the coast of the captives from Oyo's wars. For the Europeans the stabilization of Dahomey ensured a rising number of slaves during the second half of the century, but they also had to deal with a more powerful state. By 1800 the *comey* that the captain of a large ship had to pay for the right to trade had increased to the value of twenty-one slaves.[23]

At the eastern end of the Slave Coast, the eighteenth-century rulers of Benin continued to exercise a monopoly over the trade and its profits. The Dutch West India Company's agent in Benin wrote a long letter in 1724 complaining how difficult it was to conduct the trade there, partly because of rising prices and competition from the English, but notably because of African resoluteness:

> ... [T]he natives here so carefully regulated the trade at the time the factory was established, that it is now impossible to move them to pay more for the merchandise. For if I tell them that the merchandise now costs more [in Europe], they answer me that it does not concern them, that they concluded the trade on those terms at the time, and that they will now continue to trade in the same manner. They say too that they would rather do no trade than to be forced to abandon their old rights and customs.[24]

For these reasons the Dutch soon withdrew from Benin, but the French, English, and other Europeans continued to frequent the Benin River despite a system in which royal officials unilaterally set the value of all imported goods and exports. State control may have been the reason why the prices for slaves rose only moderately in Benin in contrast to other ports during the eighteenth century, but the benefit for Europeans was offset by sky-rocketing "customs" duties to the oba and senior palace officials. One captain in 1778 had to pay goods equivalent of 150 slaves over and above the purchase price of his cargo of 410 slaves and some ivory. Little wonder that this period is remembered in the kingdom's histories as a time of particular prosperity, even if only a small part of the kingdom's wealth came from its revenues from the Atlantic trade.[25]

Benin's overseas trade was modest in the eighteenth century compared to its tremendous growth in the eastern Niger Delta. The much smaller city-states there were still able to regulate commerce and increase the charges paid by all European ships for the right to trade, much as in Benin and Whydah. In June 1699, for example, the merchant known as Captain Pepple of Bonny, a brother of that city-state's king, politely declined a visiting French trader's initial offer for the purchase of slaves. Characterized by the French as "a sharp blade, and a mighty talking Black," Captain Pepple fulsomely proclaimed his "great esteem and regard for the Whites, who had much enriched him by trade." Such esteem did nothing to diminish Pepple's hard bargaining over the prices to be paid for slaves and provisions, the goods that would be accepted, and the valuation placed on such imports in the local currency of iron bars. In addition, Pepple and several other Bonny notables each demanded and received presents of "two fire-locks, eight hats, nine narrow Guinea stuffs," as well as other "dashes," on top of which the Europeans also had to make loans to the king of Bonny and his principal men in goods to a total value of three hundred iron bars (about £40).[26] In the late eighteenth century, when the Bight of Biafra became the center of the West African slave trade and Bonny its premier port, the *comey* being charged at Bonny had risen to £150 and as much as £250 at the port of Old Calabar to the east.[27]

South of the equator, Angola and other parts of West Central Africa was another major trading area responsible for the sale of over two million slaves during the eighteenth century. As in the Bight of Biafra, merchant princes in the small coastal states north of the Congo River were linked to autonomous inland trading networks, but trade along the Angolan coast from Luanda southward was under the control of the Portuguese. Not just a coastal toehold like the factories of the Gold Coast, this substantial colony exercised a measure of control some two hundred miles inland to a string of forts defending the colony's frontier. Although the degree of European occupation in Angola far exceeded any trading coast to the north, African trading partners still played a substantial role. Some of these were the wealthy women of Luanda and the itinerant peddlers known as *pombeiros* who hawked imported goods on behalf of the big Portuguese merchants in the small markets for slaves, whose position is described later in this chapter.

The most important partners in the eighteenth century, however, were Africans outside the colony: the independent African kings of Kasanje, of the Lunda empire in the middle of the continent, and of the Ovimbundu kingdoms to the south, whose wars produced captives for sale, and the coalitions of African entrepreneurs who organized the trade in slaves and ivory across an area the size of Western Europe. Expanding African states contributed their prisoners of war, dependants culled from subservient populations, as well as refugees of periodic droughts that ravaged the southern part of the region. Like the traders of the hinterland of the Bight of Biafra, but on a much larger scale, various African trading communities guided inland the caravans of goods financed by European capital and shepherded the caravans of slaves and ivory to the coast through networks of allies strategically placed along routes that stretched for hundreds of miles. As the slave exports of West Central Africa rose in the eighteenth century to as many as 40,000 a year during the great droughts of the 1780s and 1790s, prices also moved generally higher, doubling in the 1750s and increasing again in the 1770s. While exempt from the hefty customs duties of West African ports, Portuguese merchants had to advance great quantities of goods on credit to regional rulers and heads of trading communities to secure access to the scarce and expensive captives. Because much of this credit was never recovered, it constituted in effect a tribute payment similar to the West African *comey*.[28]

Despite the many variations from coast to coast, it seems possible to conclude that during the eighteenth century African kings and merchants not only took the expansion of the Atlantic trade in stride but actually increased both their degree of control and their share of the trade's financial rewards. The cost and benefits for more ordinary coastal Africans and for inland African communities will be examined in the next chapter. But before leaving the trading ports it is worthwhile to examine the cultural changes resulting from these commercial relations.

LANGUAGE, TRADE, AND CULTURE

The potential for misunderstanding and conflict is great when members of different cultures meet. As African contacts with Europeans multiplied, both sides needed to be able to communicate effectively if they were to succeed commercially. As in other parts of the world, some individuals became linguistic and cultural brokers.[29] In every era and on every coast it was Africans, not Europeans, who took the lead as translators and culture brokers. Although during the earliest decades of contact some Africans were coerced into the role of intermediaries, the speed with which this became a voluntary choice is indicative of the Africans' commitment to expanding their participation in the Atlantic trade.

A royal standing order instructed Portuguese explorers encountering an unknown African language to persuade a native speaker to come back with them or, failing that, to take one captive. The important expedition of 1455 carried several such African interpreters, who had been acquired on earlier voyages and trained in Portuguese speech and customs. Encountering a new African language area sixteen miles beyond Cape Mesurado, the expedition took a captive, who was transported back to Lisbon where they located an African woman who shared a language with him to interrogate him about his country. In this case, after some months the captive was returned home with rich presents as a good-will gesture. Some captive linguists were given their freedom after making four voyages, but many others remained permanently attached to the Portuguese explorers' retinues. A few were killed by hostile Africans. The forced recruitment of interpreters continued into the seventeenth century, at least informally, since in 1614 a Dutch trader along the Cameroon coast purchased four handsome young boys, who at the Dutch fort on the Gold Coast soon became fluent in Dutch.[30]

Once Africans saw what they might gain, they were quick to seize the initiative in learning European languages and national traits. Large numbers of coastal African rulers and traders became conversant in Portuguese and then in other European languages. As we saw in Chapter 2, the king of Benin surprised the first English visitors to his kingdom by speaking Portuguese, a language the king "had learned as a child." In 1614 the African ruler at Cape Mount on the upper Guinea coast was able to speak French, while his wife "spoke good Dutch," which she had learned while the companion to a Dutch factor. A ruler in Sierra Leone in 1666 entertained a French explorer in Portuguese. Later, after the visitor proposed a toast to the health of one of his son's wives, the lady answered in French, "Monsieur, je vous remercie" and told him afterwards, in Portuguese, that from experience she could easily pick out the French members of his party by their manners. Indeed, the Frenchman noted, most of the inhabitants could "speak a kind of corrupt Portugais." An early German visitor to the Windward Coast of West Africa had similar experiences. At Cape Mesurado in 1682 he conversed in a simplified Portuguese. Further south at Rio Cestos, the African king was able to greet him in a smattering of German, mixed with Portuguese, while the ruler's interpreter delivered what the German visitor sarcastically called "an elegant speech" in German. Even if the German was as fractured as the segment they recorded, it is noteworthy that an African even in less frequented coastal area could converse in a variety of European languages.[31]

When the linguistically adept Dutch displaced the Portuguese as the main European traders in the seventeenth century, African linguists continued to play the dominate role in cross-cultural relations. The pioneering Dutch settlement at the Cape of Good Hope, founded in 1652, was entirely dependent on the local Khoikhoi. As historian Richard Elphick points out, "The Dutch presence was a superb opportunity, not only for Khoikhoi tribes, but also for individual Khoikhoi who had the wit to seize it." Khoikhoi clever enough to become interpreters of local languages and customs for the Dutch were prominent among those turning the encounter to their advantage. One of the first was Haddot, known as "Harry." A member of an impoverished, cattleless Khoikhoi group on the Cape Peninsula, Harry recognized the opportunity for personal advancement presented by the growing European visits to the Cape. In the early 1630s he picked up a working knowledge of English while accompanying an English ship to Java. Harry and his helpers operated a kind of postal service for the English and Dutch, passing along letters from ship to ship, in the 1630s on Robben Island and then on the mainland. After the Dutch set up a permanent outpost at the Cape in 1652, Harry (still using English) became their chief interpreter.[32]

Harry's niece, Krotoa (ca. 1642–1674), known as Eva, followed in his footsteps. Employed as a servant by the head of the Dutch settlement, Eva was soon fluent in Dutch and later gained a working knowledge of Portuguese. Her role as interpreter was crucial for Khoikhoi negotiating with the Dutch, and vice versa. By the age of fifteen Eva had a comfortable familiarity with Dutch culture, wore their clothes (brought from India), was fond of their food, and had become the first native South African Christian. Yet she also maintained her Khoikhoi identity and when she entered puberty she absented herself from the Dutch settlement to undergo traditional rituals associated with becoming an adult woman. Her cultural duality was not duplicity. Bilingual and bicultural, Eva sought to harmonize her worlds, sharing her Christian experiences with her Khoikhoi relatives and changing her clothing to suit her situation.[33]

Eva was fully fluent in Dutch but, as the earlier references to corrupt or simplified Portuguese suggest, the trading languages that came into most regular use along coastal West Africa were "pidgins," rather than standard European languages. The vocabulary of these simplified languages was derived from European languages, but their underlying grammar reflected the constructions of African languages. From the sixteenth century a Portuguese-based pidgin was used along the coast and many Portuguese words and names crept into local usage. For example, Africans told an English visitor to the San Vincent river in 1555 that their word for peppercorn was *manegete* (apparently from the Portuguese *malaguetta*) and that their chief was named Diago (a variant of the Portuguese Diogo or James). Along the Gold Coast the Portuguese words were more numerous, such as the *bassina* for basin (Portuguese *bacia*).[34] As British traders assumed the leading position in Atlantic trade in the eighteenth century, a new trading pidgin using English words came into widespread use in West Africa, although the Dutch, Portuguese, and French languages remained important in particular parts of Africa. Although pidgin English was primarily an oral language, Antera Duke, an eighteenth-century trader of Old Calabar, wrote entries in his diary in it. Here is his original entry for March 3, 1787 (whose spelling and punctuation are only slightly more eccentric than those of some contemporary English traders), along with a modern rendering:

about 5 wee go on bord Captin Fairwether for tak Ephrim aqua & Ephrim
coomy and Coffee & Arshbong coomy and we com ashor with all captin so
everry ship firs guns so one great guns com up and cut one Captin Tatam
whit men head off [About 5 a.m. we went on board Captain Fairweather's
ship to take *comey* for Ephraim Aqua and Ephraim, and *comey* for Coffee and
Archibong, and we came ashore with all the Captains. Then every ship fired
its guns. One great gun came up and cut off the head of one of Captain Tatam's
white men.][35]

Antera Duke must have had quite personal reasons for keeping a written
diary, for, as many visitors to the coast reported, African traders appeared
to have no problem keeping track of complicated business deals in their
heads. For example, John Africa, a prominent trader in Bonny in the last
third of the eighteenth century who had been several times to England, was
reported to have "an extraordinary memory," able to keep in his head accounts of his dealings with fourteen or fifteen vessels and "tell to a bunch
of beads the exact state of each account when he came to settle it, although
he could neither read not write."[36]

African rulers up and down the coast designated important officials to
take charge of dealings with Europeans. For example, the post of Yevogan,
or "Chief of the White Men," in Whydah by the 1720s had developed into
three separate offices, one for the French, one for the English, and one for
the Portuguese. Dahomey later had six such "Captains of Trade."[37] Such
officials were charged with conducting royal trade, but they and their assistants also functioned as linguistic and cultural brokers. European trading
companies also employed Africans to conduct their business transactions,
and rather more is known about how these brokers functioned. In the European commercial enclaves on the Gold Coast, for example, the official
"linguist" was a key African employee. Linguists had to be skilled in both
European and African languages, but they were more than translators. In
delicate negotiation with African rulers they were virtual diplomats and
were accordingly well compensated.

In the early years linguists picked up their knowledge of language informally, but, as trade grew, the practice of Africans attending formal classes in schools both in Europe and in Africa that had begun with the early
Portuguese gained renewed attraction—this time primarily in English. In
1694, the Royal African Company provided a schoolmaster for the African
and Eurafrican children living around Cape Coast Castle, who opened what
is likely the first English-medium school in sub-Saharan Africa. Britain's
first missionary to West Africa established another school at Cape Coast in
1752 at the request of the Castle linguist, Cudjo Caboceer. Among its first
pupils was Philip Quaque, who two years later at the age of thirteen went
to England, where he received an education that led to his ordination as a
priest in the Anglican church. In 1765 he returned to Cape Coast with the
double responsibility of being catechist and schoolmaster to the African
population and chaplain to the English traders stationed there.[38] Old Calabar traders also sent some of their sons to England to learn to read and

write English. Long before the establishment of Old Calabar's first mission school in 1846, such European-educated scholars had been tutoring the children of elite families in spoken and written English.[39]

Inevitably, language learning was part of a much more complex cultural encounter. Even among the Portuguese, who were more likely to assimilate African ways than other Europeans, a white person who lived as an African was likely to be disparaged as a backwoodsman (*serantejo*). Other Europeans also saw "going native" as cultural degeneration, but Africans generally saw adopting the trappings of European culture in positive terms, since familiarity with European dress, eating habits, and social graces was as useful in commercial dealings as knowing European languages. A few Africans took pride in their new culture as a way of elevating themselves above their fellows, but for most shifting from African culture to European was as natural as switching languages.

For example, in 1750 William Ansah Sessarakoo returned to home to the Gold Coast after more than a decade in Britain where he had been educated, lavishly entertained, lionized, and received by King George II. He descended from the British warship, H.M.S. *Surprise*, clothed in "a full-dress scarlet suit, with gold lace à la Bourgoyne, point d'Espagne hat, handsome white feather, diamond solitaire buttons, etc.," the consummate English gentleman. But in welcoming his son's return, John Currantee, the chief caboceer at Anomabo, also divested him of his European finery and had him dressed in the traditional Fante mode, "a piece of broad-cloth thrown over the shoulder," marking his return to Africa.[40]

Although language learning and literacy were restricted to commercial matters in most parts of Africa, in some places they opened up far broader possibilities. The letters (in Portuguese) of King Afonso of Kongo cited earlier are an early sixteenth-century example of enthusiasm for European-style correspondence. Afonso also encouraged others to acquire the kind of formal education he had received, sending several students to Portugal for schooling. Under his sixteenth- and seventeenth-century successors, Kongo children attended mission schools in their own capital. By the early seventeenth century Kongo had eight or ten schools, which taught literacy and religious doctrine, along with some Latin and other advanced subjects to the sons and nephews of the capital and provincial elite. Although some religious instruction books were prepared in the Kongo language, literacy in Portuguese was generally more highly regarded. During the sixteenth and seventeenth centuries written records were often used to facilitate the fiscal and legal operations of the Kongo central government and for communication with the provinces as well as with European powers. Kings repeatedly cited written records to disprove false statements in disputes with resident Europeans and to make appeals to Portugal through sympathetic Jesuits or other clerical couriers.[41]

Another example from the same era shows that literacy and the habit of correspondence did not necessarily go hand in hand. In the kingdom of Ethiopia literacy had existed among the upper clergy and some nobility for a millennium before their contacts with the West, but writing had remained very largely confined to liturgical and other ceremonial purposes. According to Francisco Alvares, even among literate people, communications were sent orally by means of messengers, as elsewhere in sub-Saharan Africa. However, inspired by letters from Europe, the Ethiopian elite "began to get the habit of writing" and, he reports, in 1521 the emperor's "clerks never stopped writing the letters we were to carry to the King of Portugal," not only in their own language, but in Arabic and Portuguese as well, using their translations of the Epistles of the New Testament as letterbooks from which to adapt phrases for this new venture.[42]

SEXUAL ENCOUNTERS

Most coastal Africans learned European languages and culture through social and commercial contact with visiting traders. However, for some African women contact with Europeans was on more intimate terms. Some of these sexual encounters were casual and of little historical significance, but many women entered into more lasting relationships and marriages with European men who were long-term residents in Africa. The children of such unions often became important intermediaries in commercial and cultural relations.

Because historical records contain few details of the lives and perspectives of these women, it is useful to begin with one better documented case, even though it is in many ways atypical. This is the life of Eva, the young woman discussed earlier, who served the Dutch at Cape Town as a translator. In 1659 she encountered Pieter van Meerhoff, newly arrived from Copenhagen in the Dutch East India Company's service, who became the love of her life. They embarked on a professional relationship, negotiating good relations for the company with the northern Khoikhoi, and a more intimate one that led to two children by 1663. With Eva's help Pieter became as skilled as she at working cross-culturally. Thus their Christian wedding in 1664, underwritten by the company, may be better seen as a marriage of two kindred spirits than of members of two alien races.

The marriage restored Eva's respectability in the eyes of her two communities and signaled Pieter's rise in the company service. However, their life together ended tragically after less than four years of marriage and three more children, when Pieter was killed on a visit to Mauritius. Following this tragedy, Eva's status as "an acceptable member of European society" declined as she drank heavily and abandoned her children. Her final days were spent in exile on Robben Island, making her a poor model of Afro-European assimilation at the Cape. Yet her daughter, Petronella van Meerhoff, managed a long, successful marriage to a Dutch man. They named one of their eight children Eva.[43]

In the Cape Colony cases like Eva's were confined to the seventeenth century. As the proportion of European women to men rose, marriages and public liaisons with African women could no longer survive the disapproval of European society, although the exploitation of female servants and slaves by rural Dutch males remained common. But elsewhere in Africa European males spending long periods in Africa continued to form liaisons with African women for sexual and social companionship. Europeans living on shore were rarely in a position to mistreat African women under their hosts' protection, except perhaps in the case of women slaves.

In general such liaisons were conducted on terms acceptable to both parties. The Portuguese residents at Elmina took African or Eurafrican mistresses, whom even European rivals conceded they treated very well. According to a Dutch source, such wives "always dress more ostentatiously and stand out more than any other indigenous women . . . ; they also have far more ornaments on their clothes and all over their bodies." Nor were the English any different. At Bence Island in Sierra Leone, for example, the concubines of the Royal African Company governor and of the ship captains were housed adjacent to the official buildings and went around dressed in silk gowns. The concubine of the late governor in 1682 had borne him a son and daughter, both of whom were reported to have long blond hair, which suggests that the mother may have been partly of European descent.[44] The English chief of the Tantumkweri fort on the Gold Coast in about 1770, John Cockburn, had an African wife named Ambah and several children, whom his successor looked after in a fatherly fashion, while Ambah supported herself making *canky* (bread) and renting out her slaves.[45] Frenchmen resident on the Ile Saint-Louis in Senegal also acquired "country wives" from among what one French resident of the 1780s characterized as "sensible, modest, tender, faithful, and particularly handsome" African women of the island, giving rise to a number of mulatto families with European surnames.[46]

If the motives of European men in forming such relations seem obvious, understanding the motives of the African women takes a little more effort. According to European accounts, the women were not coerced into these relationships and at least some African women were genuinely attracted to European men. At the beginning of the seventeenth century, for example, African women on the Gold Coast were said to be sexually aggressive and to "consider themselves lucky if they have had intercourse with a Dutchman—indeed they boast of it to one another," while those at Cape Lopez particularly are said to "like to fornicate with a foreigner, which they consider a great honour, for among them it is not thought shameful at all."[47] A mid-seventeenth-century German parson to the Gold Coast reported disapprovingly, "When a young man comes from Europe, unchaste women soon offer themselves . . . for a small present, even as little as a bottle of brandy. . . . They have intercourse with him so long as he lives in the country . . . and then look round for another."[48] Clearly such women did not share the moral views of this visitor, nor did the Europeans who accepted their favors. As the women in question have left no accounts of their conduct, one can only speculate about their motives. Short-term mercenary considerations are likely to have been important, for the "small presents" were not necessarily insignificant. The gifts might mount up, and the fine clothes and jewelry surely had their attractions.

Yet explaining the women's actions purely on the basis of physical attraction and mercenary considerations is too simple, for it is clear that many were not free agents but were acting at the behest of male superiors. The ruler of Abeni promised to welcome a German trader not only with gifts of "palm wine, fowls, and oxen," but also by placing one of his wives "at the service of your love," a practice the trader noted was quite common, "for they do not make a great fuss about their wives, as we Europeans do."[49] At Cape Lopez and elsewhere it was also the custom for prominent merchants and the local king to loan a visitor one of their many wives for the night. However, such promiscuity was not the norm in Africa. On the Upper Guinea Coast, Portuguese were warned that seducing African women, that is, not first obtaining their male superiors' permission, "is the greatest crime that visitors can commit, in many parts costing them their lives and in other parts their possessions."[50]

If African hospitality extended to catering to the sexual comforts of European guests, an understanding of long-term liaisons between European agents and African women requires placing them in the context of African commercial and communal relations. Marriages were a common way of creating strong ties between two extended families and were regularly used to strengthen commercial and political alliances. In this regard one should recall the marriage proposals by several elite Africans to Iberian rulers recounted in Chapter 1. Thus, in many cases what Europeans termed "country marriages," emphasizing that their significance was confined to the period they spent in country, might better, from the African side, be termed "commercial marriages," emphasizing their role in organizing and regulating the Atlantic trade. Prominent African men arranged such ties between female family members and resident European traders as part of a "landlord-stranger" relationship, a way to welcome the foreigner into the family. On the commercial side of the marriage, the European husband provided trading capital and access to the overseas trading networks, while his wife served as an interpreter of language and customs and provided an entrée to the inland families and trading networks that were also linked to the local chief by marriages.

The status of the women in such marriages is also worth probing. Although in a few cases they were the daughters or sisters of powerful men, such as the well-born African woman who married the French commandant of Gorée in 1758, George Brooks has demonstrated that most such wives in Upper Guinea came from among the slave dependants of African freeborn elite. Since marriage across class lines was rare in this region, this suggests that African elite also considered the Europeans as subordinate dependants, making this a further example of the "subordinate symbiosis" discussed earlier. This view is reinforced by Brooks, who finds that such marriages and any inheritance from them followed African, not European, customs.[51]

If a woman entering into commercial marriages may have been less than a free agent, she would have been aware of the personal profit she might derive from such an arrangement. In the first place, she generally improved her economic status, since the European husband was expected to provide his African wife with housing, clothing, and furnishings that were in keeping with European standards and the tastes of the emerging African elite. Beyond such domestic considerations, Brooks points out, such relationships also "provided unprecedented commercial opportunities for many women." Given the high European death rate in tropical Africa, many African wives were soon widows. With the wealth they inherited from one or more marriages to Europeans many became highly influential "commercial intermediaries and culture-brokers." Termed *signares* in Senegal and *nhara* in Portuguese Guiné, they also profited from their own trade, including ventures that violated European trading company monopolies, which their connections made it hard to prosecute.[52]

Many such women commanded considerable wealth and power at the peaks of their careers. At mid-century *signares* owned most private properties on Gorée; in 1767 the richest of them, Caty Louette, owned sixty-eight domestic slaves. Of government-owned residences, a dozen years later, eleven of eighteen were occupied by *signares*. Something similar was happening in the British trading settlement on the Ile Saint-Louis, taken over by the French in 1779, and in the Portuguese enclaves at Cacheu and Bissau further south, where the son (Honório Pereira Barreto) of one very powerful *nhara*, Rosa de Carvalho Alvarenga, became governor of Portuguese Guiné. Mãe Aurélia Correia, the African wife of a Cape Verdian of Italian and Portuguese descent, managed a considerable estate in Guinea-Bissau in the 1830s and 1840s that included land, cattle, buildings, a schooner, and other goods derived from trading in slaves, salt, and agricultural commodities.[53]

The children of such marriages might inherit the wealth and skills of their parents and, like the European-educated children of African traders, might play important roles as culture brokers. Down the coast from Guiné-Bissau, for example, Betsy Heard, the daughter of an African woman and an English merchant who sent her to England for education, used her considerable talent and inherited wealth to become the major trader in Bereira in the 1790s and 1800s. In the same area, another upwardly mobile woman, Elizabeth Frazer, was the daughter of an African-American settler and one of his African wives. After her marriage, in 1826, to William Skelton, Jr., son of an African mother and an English father, she became wealthy in slave trading in the Rio Nuñez. Another prominent entrepreneuse was Mary Faber, the daughter of African-American settlers and wife of an Anglo-American ship captain.[54]

In some places, the bicultural descendants of such mixed marriages formed distinctive dynasties that were important as power brokers and intermediaries. The well-born African known as "Seniora Doll, Duchess of Sherbro," had two sons by an RAC official, from whom descended the prominent Corker/Caulker family of Sierra Leone.[55] Another enduring lineage were the Brews of the Cold Coast. The eponymous founder of the family, Richard Brew, an Irishman who first came to the Gold Coast in 1745, was stationed at the Fante post of Tantumkweri from 1751 to 1754 and became governor of the new fort at Anomabo from 1756 to 1764. In the early 1750s Brew began a relationship with Effua Ansah, a daughter of John Currantee, the dominant African trader of Anomabo and a brother of "Prince" William Ansah, who after his return from England worked as a clerk and "linguist" at the Anomabu fort. Effua Ansah had two daughters by Richard Brew, who were baptized in 1767 by the Rev. Philip Quaque, another bicultural resident of entirely African descent. While one daughter went by her European name, Eleanor, the other used her Fante name, Amba. It is unclear if Effua Ansah or an earlier Fante country wife was the mother of Richard Brew's older two sons, Richard Junior and Henry ("Harry"). After a period of education in England, Harry Brew married Abba Kaybah, a member of Philip Quaque's family. From the union of these two bicultural families sprang the long prominent Brew family of the Gold Coast. It would appear that Harry subsequently obtained the important position of linguist at Cape Coast Castle through his wife's family connections. It is noteworthy that in this matrilineal area, the Brews preserved their family identity by tracing descent patrilineally.[56]

Similar dynasties also emerged in the Portuguese colonies in southern Africa. In Angola, the Portuguese soldiers brought from São Tomé in 1571 and from Luanda after 1575 to defend the Kongo kingdom from invaders "took Kongo concubines, and they and their mulatto children formed a distinct trading community" known as *pombeiros.*[57] By the early seventeenth century *pombeiro* colonies dominated the trade routes into the interior. In the eighteenth century a second Eurafrican community developed in the port city of Luanda, whose sons controlled most of the political offices and trading positions outside of the city of Luanda and whose daughters regularly entered into marriages with European traders. Catholic rules did not recognize these liaisons, but they had the sanction of "local custom," that is, African traditions that recognized plural marriage and divorce.

For an African or Eurafrican family, marriage to a Portuguese trader was a means of obtaining trade goods, but there were risks. Portuguese husbands often abused these alliances both by taking concubines from among their numerous female slaves and by attempting to use Portuguese law to seize the assets their wives brought into the marriage. Nevertheless, commercial wives and widows became a powerful force in eighteenth-century Angola just as in West Africa. In one Luso-African parish of Luanda in 1773, women owned 68 percent of the enumerated domestic slaves. The proportion of slaves owned by women in the entire city was much lower, but Afro-European women were still a distinguished element of the city. The more successful lived discrete lives of wealth and ease. Indeed as the eighteenth century progressed, Miller concludes, "Commercialization of the slave trade eroded the immigrant [European] male shell of the Luso-African community to expose the Angolan-born women at its heart."[58]

African women also formed relations with the Portuguese *sertanejos* (backwoodsmen) on the Zambezi beginning in the sixteenth century and with the small stream of Portuguese and Goan Indian men who later migrated into the region. The key attraction was the system of quasi-feudal estates along the banks of the Zambezi known as *prazos*, over which Portugal claimed authority. The estates functioned in many ways like African chiefdoms but also were tied to the Portuguese trading empire. The *prazo*-holders intermarried among their own class when possible, but the high mortality among the small number of Europeans (and tiny number of European women) meant that the dominant pattern, in Malyn Newitt's phrasing, was "for the Portuguese men . . . to marry dark-skinned local girls and their children grew up with strong attachments to Africa and only weak and flickering loyalty to Portugal." As elsewhere in Africa, the acclimatized local women tended to outlive their immigrant husbands and become a powerful force in the region. In the eighteenth century, in an effort to lighten and re-Europeanize the population, Portugal even decreed that the *donas* who held *prazos* were to marry only European men.

Yet the preoccupation with "racial" categories that was evident in Portugal and among the European elite on the Zambezi should not obscure underlying cultural realities. Given their blood ties to the African elite and the absence of functioning European schools or Christian churches, Allen Isaacman argues, *prazo* residents lived, thought, and communicated much more in African idioms than in European ones. His rightful emphasis on the "Africanization" of these communities needs to be balanced by an understanding that, for Africans, there was also a meaningful process of "Europeanization" underway. As elsewhere, it was precisely the commitment to maintaining a position in both of those worlds that gave the Eurafrican elite their power. The key to meaningful autonomy was maintaining formal ties to Portugal's shadowy empire while evading its strictures and maintaining even closer terms with local African rulers without slipping too completely under their power. It is instructive of their success in finding a middle way that other Africans tended to refer to these people as *muzumgu* (Europeans), while somewhat later officials in Portugal used precisely the same word to describe them but with a nearly opposite meaning: nominal Christians who lived like Africans. On his explorations up the Zambezi in 1856, David Livingstone described the situation at the half-ruined Portuguese fortress of Sena: The Ngoni "consider the Portuguese a conquered tribe," and, despite official orders to the contrary, the mixed population acknowledged this de facto status by paying the Ngoni tribute.[59]

CONCLUSION

This chapter has argued that anyone seeking to understand Africa's commercial encounters with Europe must put away images of simple-minded Africans being easily duped out of their gold, ivory, and people in exchange for handfuls of trinkets. In reality, as the volume of trade with Europe increased, Africans drew upon their social and political networks to counterbalance the Europeans' organizational advantages. At the personal level, Africans' knowledge of European languages and customs gave them an additional advantage. For European traders, success required accommodating African customs and desires.

Conflict and confrontation, sharp deals and double-dealing were a part of the commercial relations. Just as elsewhere in the world, differences of culture may have made it easier to justify cheating one's trading partners— and certainly made it easier to project invidious stereotypes on them. Thus European accounts are full of denunciations of Africans as thieving, deceitful, and unprincipled. But it is clear that Africans held similar views of European traders—and with equally good reasons. In one case, Africans denounced suppliers of inferior copper rings as white devils; in another, an African accused of dishonesty retorted indignantly, "What! Do you think I am a white man?"[60] But the commercial relationships whose importance grew steadily over several centuries were not (and could not have been) based on such rough extremes. Large-scale trade required partnerships that satisfied both sides most of the time. Two examples from the second half of the eighteenth century may serve to illustrate such partnerships at their best and suggest how sophisticated some Africans had become in their relations with European traders since the fearful and the tentative early contacts recounted at the beginning of the chapter.

The first shows the fondness an African might have for his European trading partner. John Africa was one of the leading traders of eighteenth-century Bonny. He had sailed several times to England and had excellent relations with many English traders. As one of them was preparing to sail away, John Africa went on board the English ship to wish his friend farewell. Then, regaining his canoe, he pushed three ivory tusks weighing at least forty pounds each through the porthole of the captain's cabin and before beating a hasty retreat, called out in pidgin English, "Da something for buy your woman cloth" (roughly, "Here's something to buy your wife a new dress with"). Another Englishman who observed this scene commented that this substantial present was bestowed "in so delicate a manner, as would have done honour to an European of refined sentiment."[61]

The second example shows the high regard two different Europeans had for a successful Sierra Leone trading partner known as Henry (Harry) Tucker. Of mixed descent, Harry had sailed to England, Spain, and Portugal; was fluent in English; and had a so large a family by his several wives and so many domestic slaves that his town was immune to assault by rivals. One Englishman described Tucker as "my friend," a man "with whom I have had the largest connexion in business and by whom I was never deceived." The other echoed that estimation of Tucker's character and highlighted both the commercial and cultural dimensions of his role as middleman:

> This man bears the character of a fair trader among the Europeans, but to the contrary among the blacks . . . almost all [of whom] owe him money, . . . so that he is esteemed and feared by all who have the misfortune to be in his power.

He's a fat man and fair spoken, and lives after the manner of the English, having his house well furnished with English goods and his table tolerably well furnished with the country produce. He dresses gaily and commonly makes use of silver at his table, having a good side board of plate."[62]

Important coastal traders like John Africa and Harry Tucker, who dealt directly with the Europeans, were more profoundly altered than others. Not only did they possess great quantities of imported material goods, but they also adopted European culture and names, although in different degrees. If, as was seen in the previous chapter, African interest in Western Christianity largely failed to endure, European languages or their pidgins became a permanent feature of coastal communities. For a small number of coastal Africans the cultural impact of Europe might be very intense. Linguists needed to understand more than language; successful African merchant princes like Africa and Tucker could set a European table, tell a joke, and understand the Western psyche. African women who became the wives and lovers of resident Europeans often adopted Western dress, manners, speech, and values. For some young Africans the introduction to European culture was more formal. Locally, schools or long residences abroad molded their formative years, sometimes quite profoundly.

Yet it needs to be kept in mind that familiarity with European ways need not necessarily involve a loss of African customs. Most added a second culture the way they learned a second language—without displacing what was already there. Some individuals preferred to mix European and African ways. Harry Tucker furnished his house in an English way but followed African social customs in marrying six or seven wives. A very few, such as Philip Quaque, went further, adopting the dress, beliefs, and mores of Europe, while still choosing to live in Africa. Are such cases to be seen as progress or condemned as corruption? There is room for debate, but modern commentators must be cautious about drowning out the evident if ill-articulated perspectives of those Africans involved with amplified agendas from modern cultural wars. For a variety of reasons, Africans chose to continue and expand the commercial and cultural encounter that Europeans had initiated.

All of this is not to say that in forging commercial ties to Europe Africans always chose wisely or escaped destructive consequences. No one who participated in the export trade in slaves during those centuries could be blind to the sufferings it involved. Both Africans and Europeans hardened themselves to the pain of the trade's victims, and precious few Africans or Europeans before 1800 believed that slavery was morally wrong. Those who were sold away were victims and those that sold them were not—except in one sense: They were at the mercy of their desire for the goods Europeans supplied. To obtain these goods, powerful rulers and their merchant allies were willing to go to great lengths to accommodate their European trading partners. From the perspective of the present, it is easy to question what they did, but it is impossible to read the historical record and deny Africans a powerful role in forging and building these relationships and in thinking that they were the better off because of them. Some broader African perspectives on the Atlantic trade are the subject of the next chapter.

Notes

1. Philip D. Curtin, "Ayuba Suleiman Diallo of Bondu," in *Africa Remembered: Narratives by West Africans from the Era of the Slave Trade*, ed. Philip D. Curtin (Madison: University of Wisconsin Press, 1968), pp. 17–59; Peter Fryer, *Staying Power: The History of Black People in England* (London: Pluto Press, 1984), pp. 421–23.

2. Walter Rodney, *How Europe Underdeveloped Africa* (Washington: Howard University Press, 1982), p. 102.

3. A. Adu Boahen, *Topics in African History* (London: Longman, 1966), pp. 110, 112.

4. James A. Rawley, *The Trans-Atlantic Slave Trade* (New York: W. W. Norton, 1981), p. 261.

5. Philip D. Curtin, *The Atlantic Slave Trade: A Census* (Madison: University of Wisconsin Press, 1969), pp. 282–86, reviews evidence that suggests participation in a tropical African voyage cost the life of one sailor in five and one of every two Europeans sent out to man trading stations in Africa.

6. For example, Joseph E. Inikori and Stanley L. Engerman state, "It is generally agreed that those who raided and took captives, and the African traders who bought and sold captives, all realized private gains," in their "Introduction: Gainers and Losers in the Atlantic Slave Trade," in their jointly edited *The Atlantic Slave Trade: Effects on Economies, Societies, and Peoples in Africa, the Americas, and Europe* (Durham, NC: Duke University Press, 1992), p. 2.

7. For a stimulating overview of this issue, see Frederick Cooper, "Africa and the World Economy," in *Confronting Historical Paradigms*, ed. Frederick Cooper et al. (Madison: University of Wisconsin Press, 1993), pp. 84–201.

8. G. R. Crone, trans. and ed., *The Voyages of Cadamosto and Other Documents on Western Africa in the Second Half of the Fifteenth Century* (London: Hakluyt Society, 1937), pp. 68–69.

9. Jerónimo Lobo, *The Itinerio of Jerónimo Lobo*, trans. Donald M. Lockhart (London: Hakluyt Society, 1984), pp. 329–32. Keys were once a popular item on the Gold Coast, where Africans "used to put many together in a bunch and hang them on their bodies," according to Pieter de Marees, *Description and Historical Account of the Gold Kingdom of Guinea (1602)*, trans. and ed. Albert van Dantzig and Adam Jones (Oxford: Oxford University Press for the British Academy, 1987), p. 54.

10. Alan Ryder, *Benin and the Europeans, 1485–1897* (London: Longmans, 1969), pp. 32–45, 76–78.

11. Translated excerpts from Afonso's early letters may be found in Basil Davidson, ed., *African Civilization Revisited* (Trenton, NJ: Africa World Press, 1991), pp. 223–26; Anne Hilton, *The Kingdom of Kongo* (Oxford: Clarendon Press, 1985), pp. 57–60. John Thornton, "Early Kongo-Portuguese Relations," *History in Africa* 8 (1981): 193, suggests that in 1526 Afonso was referring to the nobles not of his own kingdom but of the vassal state Ndongo.

12. Shula Marks and Richard Gray, "Southern Africa and Madagascar," in *The Cambridge History of Africa, Volume 4: from c. 1600 to c. 1790*, ed. Richard Gray (Cambridge: Cambridge University Press, 1975), pp. 385–86.

13. Ryder, *Benin*, pp. 35–40.

14. Ruy de Pina, "The Foundation of the Castle and City of São Jorge da Mina," in John W. Blake, ed., *Europeans in West Africa, 1450–1560* (London: Hakluyt Society, 1942), 1:71–75; Marees, *Description*, pp. 82–83, 85, 91.

15. The quotation is from de Marees, *Description*, p. 178; cf. Kwame Yeboa Daaku, *Trade and Politics on the Gold Coast, 1600–1720* (Oxford: Clarendon Press, 1970), pp. 48–95.

16. De Marees, *Description*, pp. 51–56; Wilhelm Johann Müller, "Description of the Fetu Country," in Adam Jones, ed., *German Sources for West African History, 1599–1669* (Wiesbaden: Franz Steiner, 1983), pp. 248–53.

17. Ray A. Kea, *Settlements, Trade, and Politics in the Seventeenth-Century Gold Coast* (Baltimore: Johns Hopkins University Press, 1982), pp. 223–26, 229–36; David Henige, "John Kabes of Komenda: An Early African Entrepreneur and State Builder," *Journal of African History* 18 (1977): 1–19; K. G. Davies, *The Royal African Company* (New York, Atheneum, 1970), pp. 280–81.

18. For the calculations, see Eltis, "Precolonial Western Africa," table 1; Ernst van den Boogaart, "The Trade between Western Africa and the Atlantic World, 1600–1690: Estimates of Trends in Composition and Value," *Journal of African History* 33 (1992): 369–85; and David Eltis, "The Relative Importance of Slaves and Commodities in the Atlantic Trade of Seventeenth-Century Africa," *Journal of African History* 35 (1994): 237–49.

19. David Richardson, "The British Empire and the Atlantic Slave Trade," in *The Oxford History of the British Empire: The Eighteenth Century*, ed. P. J. Marshall (Oxford: Oxford University Press, 1998), pp. 444–50. For the background to this, see David Eltis, "The Transatlantic Slave Trade to the British Americas before 1714: Annual Estimates of Volume and Direction," in *The Lesser Antilles in the Age of European Expansion*, ed. Robert L. Paquette and Stanley L. Engerman (Gainsville: University Press of Florida, 1996), pp. 182–205.

20. Richardson, "British Empire," p. 463.

21. Willem Bosman, *A New and Accurate Description* (London: James Knapton, 1705), p. 363 verso.

22. John Atkins, *A Voyage to Guinea, Brazil, and the West Indies* (London: Caesar Ward and Richard Chandler, 1735), p. 168.

23. Robin Law, *The Slave Coast of West Africa: The Impact of the Atlantic Slave Trade on an African Society* (Oxford: Clarendon Press, 1991), pp. 261–344; Robin Law, "Royal Monopoly and Private Enterprise in the Atlantic Trade: The Case of Dahomey," *Journal of African History* 18 (1977): 560.

24. Gerrit Ockers to Pieter Valckenier, Director-General of the DWIC, Ughoton, November 1724, in Ryder, *Benin*, pp. 331–34.

25. Ryder, *Benin*, pp. 196–212.

26. From the journal of James Barbot, in *Barbot on Guinea: The Writings of Jean Barbot on West Africa 1678–1712*, ed. P. E. H. Hair (London: Hakluyt Society, 1992), II:688–89.

27. Captain Heatley, in Davidson, *African Civilization*, p. 267; Capt. John Adams, *Sketches*, cited in G. I. Jones, *The Trading States of the Oil Rivers* (Oxford: Oxford University Press, 1963), p. 46.

28. Joseph C. Miller, *Way of Death: Merchant Capitalism and the Angolan Slave Trade* (Madison: University of Wisconsin Press, 1988), pp. 173–244 and passim.

29. For a larger discussion, see Philip D. Curtin, *Cross-Cultural Trade in World History* (Cambridge: Cambridge University Press, 1984).

30. Crone, *Cadamosto*, pp. 55–56, 84; A. C. de C. M. Saunders, *A Social History of Black Slaves and Freedmen in Portugal, 1441–1555* (Cambridge: Cambridge University Press, 1982), p. 12; "Samuel Brun's Voyages of 1611–20," in Adam Jones, ed., *Brandenburg Sources for West African History, 1680–1700* (Stuttgart: Franz Steiner, 1985), p. 69.

31. Brun, "Voyages," p. 76; Nicholas Villault, *A Relation of the Coasts of Africk Called Guinee* (London: John Starkey, 1670), pp. 62, 65–66; Von der Groeben, in Jones, *Brandenburg Sources*, pp. 31–34.

32. Richard Elphick, *Khoikhoi and the Founding of White South Africa* (Johannesburg: Ravan Press, 1985), pp. 82–86, 103–6, quote p. 103.

33. Ibid., pp. 106–8.

34. "William Towerson's First Voyage to Guinea," in John William Blake, trans. and ed., *Europeans in West Africa, 1450–1560: Documents to Illustrate the Nature and Scope of Portuguese Enterprise in West Africa, the Abortive Attempt of Castilians to Create an Empire There, and the Early English Voyages to Barbary and Guinea* (London: Hakluyt Society, 1942), II:370, 383.

35. Cyril Daryll Forde, ed., *Efik Traders of Old Calabar* (London: Oxford University Press, 1956), p. 105.

36. John Adams, *Remarks on the Country Extending from Cape Palmas to the River Congo* (1823), in Hodgkin, ed., *Nigerian Perspectives*, p. 234; over two centuries earlier Müller, "Description," p. 154, had reported that although the Afutu merchants on the Gold Coast in 1660s "had no books or writings, they knew how to work out in their head their trading account, which often ran into several thousands, and to retain it."

37. Law, "Royal Monopoly," pp. 558, 563.

38. Margaret Priestley, *West African Trade and Coast Society: A Family Study* (London: Oxford University Press, 1969), pp. 16, 19–23; Davies, *Royal African Company*, p. 280; F. L. Bartels, "Philip Quaque, 1741–1816," *Transactions of the Gold Coast and Togoland Historical Society* 1.5 (1955): 153–77.

39. Christopher Fyfe, *A History of Sierra Leone* (London: Oxford University Press, 1962), p. 11, citing *Report of the Lords of the Committee of the Privy Council. . . . Concerning the Present State of the Trade to Africa, and Particularly the Trade in Slaves*, I:4–5 (James Penny); Adams, *Remarks*, in Hodgkin, *Nigerian Perspectives*, pp. 234–35. Scottish Presbyterians established the first mission school in Old Calabar in 1846; Hope M. Waddell, *Twenty-Nine Years in the West Indies and Central Africa*, 2d ed. (London: Frank Cass, 1970), pp. 266–67.

40. Priestley, *West African Trade*, pp. 20–21. See Chapter 6 for some contrary examples.

41. Hilton, *Kingdom of Kongo*, pp. 79–83; Brun, in Jones, *Brandenburg Sources*, p. 62.

42. Francisco Alvares, *The Prester John of the Indies: A True Relation of the Lands of Prester John, being a Narrative of the Portuguese Embassy to Ethiopia in 1520*, trans. Lord Stanley of Alderley, ed. C. F. Beckingham and G. W. B. Huntingford (London: Hakluyt Society, 1961), p. 376.

43. Julia C. Wells, "Eva's Men: Gender and Power in the Establishment of the Cape of Good Hope," *Journal of African History* 39 (1998):430–36; Elphick, *Khoikhoi*, pp. 103–8, 200–5.

44. Von der Groeben, in Jones, *Brandenburg Sources*, p. 27; Davies, *Royal African Company*, pp. 256–57.

45. George Metcalf, "A Microcosm of Why Africans Sold Slaves: Akan Consumption Patterns in the 1770s," *Journal of African History* 28 (1987): 392.

46. J. P. L. Durand, *A Voyage to Senegal* (1806), excerpted in *France and West Africa: An Anthology of Historical Documents*, ed. John D. Hargreaves (New York: St. Martin's Press, 1969), pp. 65–67.

47. De Marees, *Description*, pp. 37, 216–17, 238.

48. Müller, "Description," p. 157.

49. Von der Groeben, in Jones, *German Sources*, p. 37.

50. George E. Brooks, *Landlords and Strangers: Ecology, Society, and Trade in Western Africa, 1000–1630* (Boulder, CO: Westview Press, 1993), pp. 168–69, quoting Francisco Coelho. Brooks also quotes (p. 235) André Donelha's observation concerning the Cacheu River in 1585: "In Cazamansa it is the law that the black man who forces a married woman must die for this, but a white man is fined the value of a slave."

51. Brooks, *Landlords and Strangers*, pp. 135–41; George E. Brooks, Jr., "The *Signares* of Saint-Louis and Gorée: Women Entrepreneurs in Eighteenth-Century, Senegal," in *Women in Africa: Studies in Social and Economic Change*, ed. Nancy J. Hafkin and Edna G. Bay (Stanford, CA: Stanford University Press, 1976), pp. 19–44. The term "commercial marriage" is used by Miller, *Way of Death*, p. 290.

52. George E. Brooks, "A Nhara of the Guinea-Bissau Region: Mãe Aurélia Correia," in *Women and Slavery in Africa*, ed. Claire C. Robertson and Martin A. Klein (Madison: University of Wisconsin Press, 1983), p. 296.

53. Brooks, "*Signares* of Saint-Louis," pp. 30, 43; Brooks, "Nhara of Guinea-Bissau," pp. 295–313.

54. Bruce L. Mouser, "Women Slavers of Guinea-Conakry," in Robertson and Klein, eds., *Women and Slavery in Africa* (Madison: University of Wisconsin Press, 1983), pp. 321–33.

55. Fyfe, *History of Sierra Leone*, p. 10 and passim.

56. Priestley, *West African Trade*, pp. 106–09, 121–26.

57. Hilton, *Kingdom of Kongo*, p. 71.

58. Miller, *Way of Death*, pp. 289–95, quote p. 294.

59. M. D. D. Newitt, *Portuguese Settlement on the Zambezi: Exploration, Land Tenure and Colonial Rule in East Africa* (London: Longmans, 1973), pp. 131–86, quote p. 144; Allen F. Isaacman, *Mozambique: The Africanization of a European Institution, the Zambezi Prazos, 1750–1902* (Madison: University of Wisconsin Press, 1972), pp. 43–63; H. H. K. Bhila, "Southern Zambezia," in *UNESCO General History of Africa*, vol. 5: *Africa from the Sixteenth to the Eighteenth Century*, ed. B. A. Ogot (Los Angeles: Uni-

versity of California Press, 1992), pp. 648–56; David Livingstone, *Missionary Travels and Researches in South Africa* (New York: Harper & Brothers, 1859), 703.

60. "Andreas Josua Ulsheimer's Voyage of 1603–4," in Jones, *German Sources,* p. 27; John Newton, *Journal of a Slave Trader (John Newton), with Newton's Thoughts upon the African Slave Trade,* ed. Bernard Martin and Mark Spurrell (London: Epworth Press, 1962), pp. 106–7.

61. Adams, *Remarks,* in Hodgkin, *Nigerian Perspectives,* p. 234.

62. Newton, *Journal,* p. 15; Nicholas Owen, *Journal of a Slave-Dealer, "A View of Some Remarkable Axcedents in the Life of Nics. Owen on the Coast of Africa and America from the Year 1746 to the Year 1757,"* ed. Eveline Martin (London: George Routledge and Sons, 1930), p. 76. Owen's spelling and grammar have been standardized.

Suggested Readings

Brooks, George E. *Landlords and Strangers: Ecology, Society, and Trade in Western Africa, 1000–1630.* Boulder, CO: Westview Press, 1993.

Priestley, Margaret. *West African Trade and Coast Society: A Family Study.* London: Oxford University Press, 1969.

Thornton, John K. *African and Africans in the Making of the Atlantic World, 1400–1800.* Cambridge: Cambridge University Press, 1998.

ATLANTIC IMPORTS
AND TECHNOLOGY

The Ikiri market, some 250 miles up the Niger River, was a very busy place in the 1830s. One of a string of large markets spaced out along the lower Niger, Ikiri was sited on a large sandbank and framed by the rolling hills on either side. The beauty of its setting was not what made Ikiri a center of intense commercial activity but its location in a neutral zone abutting several communities and the ease with which these in attendance might withdraw in their canoes should any disturbance threaten. The hundreds of canoes that converged on Ikiri every ten days came from near and far. From the north came traders from the kingdom of Nupe, from the Igbirra city of Panda, and from the Hausa cities of further north. Igbo and Igala traders from the east bank joined Yoruba from the west. They set up their stalls alongside traders who came up river from the Igbo towns of Onitsha and Aboh and from the more distant communities of Benin and Bonny in the Niger Delta. Each set of traders brought items to trade with those other regions. The northerners came laden with "cloths of native manufacture, beads, ivory, rice, straw-hats, and slaves" as well as horses, bridles, and saddles; the coastal traders filled their trading canoes with imported cloth, beads, and hats, as well as hardware, gunpowder, Venetian looking-glasses, and snuff-boxes. Local farmers displayed live animals and fresh vegetables.

Traders erected temporary stalls to use during market sessions that stretched over three days. Men sold the imports and other goods of high value, while women did a lively commerce in small livestock and fowls, fish, a variety of agricultural produce, and numerous other local goods. One European witness estimated the market crowd at six thousand; another reckoned that eleven thousand slaves passed through Ikiri in the course of a year; a third believed that the volume of commercial traffic on this part of the Niger was twice that of the busy upper Rhine River in Europe.[1] The network of large markets and fairs to which Ikiri was joined spread across the inland regions of Atlantic Africa. Many markets thrived because, like Ikiri, they were free of any single political control; others flourished because of the protection of an African state, such as Asante and Dahomey, which also taxed the wealth the markets brought.

Despite such variations, Ikiri may serve to illustrate three significant features of inland Africa's indirect encounters with Europeans through the goods they brought. First, the flow into Africa of goods imported through the Atlantic was basic to the export of slaves, ivory, gold, and other goods. While coastal middlemen took a large cut of the imports and reserved some finery for themselves, they had to work hard to keep their inland customers satisfied by supplying them with a variety of imports.

Second, the inland marketing system was dynamic and responsive to the new circumstances, both regional and overseas. Already in existence when the first Portuguese visited the Niger Delta, the network of large markets along the lower Niger had probably served neighboring and distant peoples for centuries before 1500, even if the sites of particular markets sometimes shifted. The market network responded to the growth in trade to and from the Atlantic by shortening the intervals between large markets or increasing the number of days they met, by creating new links with more distant areas, and by attracting more trading professionals. The impact of the Atlantic economy can also be seen on the financial underpinnings of the markets. The cowry shell currency at Ikiri had been in use in West Africa before the arrival of the first Europeans, but the volume of cowries Africans obtained from European ships facilitated the expanding volume of the inland trade. Elsewhere, Africans had used currencies based on metal, notably gold and iron. Under the stimulus of the Atlantic economy Africans adopted new currencies based on copper and iron rods or bracelets (*manillas*), which spread inland, displacing or supplementing preexisting metal currencies. Historians generally agree that the volume of imports before 1850 was sufficient to stimulate commercial activity in Africa but not large enough to have transformed the economy in a major way, although the impact varied with the intensity of the trade.[2]

Third, as imported goods moved inland they supplemented and competed with domestic manufactures. Imported products that were notably different, better, or cheaper did well, but the ability of African goods to survive this competition is evident in that fact African-made cloth, beads, and hats at Ikiri were still sold alongside imported versions of the same items centuries after the Atlantic trade began. Modern research in African history has largely discredited the once popular notion that African production collapsed in the face of foreign competition, but the various ways in which Africans responded to different products need to be evaluated carefully.

EVALUATING INLAND TRADE

A balanced consideration of the larger meaning of these three points is elusive. One must steer between the exaggerations of older histories that assumed European dominance in the Atlantic trade and ignored or under-

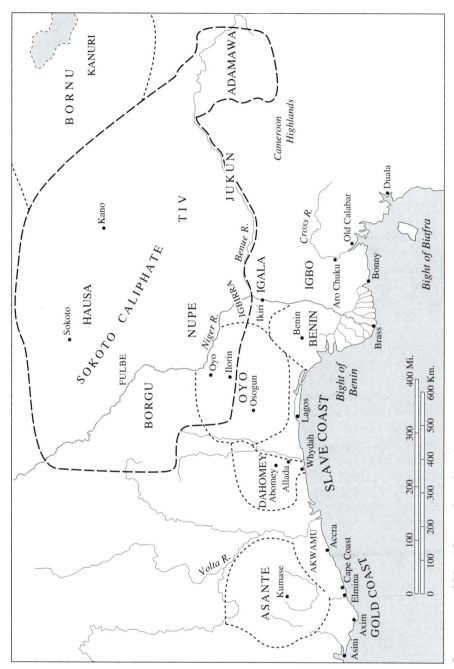

Eastern states of West Africa in the eighteenth century.

estimated the abilities of African consumers and producers and the tendency of some modern histories to pay too little attention to the changes stimulated from without. In addition, one must work with evidence that is thin and indirect until near the end of the period under consideration. Putting African perspectives and interests in the foreground helps, but the analysis that follows is more suggestive than definitive.

Much misunderstanding is promoted by the common practice of labeling these exchanges "the Atlantic slave trade." African coastal traders were well aware that slaves dominated their exports after 1700, but from their perspective two other features of the trade were at least as important. One was their other exports, such as gold, ivory, and forest products, and the other was the great volume of imports they received in exchange. Much attention has been focused on the probable impacts of the export of slaves on Africa (although the lack of hard evidence makes this quest elusive),[3] but the impact of the imports (also difficult to assess rigorously) has been given much less attention.

A second distortion with regard to the Atlantic exchanges stems from speaking of the imports as "European goods." To be sure, the majority were from Europe and all arrived in European ships, but it is important to stress that inland Africa's encounter with the Atlantic economy was a global encounter. Although Europeans would naturally have preferred to supply only products of their own countries, African preferences and other factors assured that inland Africa's imports came from Asia, the Americas, and other parts of Africa, as well as from different parts of Europe.

The diversity of the imports is apparent from the first decades of the trade. When the Portuguese first ventured along the coast of West Africa, they brought with them an assortment of goods from their own country and from other parts of Western Europe: Portuguese woolen caps and blankets, English and Irish textiles, copper and brass vessels, and tin bracelets. To meet African demand they soon added a variety of goods from other parts of Africa. From North Africa they brought a variety of textiles and clothing, grain, and horses. According to a leading historian of Portuguese expansion, the most popular item they sold at São Jorge da Mina in 1509 was striped Moroccan cloth known as *alambéis* (from the Arabic *hambel*). Other Moroccan goods topping the list included table cloths, cloaks, and *jellabas*, long, loose, hooded garments.[4]

North African goods remained important to the Atlantic trade for many decades, but Europeans also carried goods from one part of sub-Saharan Africa to another. From the early 1500s, Portuguese traders wanting to purchase gold from the Gold Coast found it desirable to supplement their goods with beads, cotton cloth, leopard skins, and palm oil purchased from the kingdom of Benin and its neighbors in the Niger Delta. During the seventeenth century Niger Delta traders sold Dutch and English traders large quantities of cotton cloth for resale on the Gold Coast. The Dutch purchased at least sixteen thousand Benin cloths between 1644 and 1646, and they believed the English purchased even more, which is likely since a single English ship is known to have purchased some four thousand pieces of the prized cloth in 1646. From the seventeenth century into the nineteenth, cloth producers on the Senegal and Gambia rivers also sold substantial quantities of their textiles to Europeans traders, who found such "country cloths" indispensable for making purchases elsewhere in West Africa.[5]

Africans also received very large quantities of goods from other continents through the Atlantic trade. Essential to the success of the trade was the growing volume of Indian cotton textiles Europeans brought from South Asia. Indian cottons became more important than European-made textiles in volume until machine-made British cottons cut into their dominance in the nineteenth century. Tobacco and rum from the Americas also became important after the development of a significant trans-Atlantic trade to Africa from Brazil at the end of the sixteenth century and from the West Indies and North America in the course of the next century.

What were the effects on inland Africa of the diverse and ever-changing assortment of goods received from the Atlantic economy? Keeping in mind that trading imports came from many sources and were exchanged for a variety of exports, not just slaves, helps to temper extreme assessments, such as that cited earlier by the late radical critic Walter Rodney, who, in his anger over the slave trade, asserted it was a proven "fact that the majority of the imports were of the worst quality even as consumer goods—cheap gin, cheap gunpowder, pots and kettles full of holes, beads, and other assorted rubbish," teamed with the improbable corollary that such valueless goods somehow managed to undermine African craft industries.[6] Few scholars today cling to the notion of ignorant Africans being easily duped by worthless trinkets. There is also a retreat from the more extreme ideas of African economies being undermined by the trade goods, although one has to guard against leaning too far in the other direction. One influential recent historian, for example, asserts that, in the period before 1680 and for some time thereafter, "Europe offered nothing to Africa that Africa did not already produce."[7] This statement rightly emphasizes that African manufacturing was already well established, but it understates the novelty of tobacco, distilled alcohol, and firearms. As will be explained later, these imports were incorporated into existing customs of smoking, drinking, armed combat, and hunting, but they also introduced significant changes in African life.

Both continuity and change were characteristic of African consumption patterns. As African exports went from gold and ivory to slaves and then back to other nonslave goods between 1500 and 1850, it is striking how constant the larger categories of imported goods remained. Records of two hundred Dutch ships trading on the Gold Coast between 1593 and 1607 show that textiles typically constituted two-fifths of the value of the imports (including various woolens, linens, and silks in different styles, colors, and weights); following next in importance were metals and metalware, including iron bars, a variety of tools and weapons (axes, hatchets, spades, many varieties of knives, cutlasses), copperware (basins, pots, and buckets), and tinware (pots, pans, and the like). African imports from the 1680s, 1780s, and 1820s were essentially similar, except for the increased importance of firearms, alcohol, and tobacco. In all periods the imports included expensive goods intended for the coastal and inland elite and cheaper goods aimed at the mass market. In this regard African imports differed little from those imported by Asia and the Americas in the same period.[8] Although they held quite different shares of the African market, insight into the impacts of Atlantic imports comes from examining three different groupings: utilitarian textiles and metals, psychic spirits and tobacco, and firearms.

TEXTILES AND METALS

Africans had been producing textiles and metals of very high quality since long before the advent of the first Europeans. Even though weaving and metallurgy were widespread, the eagerness with which Africans responded to new supplies from the Atlantic strongly suggests that this demand was not simply motivated by the novel designs of the imports nor by their superiority, but rather by an unmet demand for cloth and metals that imports were able to at least partially satisfy at prices consumers could afford.

Let us consider textiles first. Throughout much of West Africa cotton textiles were woven, mostly on narrow looms, and often dyed with local indigo dyes. Cloth was also made from the leaves of the raffia palm in forested areas, notably in the West Central Africa, where palm cloths often served as a currency. In more remote areas cloth was made by pounding the bark of certain trees into a soft cloth. Despite these local supplies, the demand for imported textiles was tremendous. Part of their appeal was due to the variety of designs, colors, sizes, and textures imported textiles came in, but novelty was not their main attraction. Nor, for the most part, did domestic production disappear. In some places, the Atlantic trade actually stimulated local production, as in the cases of African textile exporters cited earlier. It also introduced new crops, as in Senegambia, where an American cotton plant became the most commonly grown variety.[9]

In Africa, as elsewhere, clothing served three complementary purposes: for warmth, for display, and for modesty. Even in the tropics, people sought warmth from clothing, sheets, and blankets on chilly nights and in the cooler seasons. The uses of clothing for display and modesty were more likely to be governed by cultural norms than practical considerations. As a general rule, the higher a person's status and wealth, the more clothing he or she wore. A Dutch account, for example, noted that in the kingdom of Benin in the early seventeenth century, "people of wealth . . . wear two and sometimes four cloths on top of each other," while common "people wear a single cloth over their naked bodies." It further reported that no man could wear any clothing at all without the king's permission and that women went naked until they married.[10] The last assertion may not be completely accurate, but it was certainly common throughout much of sub-

Saharan Africa during these centuries for children of both sexes to go naked before puberty and for custom to dictate who might wear what sort of clothing. Besides reflecting cultural norms based on age and sex, clothing was a popular way of displaying wealth.

To satisfy their practical and prestige desires, Africans imported such an array of different fabrics and designs that anyone today reading the shipping invoices needs a lot of help in sorting out the numerous textiles listed. One European-made cloth very popular before 1750 was the *perpetuana*, a durable wool serge made in the Low Countries and England that was specially dyed for African tastes. Another, generally lighter weight cloth, the *silesias*, was made originally in Silesia (a region of Central Europe later divided among Poland, Germany, and Czechoslovakia) and then in England. *Silesias* were extremely popular as clothing on the Gold Coast, whose inhabitants bought thirty million yards from the Dutch during the seventeenth century. Africans also bought millions of used linen bed sheets from Europe; their large dimensions (five feet by ten feet) made them useful as cloaks and for wrapping oneself up in at night.

In the course of the eighteenth century, cotton textiles from India flooded into Europe and from there into Africa. Both men and women wore untailored Indian cotton pieces as body "wrappers," the customary article of clothing. The textiles came in many coarse and fine varieties. Africans bought large quantities of dyed *calicos* as well as more expensive *nicanees*, woven from dyed thread in blue and white stripes. Some shipping invoices refer to "Guinea stuffs," which were cloths made in India expressly for the African market. Also very popular for wrappers was *chintz*, which came in a variety of colors and designs. There were many, many others.[11]

The period of greatest expansion in imported cloth came in the first half of the nineteenth century, associated with rising West African exports of palm oil and falling prices for mechanically spun and woven cottons from industrial mills. West African imports of British cottons increased nearly fifty-fold, from 350,000 yards in 1820 to 17,000,000 yards in 1850. Imports from France also grew substantially.[12] While not entirely typical of the whole trading period, the nineteenth century provides the best evidence by which to judge was happening in the interior, as these textiles passed through a mature inland marketing system to great numbers of African customers.

Coastal communities in direct contact with the Atlantic were more inclined to define prestige in terms of imported cloth, but in inland markets imported textiles had to compete with locally made cloth and cloth brought overland from other regions of Africa. As in markets everywhere, price and prestige greatly shaped consumers' choices. In 1817, the prices of luxurious Indian silks and glazed cottons (*sastracundas*) doubled and quadrupled as they moved from the coast to the markets of the Asante kingdom's capital Kumase, which suggests wealthier consumers were willing to pay a much higher mark-up to get these prestige goods. In contrast, the ordinary textiles that made up the bulk of imported cloth had risen in value by only 50 percent by the time they reached the Kumase markets, the lower mark-up suggesting that Africans purchasing ordinary cloths were price sensitive and inclined to buy imports only if they were cheaper than locally made cloth of comparable quality. It is possible that some domestic weavers of specialty cloth lost customers to the luxurious imports, but it seems more likely that the rich purchased imported cloth in addition to that made locally. Some African weavers also adapted to evolving consumer tastes by unraveling imported silks and reusing the rare yarns in their own weaving.[13] Down the coast in Angola, the impact of imported cotton textiles may have had somewhat different effects than in the Gold Coast hinterland, since there were few locally made cotton textiles. The cooler temperatures of the inland plateau made clothing a practical necessity that the dense population seems to have found insufficiently satisfied by local animal skins, bark cloth, and palm-fiber textiles. The unmet demand led to large imports of cotton textiles, whose attraction was enhanced by the prestige that eye-catching dyes, weaves, and patterns from the Atlantic could offer.[14]

Mining and metallurgy were another set of African industries that had great practical as well as cultural significance. Africans had also been proficient in the production of iron, copper, and gold for centuries before 1500. Although iron production was widespread in tropical Africa and employed diverse ingenious and highly effective techniques, it is likely that the amount of iron produced by these small smelteries was insufficient to meet all the needs of the population. Some areas may have been well supplied, but others were not, especially in regions that lacked iron ore to smelt. In places, Africans also mined and smelted copper and gold on a large scale, but deposits of these ores were far less widely distributed than iron. Copper mining was concentrated in the highlands on either side of the upper Zambezi and Congo rivers with smaller areas of production in the Sahara and the desert's southern fringes, where the shortage of water limited how much ore could be processed. Gold production was common along the Zambezi and in parts of West Africa. The high value of gold had fed a steady export of gold across the Sahara and across the Indian Ocean, as well as to European markets, as earlier chapters have shown. As a consequence, gold was very rare in Africa's non-gold-producing areas. Copper found a much more widespread market among Africans, who often used it for jewelry. Even so, in much of Africa copper was scarce and costly before the arrival of the Europeans.

Africans obtained large quantities of iron and copper from the Atlantic because innovations in mining and metallurgy had greatly expanded European production and lowered costs. Europe's "gunpowder revolution" in the late Middle Ages had greatly stimulated the production of copper and brass for cannon. Iron production for military and other uses had also expanded, especially in areas of Scandinavia, Germany, and Russia, where dense forests could supply the vast quantities of charcoal that iron smelting required. During the eighteenth century the use of coke from coal for charcoal in the smelting process in Britain further expanded iron and copper production. As European production grew it also became more efficient. It is thus not surprising that African consumers increased the volume of their metal imports as the metals of iron and copper declined.[15] Thus, Africa's hunger for these metals matched Europe's capacity to supply them, just as Africa's production of gold helped satisfy Europe's insatiable demand for that item.

Demand for copper and brass was nearly insatiable in some parts of West Africa in the first half of the sixteenth century, averaging at least forty-five tons a year, or a third of the total goods Portuguese traders supplied. On the Gold Coast between a third and a half of African gold exports were paid for with copper or brass. The kingdom of Benin imported copper or brass *manillas* (wristlets) by the tens of thousands along with copper and brass basins of various sizes. The strong demand for copper continued after 1650, but iron became the metal most sought by Africans, as European production soared, while African production could not because of shortages of trees to make the charcoal needed for smelting. During the eighteenth century iron bars became a staple of the African trade with British production taking the lead. The copper and brass supplied also rose, with the British trades alone going from an average of 325 tons a year in the period of 1701–1710 to 2,860 tons a year in 1791–1800. African copper and brass imports continued to be strong during the first half of the nineteenth century.[16]

While the volume of textile and metal imports grew rapidly, researchers have pointed out that it was not enormous in proportion to the population of the regions of Africa that purchased these goods. Walter Rodney's idea that textile and metal imports deliberately strangled and destroyed African production of cloth and iron is certainly not true for the period before 1850 and severely underestimates both the skill and the resilience of African craftspeople. On the whole, imports of textiles and metals appear to have supplemented African production rather than replaced it. Nevertheless, it is clear that African producers in some places were adversely affected by the flood of imported cloths and metals. For example, producers of bark cloth in the Gold Coast hinterland and of palm cloth in Central Africa both lost markets to imported textiles during the two centuries after 1500. Similarly, iron makers in coastal areas of Central Africa and elsewhere also lost ground to the cheaper imports, but further from the ocean African producers held their own. On his journey down the Congo River in 1876–1877, Henry M. Stanley remarked often on the abundance and high quality of locally made iron knives, spears, gongs, and hoes in a vast region of Africa where external trade seemed not to have penetrated.[17]

Moreover, some inland African producers found new opportunities in the expanding distribution networks and political changes of these centuries. For example, the formation of the new Islamic African empire known as Sokoto Caliphate in the central Sudan in the early nineteenth century created a large area of trade that brought a golden age to the weavers, dyers, and merchants of the Hausa cities of Kano and Zaria. Intensive production techniques and aggressive marketing enabled Hausa cloth, in historian John Iliffe's words, "to destroy [the neighboring kingdom of] Borno's textile industry, capture the Timbuktu market, outsell local textiles a thousand kilometres away, and find outlets as distant as Egypt and Brazil." The situation was similar for cotton textile makers in Senegambia, who not only held their own but, as we have seen, also sold locally made cloth, often in considerable quantities, to European traders for resale elsewhere in Africa.[18]

The case of iron is different because most of it was imported as iron bars rather than in the form of finished products. This must have been a boon to African blacksmiths, who turned these bars into every sort of useful object. In turn, the iron objects the smiths turned out must have been greatly welcomed by consumers, who would have had greater access to hoes, knives, nails, and the like. Although there is no way to measure the change, it is likely that more abundant iron hoes and axes served to increase agricultural output by speeding the clearing and tilling of the fields, and more numerous spears and knives for hunting and butchering may also have expanded the availability of animal protein. Greater supplies of copper and brass would also have been a boon to smiths, but the impact of these metals on economic development was less because they were used more for decoration than for tools. Finally, the use of both iron bars and brass *manillas* as currencies would have helped promote economic growth.[19]

Change is the very essence of an expanding economic system, for customer preferences permit the more efficient producers and desirable goods to prosper, even if this is at the expense of others. However, the negative effects of change for African producers during the centuries before 1850 were limited by several circumstances. In the first place, African demand for textiles and metals exceeded internal supplies, and the quantities of imports was too small to saturate—or even satisfy—the market. Second, the price advantage imported textiles and metals enjoyed at the coast, versus African-made products, declined or vanished as the goods moved inland because of the costs of transport and the profit taken by African middlemen. Third, many Africans retained a strong preference for locally made goods, both because of their greater durability and because of ritual considerations associated with the methods of production. As one modern historian puts it, among those who could afford it

> these imports . . . no more replaced the prestige accorded to the original items than trendy plastic furniture substitutes for an heirloom oak chest today. In fact, as in the modern analogy, the spread of inexpensive substitutes for the masses may have stimulated demand among the wealthy for the authentic local equivalents.[20]

Under these circumstances, overall local production did not falter until the volume of imports increased sharply under conditions of colonial rule beginning in the late nineteenth century. Thus, one study concludes, it was "not until the end of the nineteenth century [that] imported iron became sufficiently cheap to and plentiful in these internal markets to outweigh the prejudices against it." In many places African iron smelting continued well into the twentieth century.[21] Similarly, African-made cotton textiles "maintained their popularity on the West Coast itself and were traded far and wide from the River Gambia to Lake Chad" well into the twentieth century and in places were used as currency and even for payment of colonial taxes.[22]

TOBACCO AND DISTILLED SPIRITS

Tobacco and distilled spirits were a different kind of import from textiles and metals and serve to illuminate different aspects of African consumer demand. From an economic point of view these were luxury goods, goods serving no demonstrably utilitarian purpose, but they can also be viewed as psychic goods, that is, their appeal was based on the effects they had on the mind and emotions. Although tobacco and spirits were new products, Africans tended to fit their use into already existing social contexts. Thus some researchers have found them a useful illustration of the African capacity to adopt new customs and products while continuing with older traditions.

Tobacco was a Native American crop that European voyagers introduced to Africa at much the same time that they introduced it to Europe. It found a ready market (as well as some opposition) in both lands. Africans may have taken up the use of tobacco more readily since the practice of smoking other plants (including marijuana in places) and chewing other stimulating leaves was already well established. Native Americans had prized tobacco for its medicinal and mystical uses as well as its recreational ones, and these aspects of tobacco use followed the plant across the Atlantic.

The Portuguese had been the first to introduce modest amounts from Brazil, but it was Dutch traders who capitalized on African demand in the late 1600s—much to the traders' profit. Other Europeans followed suit. According to a German observer, in the mid-seventeenth century Africans of all ages and both sexes on the Gold Coast avidly sought tobacco, smoking it during the day and hanging little bags of it around their necks at night "as if it were a precious jewel." Africans also purchased tobacco horns and snuff boxes. At Benin in the early 1700s Africans were willing to pay as much as a pound of ivory for ten pounds of Brazilian tobacco. Two centuries later inland Africans along the Niger were reported to be "greatly addicted to smoking."[23] While the Brazilian government tried to restrict the quality of its tobacco exports to the lowest grade, which gradually established a market on the Gold Coast, it was not entirely successful in blocking the sale of higher grades. In West Africa, American traders learned, "Only premium grade tobacco would do," although this may have been true of tobacco intended as gifts for their African partners rather than of tobacco meant for general sale.[24]

Over time, Africans in many areas became proficient in supplying their own demands for tobacco. Tobacco was widely grown in Senegambia, but imports still rose in the nineteenth century, constituting 10 percent of the region's Atlantic imports in the 1830s. By that date Africans on the lower Niger, Angola, and elsewhere in Africa were also satisfying much of their desire for tobacco from locally grown crops.[25]

Distilled alcoholic beverages were another novelty brought by the Atlantic trade. Africans in many places were brewing various grain-, honey-, and fruit-based alcoholic beverages long before the arrival of Europeans, but the high alcoholic levels of imported brandy, rum, gin, and whisky set them somewhat apart from these older beverages. Wine made from grapes was also an innovation that found a limited market in Angola and other places. African taste for such products took some time to establish itself, but by the late eighteenth century barrels and bottles of distilled spirits formed as much as a fifth of overseas imports in some places.

A Lutheran pastor on the Gold Coast commented on African enthusiasm for distilled spirits, especially French brandy. He noted their distaste for Dutch gin and Barbadian rum in the 1660s, but by the end of the century Africans had acquired a taste for these, too. David Eltis estimates that western Africa "absorbed at least two million gallons of alcohol between 1680 and 1713 . . . , two-thirds of it sold on the Gold Coast." African imports of spirits increased still more over the next century. Spirits feature prominently in the goods brought by American traders from Rhode Island, who sold eleven million gallons of rum to Africa between 1709 and 1807, a colossal 830,000 gallons of it in the peak year, 1806.[26]

The effects of this trade in Africa have been variously interpreted. Today, awareness of the serious long-term health issues associated with tobacco smoking may incline one to see its introduction to Africa as a step backward. Similarly, a century ago, European assumptions of African incapacity and a growing Anglo-American outcry against the evils of drink at home combined to reinforce beliefs that the growing alcohol trade was undermining African society. However, the contemporary West African explorer Mary Kingsley challenged the factual basis of the latter claim:

> . . . [T]he cry against alcohol is at present a popular one in England, and it has the advantage of making the subscribers at home regard the African as an innocent creature who is led away by bad white men. . . . I should rather like to see the African lady or gentleman who could be "led away"—all the leading away I have seen on the Coast has been the other way.[27]

Kingsley went on to show, by laboratory analysis, that the trade gin of the late nineteenth century was safe to drink, that the quantities being imported were moderate in terms of the population, and that drunkenness was much rarer in western Africa than in England.

More recently, Harvard historian Emmanuel Akyeampong has sought to reconstruct precolonial alcohol usage in the Gold Coast hinterland. Although the evidence available is limited, he makes the case that the consumption of mildly alcoholic palm wine was widespread and had profound symbolic and ritual significance. Senior men "incorporated the ritual use of palm wine into all important social contracts and occasions," restricting its normal use to themselves and reinforcing their authority by denying it to junior males and women. He notes that "alcoholic drinks were treasured fluids that, through frequent libations on the ground to the ancestors, bridged the gap between physical and spiritual worlds." Beginning sometime in the seventeenth century imported alcoholic drinks came to be used ritually alongside palm wine, and the new products' higher economic value, stronger alcoholic content, and foreign origins added to their symbolic value. In time, imported alcohol became an essential component of naming ceremonies, initiation rights, marriages, deaths, and funerals. One of his informants relates that in former times, "if a warrior brought home an enemy's head, he was given rum mixed with some drops of the enemy's blood, to drink. This, they say, not only protected him against the avenging ghost of the beheaded, but also made him braver." Finally, Akyeampong argues, alcohol and other imported goods were important in status changes. Enriched by trade, ordinary men might become "big men" whose higher status was "distinguished by generosity, the use of imported drinks, rich cloths, gold ornaments, and a large number of wives, children and other dependents."[28] As Chapter 3 detailed, the Atlantic trade also empowered some women, and they too used foreign goods to display their new status.

Such social transformations took place up and down the Atlantic Coast. In Angola, Miller suggests that initially alcohol imports "enhanced the powers of lords and elders to contact ancestors or other spirits on behalf of the communities they represented" and later facilitated the rise of new men. However, ritual use was not necessarily equivalent to temperate use. A missionary in Old Calabar noted that "not less than eight puncheons" of rum, perhaps eight hundred gallons, were consumed at one big man's funeral, this well before the inflow of cheap gin took off in the 1860s.[29] Akyeampong cites an old Asante ceremony in which an extravagant quantity of rum was poured out in brass pans to be consumed by slaves, women, and children, whose inebriation was a ceremonial release of social tensions.

In addition to socially controlled ritual situations, imported alcohol was widely consumed in nonritual settings. Kingsley estimated that only about an eighth of all imported liquor was used ceremonially in libations, shrines, and burials—"spirits to the spirits," in her phrasing. As the amount of liquor increased, drunkenness became a growing social problem for some, as Miller notes it did in Angola in the nineteenth century. One may also recall the unfortunate case of the widowed Eva van Meerhoff in Cape Town recounted in Chapter 3. However, Akyeampong's study suggests that unbridled use could also be restrained. As a colonial anthropologist observed, "No people in the world is more cognizant of the evils of alcoholic excess than the [Asante]."[30]

Precise measures of the impact of alcohol and tobacco in Africa are impossible, but it seems reasonable to observe that Africans were certainly not more likely to abuse alcohol than were contemporary Europeans, and Africans were more likely to exercise social control over its consumption, although control was not always equivalent to moderation. In some places

Africans also appreciated that distilled spirits in glass or ceramic containers could be stored indefinitely in a tropical climate, providing a way to amass wealth that could be dispensed as needed. Likewise, despite tobacco's addictive properties, there is no evidence that Africans suffered harmful effects from its use during these centuries, when life spans were much shorter than they are today.

GUNS AND POLITICS

Firearms occupy a special place in the history of Africa's imports for two reasons. They were arguably the most significant technical innovation to arrive from the Atlantic, and their impact on the continent has been hotly disputed. As Chapter 2 recounted, the Portuguese had been quick to show off the power of their weaponry, and Africans quickly recognized the value of the new technology. Up until the first half of the seventeenth century, Africans had gained access to firearms largely through forming alliances with Europeans trained in their use. Thereafter, changes both in Europe and in Africa led to Africans purchasing ever-growing numbers of firearms and training their own soldiers in their use.

On the European side, there was a greater willingness to sell firearms and great improvements in their design and manufacture. Unlike the Portuguese, the northern European Protestants who were dominant in the coastal trade of seventeenth-century West Africa were free of prohibitions against selling arms to non-Christians. In this changed climate, even the Portuguese had to sell firearms in Angola in order to retain a competitive position. In addition, European manufacturers introduced technical improvements, including a more reliable flintlock firing mechanism and more accurate long barrels, which gave firearms a greater edge over traditional African weapons. On the African side, profits from the Atlantic trade enabled more rulers to purchase large quantities of firearms and to train military units in their use. As a consequence, firearm imports grew substantially in many parts of Africa during the eighteenth century. Africans purchased at least twenty million guns between 1750 and 1807, and annual sales continued to rise in the following decades. Moreover, fierce competition among European nations for access to African markets drove prices for guns steadily downward, especially when measured against the rising prices for slaves. Thus, African traders who got two guns for every slave in 1682 were getting between twenty-four and thirty-two guns per slave by 1718. Although the Dutch remained active in this trade, it was the English who became most adept at manufacturing cheap guns for the African market.[31]

The uses to which guns were put varied considerably from one part of Africa to another. Many African societies had none at all. In the mid-1820s, for example, the Zulu king Shaka, founder of the most powerful and feared military forces in southern Africa, could still regard "with ridicule the power of European firearms, urging that native *assegais* [short-handled spears] were far superior" both for hunting and battle.[32] However, many emerging and expanding states that were well connected to the Atlantic trade were eager to equip some part of their armies with the latest weapons. As in other parts of the world, firearms had other uses besides warfare. They facilitated the hunting of large animals such as elephants and provided a measure of protection from human attacks in these troubled times.

Despite these variations, there has long been a tendency to assess the significance of firearms in Africa in a monolithic and negative way. British abolitionists appear to have begun the tradition of seeing the weapons as a menace to African societies. They argued that the importation of guns was the principal reason for warfare within Africa and that it was by means of such wars that guns-toting Africans supplied the Atlantic economy with slaves. The bias inherent in such blanket generalizations is apparent when one considers that such critics did not view the much larger number of guns in Western societies as inherently destructive. Nevertheless, a negative interpretation remained popular, with many historians in the mid-twentieth century positing the existence of a "guns-for-slaves" cycle, in which Africans sold slaves to get guns and then used the imported guns in wars to obtain more slaves. Many societies, it was argued, found themselves trapped in a vicious cycle from which there was no ready escape. Some Marxist historians also posited the existence of a slave-raiding "mode of production," in which an economy rested on slave raids and exports, much as a modern economy rests on an industrial "mode of production."

While it is undeniable that guns came to feature prominently in the bundles of goods for which slaves were sold, there are three problems with theories that propose a strong link between guns and slaves. First, one also needs to keep in mind that firearms became a significant trade item rather late in most parts of Africa, so that the guns-for-slaves cycle could not have existed before the eighteenth century. Second, more recent scholarship on African political development in this period finds that the blanket application of such general theories simply does not fit the facts. A few societies may have come close to having a guns-for-slaves cycle, but in most getting firearms was not the reason for participation in the slave trade, nor were guns a major factor in warfare or in enslavement. Third, such theories do not reflect the way contemporary Africans viewed what they were doing. An examination of the role of guns in several different Atlantic coasts will demonstrate the complexity of gunpowder's impact in Africa.

As Philip D. Curtin has shown, coastal societies along the Senegal and Gambia rivers began importing guns at the end of the seventeenth century. Despite efforts of the French traders to curtail the sale of guns to the interior peoples, the gun frontier proved impossible to stop. Rulers in the inland region of Futa Toro converted their armies to firearms in the mid-eighteenth century. One enterprising chief even seized some cannon from a French ship and hired an Afro-Frenchman to command them. By the middle of the nineteenth century even more distant states in the interior were using guns. Yet Curtin finds that a "guns-for-slaves" theory fits Senegambia poorly both chronologically and geographically. He notes that export of slaves from Senegambia actually declined from the 1730s as imports of guns grew and that most of the slaves exported into the Atlantic came from wars among the Bambara in the deep interior, where guns did not play a major role in warfare, "in part because coastal trading states there and elsewhere in West Africa were eager to keep inland peoples from having quantities of firearms."[33]

Historian Ray Kea has documented an even more complex transition along the Gold Coast. Some coastal societies had bought enough muskets from Dutch traders in the 1590s and early 1600s to become adept at handling them with the aid of Dutch and Portuguese instruction, but then the Dutch halted gun sales for several decades. Despite the ban, some African rulers successfully demanded "gifts" of muskets, shot, and powder from both Dutch and English traders. In addition, European forts regularly trained some Africans whom they employed in the use of firearms to defend them from attacks by other Europeans.

Imports of firearms started growing again just before 1650 when the English began selling guns by the hundreds as a way to gain a trading advantage over their Dutch competitors. In the 1650s, several coastal rulers acquired retinues of three hundred to four hundred musketeers, and a few seemed to have amassed much larger numbers of muskets along with a few small cannon. The Dutch resumed the trade in 1660. By the 1680s and 1690s musketeers equipped with the new flintlocks had replaced archers in the armies of the coastal states; the process had gone even farther in the rapidly expanding states of Denkyira and Akwamu, which were asserting their authority over the lands just behind the coast. Nevertheless, Kea emphasizes, firearms did not cause the "military revolution" underway in these states but were simply a new technology that was conveniently incorporated into a larger transformation already underway. Rather than the importation of firearms causing the militarization of African states, he argues, militarization was well underway before firearms became available in quantity. Thus, it was the military needs of the African states that drove the demand for large quantities of firearms.[34]

By the beginning of the 1700s, Willem Bosman, the chief Dutch West India Company agent at Elmina, could write admiringly of the dexterity Gold Coast Africans exhibited in the use of their firearms. He also offered an explanation of why the Dutch had tried to restrict sales of firearms on the Gold Coast for a time before 1650 and why that policy had collapsed, referring to the firearms in African hands as "a knife to cut our own throats" yet conceding there was no alternative to including firearms if the Dutch were to retain their profitable African trade. Bosman noted that the "incredible quantities" of firearms and gunpowder that all European traders had to bring if they were to have any part of the trade "for some time have been the chief vendible merchandise here."[35] His remarks would be echoed by many others in the decades that followed.

The newly armed African communities along the Gold Coast were soon faced with the same dilemma that confronted the European traders in deciding whether to sacrifice profits or security in the face of demand for firearms by Africans further inland. As with the Europeans, once one African community agreed to sell guns, the others had to follow, so before 1700 the firearm frontier was moving north. By 1730 Gold Coast and Slave Coast Africans may have been purchasing as many as 180,000 guns a year, along with large quantities of powder and shot. At a critical point in the colossal power struggle among Africans behind the coast Akwamu supplied guns and gunpowder to the founders of the Asante kingdom, who used the weapons to win their independence from Denkyira.[36]

In addition to adopting Akwamu's fighting system, Asante took advantage of a second technological advance in firearms manufacture, the more accurate long-barreled musket, which gave its troops a decisive advantage in 1742 over armies that were armed with the short-barreled guns. However, Kea and other historians make it clear that firearms played a relatively minor role in the success of Asante armies in their massive expansion northward, partly because different organizational strategies were used and partly because the British were able to block sales inland between 1807 and 1817. For its part, Asante did its utmost to block the flow of firearms to its northern neighbors (even to those that were its allies), fearing, as a Muslim traveler noted around 1780, "that if these powerful instruments of war should reach the possession of the populous inland States, their own independence would be lost." In this Asante succeeded where its southern neighbors had failed, for European visitors found Asante's weapons blockade still in effect during the nineteenth century.[37]

If the role firearms played in Asante armies was important but not central, were these weapons critical to the export slave trade, as some have argued? A full answer would require a lengthy explanation of how the export slave trade was a by-product of Asante's political expansion, and, while profitable, it was not essential to the kingdom's commercial dealings with either the Atlantic coast or African traders to the north. Thus, the link between firearms imports and the export of slaves was at best indirect. For our purposes, the words of Asante ruler Osei Bonsu may be sufficient. In the course of trying to persuade a British delegate that Britain should abandon its abolitionist policy and resume buying slaves in 1820, Osei Bonsu characterized the connection between warfare and enslavement in these words: "I cannot make war to catch slaves in the bush, like a thief. My ancestors never did so. But if I fight a king, and kill him when he is insolent, then certainly I must have his gold, and his slaves, and the people are mine too. Do not the white kings act like this?"[38] Osei Bonsu's assumption that European monarchs still enslaved their conquered enemies was ill informed, but his larger point was well taken: Like European rulers, Asante kings made war for reasons of state, not for petty financial gain.

The western Slave Coast is a more likely candidate for a guns-for-slaves cycle. The importation of firearms there followed the general pattern of slow growth in the late seventeenth century, followed by a burgeoning arms trade in the eighteenth. Early arms traffic was directly related to the growing confrontation between the coastal trading states of Whydah and Allada, which reached such a point in 1704 that English agents at Whydah instructed the Royal African Company to make guns a third or even half of every cargo sent to the coast. As elsewhere, firearms soon penetrated further inland, reaching the growing kingdom of Dahomey, which was intent on dominating the coast and its lucrative trade. Like the other peoples of the region, Dahomeans had earlier fought with bows, arrows, and throwing clubs, but in 1726 King Agaja of Dahomey declared, "Both I and my predecessors were, and are, great admirers of firearms, and [we] have almost entirely left off the use of bows and arrows" and other "old fashioned weapons."[39] By then, skillful use of firearms had enabled his armies to gain the upper hand over coastal Allada and Whydah.

Dahomey's success in transforming its armies to the new weaponry depended on greater training, discipline, and centralized control. Like contemporary European states, Dahomey created a well-trained, specialized standing army led by professional officers, and the state supplied its soldiers with guns and powder, rather than requiring them to provide their own weapons as had once been the custom. Despite this reliance on imported weapons, Dahomey's military organization owed little to European models or instruction—indeed, the state's use of women in combat roles anticipated Western practice by several centuries.[40]

While Dahomey's military changes gave the kingdom a decisive advantage over the smaller coastal states of the Slave Coast, its firearms could not hold off the cavalry charges of the older and larger inland kingdom of Oyo, whose punitive invasion in 1726 in response to appeals by the kings of Allada and Whydah inflicted considerable losses on Dahomey. Two defensive strategies introduced by King Agaja prevented a second Oyo invasion in 1728 from inflicting as much damage, although the Oyo army did capture considerable booty. The first strategy was to withdraw his forces behind barriers the horses would find difficult to cross until Oyo's forces ran short of fodder and had to retreat before the seasonal rains made the roads impassable. Agaja's second change was the construction of defensive earth works and ditches around the capital of Abomey. On the advice of a renegade French officer, he topped the walls with cannon captured from Whydah. However, determined to impose its will on the upstart, Oyo cavalry launched protracted invasions each dry season until, in 1732, Dahomey finally agreed to pay its powerful neighbor an annual tribute to discontinue the attacks.[41]

Because a massive export of slaves paid for the guns that permitted Dahomey's expansion and defended the kingdom against Oyo's attacks, the facts appear consistent with a guns-for-slaves cycle. However, that was not Dahomey's perspective. When asked by a long-time European resident in his kingdom about 1780, King Kpengla (r. 1774–1789) unequivocally denied the connection:

In the name of my ancestors and myself I aver, that no Dahom[e]an man ever embarked in war merely for the sake of procuring wherewithal to purchase your commodities. . . . [I]f white men chuse to remain at home, and no longer visit this country, will black men cease to make war? By no means. . . . God made war for all the world, and every kingdom, large or small, has practiced it more or less.

Modern historians are less categorical. While not denying Kpengla's basic assertion, Robin Law's authoritative study points out that the predatory nature of the new Dahomean state was not a primordial or universal ethic, as Kpengla implied, but a specific response to the commercial conditions on the coast. Kpengla's view, echoed by other African rulers, that internal not external factors shaped his state's actions, merits credence as a statement of policy, but the awesome power of the Atlantic economy cannot be ignored. Law observes, "In Dahomey it is not easy to determine whether the bandit gang has turned itself into a state, or the state turned to banditry," but the effect was the same. This statement rightly emphasizes that the primary impetus for Dahomey's military actions came from within, but these events are hard to imagine outside the context of the Atlantic trade that made the adoption of European military weapons and strategies possible. As Law concludes, "If God, as King Kpengla is alleged to have said, made war for all the world, it was the impact of European 'industrialism' and the system of international commerce it created which gave war its special place in Dahomean culture."[42]

Below the Equator, Angola and neighboring parts of West Central Africa were another region where firearms and slave raids had a long history. As seen earlier, the kingdom of Kongo had made occasional use of Portuguese mercenaries in the sixteenth century, but its later leaders seem to have shunned firearms, perhaps because the inefficiency of muskets in battle could not justify the added expense. In the course of the seventeenth century, the new Mbundu warlords who came to power as a stabilizing force in the raided areas regularly found small groups of mercenary Portuguese armed with muskets and artillery valuable enough to operate joint expeditions with them for slaves. However, in the eighteenth century Africans shifted from using Europeans as allies and mercenaries to possessing their own firearms.

The transition began north of the Congo River, where African traders at Loango had exported ivory rather than slaves until about 1650. In the early eighteenth century, as the slave trade grew, Loango traders insisted that northern European traders sell them one gun (along with other goods) in return for every slave—and two or three guns per slave a few decades later. Unable to continue their long-standing policy of restricting African access to firearms in the face of such competition, the Portuguese south of the river at Luanda allowed the legal entry of fifteen hundred guns a year in the 1760s, with many more being smuggled in. By the late eighteenth century all of the West Central African ports (Loango, Luanda, and points south) were probably importing sixty thousand guns a year and exporting thirty thousand slaves. The annual imports of guns represented about two weapons per hundred adult males in the hinterland population, but, as Joseph Miller argues, the number of weapons in circulation may have grown only slowly because of the low quality of the "Angola gun" and the rigors of the moist tropical climate that shortened its useful life.[43]

Interpreting the role of guns in Angola is complex. A guns-for-slaves cycle is questionable, but a goods-for-slaves cycle clearly existed. Although African kingdoms in West Central Africa regularly raided for slaves, the role played by firearms in this process evolved slowly and never became dominant. Only during the eighteenth century did a significant number of African military leaders have sufficient firearms—and sufficient skill in their use—to maintain standing units of marksmen, who were usually specially trained slaves. According to Miller, "this modest revolution in African military technology" in Angola ended European "wars of conquest" and slave raids and further empowered Africans to expand their assaults against their neighbors as well as against Portuguese caravans. Yet he resists describing this as a guns-for-slaves cycle precisely because the guns were also used to capture goods and because, while enhancing slave raids, guns did not dominate the military process. His analysis probes the many political and economic contradictions and dilemmas faced by rulers who lived by the sword or by the gun. One can almost hear an Angolan Kpengla pleading that he too was not making war merely for the sake of procuring commodities. Yet, as on the Slave Coast, the broader dynamics of the relationship do suggest that guns were a significant lubricant of the export slave trade, as Miller concedes.[44]

Only a handful of African states that imported firearms underwent military transformations, and one major importing region, the densely populated hinterland of the Bight of Biafra, had no large states or standing armies at all. As on other coasts, the quantities of firearms imported along the Bight of Biafra rose along with the rapidly expanding slave trade of the eighteenth century, but direct connections between the weapons and the collection of slaves were few. Rather, as the next chapter shows, warfare played no significant role in obtaining slaves in the hinterland of the Bight of Biafra. Most of those sold away were victims of kidnapping or persons sold for debt or as the result of judicial processes. Coastal traders and rulers formed gun-toting entourages and sometimes engaged in short-lived skirmishes with their neighbors or engaged in raids, but there is no record of wars of state expansion and of military slave-raiding as on the Gold and Slave Coasts, Senegambia, and Angola. In this region, the major inland professional traders traveled in troupes from market to market accompanied by armed guards, and the largest of them, the Aro, had armed allies who used weapons to establish order, but rarely to secure slaves. Nor were the needs of such commercial communities adequate to account for the use of the quantities of weaponry that flowed into this region from the mid-eighteenth century, particularly the popularity of lower quality weapons.

Rather than being used by armies in warfare, most of the weapons imported by this region must have gone into the hands of common people, who used them for hunting, for self-defense, and for firing at funerals and on other ceremonial occasions, rather than for war. The high proportion of very cheap muskets manufactured explicitly for this region strongly suggests such a mass market for guns. Fully half of the weapons imported through the port of Bonny were "Bonny muskets," made exclusively for this port. Although the abolitionist literature saw the proliferation of low-quality weapons as an example of Europeans exercising their trading advantage, the facts now seem otherwise. These weapons were avidly sought by African consumers, and it is clear that the manufacturers would have preferred to sell better weapons, as the profit margin on the cheapest weapons was razor thin. Rather than European profit, the explanation for such weapons' sales must be sought in the extremely high demand for such weapons by Africans of limited means.[45]

As this survey of the role of firearms in several parts of Africa suggests, while imports of firearms closely tracked exports of slaves, a guns-for-slaves equation is too simple to describe the complexities of political transformations. Not only did guns play an ancillary rather than primary role in most African armies of this era, but for the most important states guns were a component of a process of military transformation that was already underway. While some historians are willing to speak of a qualified "military revolution" in early modern Africa, there was no general "gunpowder revolution" such as occurred in the Ottoman Empire and Western Europe.[46]

The reasons for firearms' limited impact in Africa are not hard to find. The quantity of weapons in any part of Africa was never large on a per capita basis. Except in Dahomey, they remained confined to specialized military units, while the rest of the armies continued to rely on traditional metal weapons. Partly this was due to the conservatism of African military leaders, but it is also clear that in most circumstances firearms did not ensure a clear-cut edge in battle. In the forests, dense vegetation limited the line of sight, while tropical humidity hindered the gunpowder's ignition and complete burning. In the more open northern savannas, firearms were more useful but were limited in two significant ways (also experienced by fifteenth- and sixteenth-century European armies): A well-established cavalry could overrun musketeers while they were performing the slow cleaning and reloading tasks their weapons required, and the cost of maintaining a disciplined army was high.

However, the appeal of weapons was not confined to their sharp-shooting ability. Much of warfare is psychological, and Africans were no less prone than armies elsewhere to seek to protect themselves with charms, amulets, and prayers while spooking their enemies with means possible from elaborate battle dress, blood-chilling war cries, and other displays. In this endeavor they appreciated firearms' ability to frighten their enemies with smoke, fire, and noise, a tactic that was quite reasonable given the inaccuracy and short range of muskets in use before 1850. But it is also important to realize that Africans used firearms for more than war. They used weapons for protection and hunting. In addition, many adapted the European custom of firing guns for ceremonial effect to their own cultural norms. Bosman, for example, relates that some cannon in African hands on the Gold Coast at the beginning of the 1700s only served "to shoot by way of compliment and salutation, of which the blacks are very fond."[47]

ECONOMIC AND SOCIAL CONSEQUENCES

What were the overall consequences of these imported goods for inland Africans? Generalizations are difficult since the goods themselves were highly varied and, as the chapter has argued, had different consequences in different places. Still, it seems clear that on the whole inland Africans got what they wanted, at prices they were willing to pay, and believed themselves better off for the exchanges. However, some modern historians argue that Africans' perceived self-interest is not a sufficient test of the actual consequences of the exchanges. Even when Africans made good bargains, the larger consequences of their transactions might still have been harmful. Rather than short-term satisfaction, these arguments concern issues of long-term economic development or underdevelopment. These critics point out that, while Europe's participation in the Atlantic economy promoted a pattern of economic development from commercial capitalism to industrial capitalism at the end of the eighteenth century, Africa underwent no such economic transformation, and after 1850 the continent became more dependent on external forces, eventually losing its independence to European imperialists. Although this book is primarily concerned with presenting Africans' actual perspectives, such questions are too important not to consider briefly. Three aspects of the issue of development are relevant: first, the social context of the imports; second, their relative importance in the domestic African market; and third, the question of technology transfer.

Complex group and class relationships were involved in African relations to the Atlantic economy, so it is to be expected that gains and losses in Africa varied by class and location. African coastal middlemen were in a position to claim the most desirable goods for themselves and to exact a considerable profit from the goods they took inland. Nevertheless, as we have seen, such middlemen also had to satisfy the inland traders with whom they dealt, and the inland traders, in turn, needed satisfied customers if they were to prosper. An example of these connections in 1699 comes from an exchange between the African middleman Captain Pepple of Bonny and his European partners. Pepple told them that he needed to raise his prices for slaves because the inland people, aware of the many large ships calling at Bonny, were demanding more goods for slaves at the large inland markets.[48] The "inland people" to whom Pepple referred were not the common masses but the political and commercial elite whose domination of the inland markets and trading networks was strengthened by their privileged access to imported goods. But if strengthening the existing elite was one social consequence, the Atlantic exchanges also enabled new men to catapult themselves from lowly origins to positions of power.

The wealth Africans gained from the overseas trade was not invested primarily in goods and investment capital, as in Europe, but in people. In inland Angola, for example, Joseph Miller has shown how both the established elite and ambitious new men used access to textiles, metals, tobacco, and alcohol as a means of strengthening their wealth in people. The imported goods that washed across this region in unprecedented quantities in the 1700s rapidly passed from the hands of rulers into those of an array of followers and hangers-on. This was no "exchange" of goods for specific services, but a looser network of patronage and clientship whose boundaries of obligation were undefined. Like the widespread payment of "bride wealth" by male suitors to their prospective in-laws, patrons were not "buying" the loyalties of their clients, but forming social compacts with symbolic and practical consequences.

One of the clearest examples of a social compact that ambitious West Central African leaders used was marriage. In addition to acquiring large numbers of wives and in-laws, they also used the wealth of the Atlantic trade to cement friendships with other powerful men. Such leaders regularly kept as retainers most of the slaves who passed through their hands, while selling the rest. They kept young women—taken or given as wives, whose labor produced food and whose offspring were added followers— and children, who swelled their dependants. Because grown men were harder to control, they were more likely to be sold away in exchange for goods. In Angola, as elsewhere, the imported goods were carefully selected to meet the needs of their purchasers. The colorful textiles that formed half of all imports were designed for mass distribution among these dependants. The alcoholic drinks and tobacco from the Americas that formed a higher share in Central Africa than in other places also helped solidify social ties.[49]

The details differed in other parts of Africa affected by the Atlantic trade, but the values and social systems evident in West Central Africa were not unique. In the highly centralized political economy that developed behind the Gold Coast rulers of Asante occupied the apex of a system of patrons and clients reaching downward through many levels of society, whereas the politically decentralized hinterland of the Bight of Biafra had many more autonomous patrons and fewer levels of clientage. Although markets were more important for redistributing goods in these West African regions than in West Central Africa, here too the exchange of goods had a strong social component. Persons who acquired new wealth were expected to share it with their communities through gifts and lavish feasts, which turned economic capital into social obligations. However much these mechanisms worked to rebuild social security in African regions damaged by the more destructive aspects of warfare and slave raiding, they did not lead Africa in the direction that produced industrialization in Europe.[50]

The larger economic consequences of the trade have also become better understood from the African side. Economic historians have shown that imports can have had only a relatively modest effect on Africa before 1850 compared to later times. Anthony Hopkins demonstrates that the volume of goods exchanged at the peak of the Atlantic trade in the late eighteenth century was only about a quarter of that a century later and one-sixtieth the volume of trade at the end of the colonial era in the late 1950s. He concludes that such a volume was not large enough to have seriously undermined local textile and metal production. Following this line of reasoning, David Eltis concludes that "the economy of western Africa remained little affected by trade with the Atlantic" during the slave trade era. He refines Hopkins's argument by taking into consideration the changing population size over time, allowing him to conclude that in the era of the slave trade imports of guns, alcohol, and tobacco were small on a per capita basis, and, in any event, the mix of goods Africans imported differed little (except for a smaller proportion of luxuries) from the goods traded to other parts of the world at this time. Indeed, one of the recurrent arguments of British abolitionists was that British trade to Africa would not be able to expand beyond these relatively low levels until the slave trade was completely extinguished.[51]

If the size of Atlantic trade was too small to have affected Africa adversely, the necessary corollary is that it was also too small to have developed the continent's states and economies in the ways visible in Europe by the early nineteenth century. Just as African planners today do not see national development as Europeanization, it seems unwarranted and rather Eurocentric to expect Africa to have followed Europe's pattern of development in earlier times. In fact, as this chapter has demonstrated, inland Africans were much less inclined to trail in Europe's wake than were some Africans in coastal communities. Instead, during these dynamic centuries, African economic, political, and social development continued along lines laid out by long-standing African traditions.

Yet there was change as well as continuity. It is notable that of the four pillars underpinning early modern European expansion—ships, state sponsorship, capitalism, and gunpowder—only the last was widely adopted in Africa. Partly this was because of the Europeans' greater reluctance to share their knowledge in these areas than they were to share religious beliefs. As we have seen, the Portuguese had stoutly resisted selling firearms to Christian allies and the Dutch and other Europeans had also been reluctant to further strengthen their already powerful African trading partners. Even after economic motives had launched the massive gun trade, Europeans were not eager to share information that could cut into their trading profits. Rodney cites the example of King Adandozan of Dahomey, whose 1804 request to the British for a firearms factory was refused.[52]

Yet a stronger case can be made for technology transfers failing to take place because of Africans' lack of interest in them. Despite the fact that many Africans rode European vessels to European ports with busy shipyards, there is no suggestion anywhere in the historical record of Africans copying the shipbuilding techniques and ship designs they observed to construct superior ocean-going vessels of their own. In addition, as we have seen, Africans found developing their own economic and political institutions preferable to imitating the banks, stock exchanges, insurance companies, and royal courts of Europe.

The widespread adoption of firearms in Africa was a notable exception to this pattern, but why didn't Africans move beyond purchasing the technology to manufacturing their own weapons? Not only did this not occur on any scale by 1850, but except in South Africa, it is rarely true today. Explanations have varied. The simplest is that Africans lacked the skill to do so.[53] Given the long history of complicated mining, metalworking, and manufacturing changes that lay behind European arms manufacturing, it would have been as challenging for Africans to manufacture early nineteenth-century weapons as to duplicate the complexities of industrial textile production.

Yet this argument is misleading for three reasons. In the first place, there were highly skilled smiths in many parts of Africa. Even at the end of the sixteenth century, blacksmiths near Accra on the Gold Coast used the large quantities of iron they imported to make what Europeans appreciated as "fine weapons," including large double-edged swords and *assegais* of various types. Second, even if some European manufacturing techniques would have been beyond African skills, most of the weapons Africans imported in greatest numbers were cheap trade guns rather than finely crafted hunting guns. Indeed, as Ray Kea has pointed out, "blacksmiths on the Gold and Slave Coasts became adept at repairing" the many defects in these cheap guns, thereby cutting down on the number of weapons that they needed to import. Finally, Africans also learned to manufacture their own gunpowder, as the explorer Mungo Park discovered in 1796 when he enjoyed the hospitality of a West African who made his living at this trade, mixing niter evaporated from local ponds with sulfur imported from across the Sahara.[54]

Indeed, in the late nineteenth century some African smiths did make complex weapons, although it was a slow technique that produced only modest numbers of guns. When a partially successful French blockade cut him off from European imports in the 1880s, the West African Islamic reformer Samuri Turé put large numbers of blacksmiths to work making breech-loading guns with some rifling in the upper barrel, along with substantial quantities of gunpowder and shot. Smiths in Dahomey were doing something similar. To upgrade his skills, one of Samuri's smiths even took a training course at the French arsenal at Saint-Louis at the mouth of the Senegal River, which may have led to the production or repeater rifles for Samori's forces near the end of his war with the French.[55] Thus Africans were capable of manufacturing their own weapons if they had to, upgrading skills through trial and error and through industrial espionage. With rare exceptions, however, the low cost of European-made products made it pointless to make their own guns. Much as in the case of iron and copper rods, it made more sense to import than to compete.

This chapter and its predecessor have tried to demonstrate that African traders and consumers took great pains to ensure that the quality and variety of the goods they received were to their satisfaction. As with people everywhere, some chose wisely, others foolishly. Gain and harm both occurred. The next chapter details the miseries suffered by the millions of Africans who were sold away as part of the exchange for such imports. Many African communities also suffered from the wars and raids associated with the slave trade, although, as the next chapter explains, it is difficult to assess how much of this damage was externally caused. The effects of the goods received in return (at least by coastal traders) also varied. If a trade gun exploded in someone's face, that was clearly harmful, but there were obviously gains when an African used the gun to defend his family against an enemy attack or to shoot game to feed them. Some perceptions were class based. A piece of cloth deemed of inferior quality by an elite African might be prized by someone of more humble status. Still other perceptions were highly subjective. One customer might, on reflection, feel cheated at a purchase, but another, paying the same price, might regard it as a good bargain. Yet on the whole, the conclusion seems inescapable that Africans got what they wanted.

Notes

1. MacGregor Laird and R. A. K. Oldfield, *Narrative of an Expedition into the Interior of Africa . . . in 1832, 1833 and 1834* (London: Richard Bentley, 1837), I:160–70; II:318–26.

2. Many of these issues for this part of Africa are discussed in greater detail in David Northrup, *Trade without Rulers; Pre-Colonial Economic Development in South-Eastern Nigeria* (Oxford: Clarendon Press, 1978). For cowries see Marion Johnson, "The Cowrie Currencies of West Africa," *Journal of African History* 11 (1970): 17–49, 331–53.

3. Patrick Manning, *Slavery and African Life* (New York: Cambridge University Press, 1990), has provided a detailed and refined model of what might have happened demographically.

4. A. J. R. Russell-Wood, *The Portuguese Empire, 1415–1808: A World on the Move* (Baltimore: Johns Hopkins University Press, 1998), pp. 131–32.

5. Alan F. C. Ryder, *Benin and the Europeans, 1485–1897* (London: Longmans, 1969), pp. 93–95; Ray A. Kea, *Settlements, Trade, and Politics in the Seventeenth-Century Gold Coast* (Baltimore: John Hopkins University Press, 1982), pp. 216, 234; Philip D. Curtin, *Economic Change in Precolonial Africa* (Madison: University of Wisconsin Press, 1975), p. 213.

6. Walter Rodney, *How Europe Underdeveloped Africa* (Washington: Howard University Press, 1972), p. 102. For a penetrating critique of Rodney's analysis, see David Eltis, "Precolonial Western Africa and the Atlantic Economy," pp. 97–119 in *Slavery and the Rise of the Atlantic System*, ed. Barbara L. Solow (New York: Cambridge University Press, 1991).

7. John Thornton, *Africa and Africans in the Making of the Atlantic World, 1400–1800*, 2d ed. (Cambridge: Cambridge University Press, 1998), p. 44.

8. Kea, *Settlements*, pp. 207–8; David Eltis and Lawrence C. Jennings, "Trade between Western Africa and the Atlantic World in the Pre-Colonial Era," *American Historical Review* 93 (1988): 947–57.

9. Curtin, *Economic Change*, p. 211. American corn (maize), cassava, and tobacco were also new crops introduced via the Atlantic economy that became extensively cultivated and traded within Africa.

10. Olfert Dapper, *Naukeurige Beschrijvinge der Afrikaensche Gewesen* (Amsterdam, 1688), translated in Thomas Hodgkin, ed., *Nigerian Perspectives: An Historical Anthology* (London: Oxford University Press, 1975), p. 162.

11. Stanley B. Alpern, "What Africans Got for Their Slaves: A Master List of European Trade Goods," *History in Africa* 22 (1995): 6–12; Eltis and Jennings, "Trade between Western Africa," pp. 949–50.

12. Colin W. Newbury, "Prices and Profitability in Early Nineteenth-Century West African Trade," in *The Development of Indigenous Trade and Markets in West Africa*, ed. Claude Meillassoux (London: Oxford University Press, 1971), p. 93.

13. Ivor Wilks, *Asante in the Nineteenth Century: The Structure and Evolution of a Political Order* (Cambridge: Cambridge University Press, 1975), pp. 442–43.

14. Joseph C. Miller, *Way of Death: Merchant Capitalism and the Angolan Slave Trade, 1730–1830* (Madison: University of Wisconsin Press, 1988), pp. 78–83.

15. Hermann Kellenbenz, "Technology in the Age of the Scientific Revolution, 1500–1700," in *The Fontana Economic History of Europe: The Sixteenth and Seventeenth Centuries*, ed. Carlo M. Cipolla (Glasgow: Collins/Fontana Books, 1974), pp. 193–96, 198–212.

16. Eugenia W. Herbert, *Red Gold of Africa: Copper in Precolonial History and Culture* (Madison: University of Wisconsin Press, 1984), pp. 125–53, 179–82.

17. Rodney, *How Europe*, pp. 101–2; Kea, *Settlements*, p. 299; Miller, *Way of Death*, p. 272; Robert W. Harms, *River of Wealth, River of Sorrow* (New Haven, CT: Yale University Press, 1981), p. 46; Henry M. Stanley, *Through the Dark Continent* (reprinted New York: Dover Publications, 1988), II:178, 222–23, 226.

18. John Iliffe, *Africans: The History of a Continent* (Cambridge: Cambridge University Press, 1995), p. 172; Curtin, *Economic Change*, pp. 213, 313.

19. Herbert, *Red Gold*, pp. 288–95; Curtin, *Economic Change*, pp. 240–53; Northrup, *Trade without Rulers*, 157–64.

20. Miller, *Way of Death*, p. 86.

21. L. M. Pole, "Decline or Survival? Iron Production in West Africa from the Seventeenth to the Twentieth Centuries," *Journal of African History* 23 (1982): 503–13, quote 512. See also Eugenia W. Herbert, *Iron, Gender, and Power: Rituals of Transformation in African Societies* (Bloomington: Indiana University Press, 1993), pp. 6–12 and passim. On the strength and weakness of iron in the Sudan, see Ralph Austen, *African Economic History* (London: James Currey, 1987), pp. 46–47. Curtin found that in Senegambia "African iron production appears . . . to have held its own relatively well in the face of European competition," especially in the inland regions that were the main producers; Curtin, *Economic Change*, p. 210.

22. Allan McPhee, *The Economic Revolution in British West Africa* (London: George Routledge & Sons, 1926), pp. 44–45.

23. Otto Friedrich von der Groeben, *Guineische Reisebeschreibung* (*Description of a Voyage to Guinea*), translated in Adam Jones, ed., *Brandenburg Sources for West African History, 1680–1700* (Stuttgart: Franz Steiner, 1985), p. 25; Ryder, *Benin*, p. 145; quote from Laird and Oldfield, *Narrative*, I:164.

24. Russell-Wood, *Portuguese Empire*, p. 141; Miller, *Way of Death*, pp. 328, 462; Jay Coughtry, *The Notorious Triangle: Rhode Island and the African Slave Trade, 1700–1807* (Philadelphia: Temple University Press, 1981), p. 87.

25. Austin, *African Economic History*, p. 39; Laird and Oldfield, *Narrative*, II:181; Curtin, *Economic Change*, pp. 230, 318; Miller, *Way of Death*, p. 329.

26. Miller, *Way of Death*, p. 75; "Wilhelm Johann Müller's Description of the Fetu Country, 1662–9," in Adam Jones, ed., *German Sources for West African History, 1599–1669* (Wiesbaden: Franz Steiner, 1983), p. 213; David Eltis, *The Rise of African Slavery in the Americas* (New York: Cambridge University Press, 2000), p. 301; Coughtry, *Notorious Triangle*, pp. 82–83.

27. Mary Kingsley, *Travels in West Africa*, 5th ed. (Boston: Beacon Press, 1988), p. 663.

28. Emmanuel Akyeampong, *Drink, Power and Cultural Change: A Social History of Alcohol in Ghana, c. 1800 to Recent Times* (Portsmouth, NH: Heinemann, 1996), pp. 1–46, quotes pp. 15, 21, 28, xvi–xvii.

29. Miller, *Way of Death*, p. 84; Hope M. Waddell, *Twenty-Nine Years in the West Indies and Central Africa, 1829–1858*, 2d ed. (London: Frank Cass, 1970), p. 358, reports that some Efik regarded this conspicuous consumption as a "fool[ish] fashion." See A. J. H. Latham, *Old Calabar, 1600–1891* (Oxford: Clarendon Press,1973), pp. 74–75, for the effects of steamship lines on the alcohol trade and Justin Willis, "*Enkurma Sikitoi*: Commoditization, Drink, and Power among the Maasai," *International Journal of African Historical Studies* 32 (1999): 339–40, for an overview of recent literature.

30. R. S. Rattray, *Ashanti* (Oxford: Clarendon Press, 1923), p. 135.

31. J. E. Inikori, "The Import of Firearms into West Africa 1750–1807: A Quantitative Analysis," *Journal of African History* 18.3 (1977): 339–68; W. A. Richards, "The Import of Firearms into West Africa in the Eighteenth Century," *Journal of African History* 21.1 (1980): 43–59.

32. Henry Francis Fynn, *The Diary of Henry Francis Fynn*, comp. and ed. James Stuart and D. McK. Malcolm (Pietermaritzburg: Shuter and Shooter, 1969), pp. 120, 130. Although Zulu power persisted through the middle of the century, thereafter the kingdom increasingly felt the impact of the Europeans' destructive firepower.

33. Curtin, *Economic Change*, pp. 323–25, quote p. 325.

34. Ray Kea, "Firearms and Warfare on the Gold and Slave Coasts from the Sixteenth to the Nineteenth Centuries," *Journal of African History* 12 (1971): 185–213; Kea, *Settlements*, pp. 154–63.

35. Willem Bosman, *A New and Accurate Description of the Coast of Guinea* (London: James Knapton, 1705), pp. 184–85; spelling has been slightly modernized. Bosman goes on to note that Africans also make great use of swords, *assagais*, and shields, and some of bows and arrows, showing that guns hardly dominated warfare and

that local technology and manufacture held its own. Here as elsewhere, guns were additive, not substitutive.

36. Kwame Yeboa Daaku, *Trade and Politics on the Gold Coast, 1600–1720* (Oxford: Clarendon Press, 1970), pp. 163–64.

37. Richards, "Import of Firearms," pp. 48, 51; Wilks, *Asante*, pp. 20, 270, 690.

38. Joseph Dupris, *Journal of a Residence in Ashantee* (London: Henry Colburn, 1824), p. 163.

39. Robin Law, *The Slave Coast of West Africa 1550–1750: The Impact of the Atlantic Slave Trade on an African Society* (Oxford: Clarendon Press, 1991), pp. 202–3, 271. Some spelling in the quotation from Agaja (p. 271) has been modernized.

40. Law, *Slave Coast*, pp. 270–72, 275–76. For the use of women in armies, see Edna G. Bay, *Wives of the Leopard: Gender, Politics, and Culture in the Kingdom of Dahomey* (Charlottesville: University of Virginia Press, 1998), pp. 134–42.

41. Law, *Slave Coast*, pp. 278–94.

42. Ibid., pp. 345–48, 350.

43. Miller, *Way of Death*, pp. 88–91.

44. Ibid., pp. 116–26.

45. Inikori, "Import of Firearms," pp. 336–37, 360–62; Richards, "Import of Firearms," pp. 52–57. The interpretation presented here disagrees with that offered by Inikori. In arguing, from the volume of guns alone, for the existence of a slaves-for-guns cycle, Inikori ignores the fact that most slaves here were the product of kidnapping, not warfare. Inikori's contention that guns were unimportant in purchases of produce and other nonslave items is also belied by the continuing importance of firearm imports after the end of the overseas slave trade. See K. Onwuka Dike, *Trade and Politics in the Niger Delta, 1830–1885* (Oxford: Clarendon Press, 1956), pp. 104–5; Latham, *Old Calabar*, pp. 24, 73–74; Northrup, *Trade without Rulers*, pp. 79–80, 89–145, 209–10.

46. Cf. Geoffrey Parker, *The Military Revolution: Military Innovation and the Rise of the West, 1500–1800*, 2d ed. (Cambridge: Cambridge University Press, 1966); William H. McNeill, *The Pursuit of Power: Technology, Armed Force, and Society since* A.D. 1000 (Chicago: University of Chicago Press, 1982).

47. Bosman, *New and Accurate Description*, p. 187.

48. In Hodgkin, ed., *Nigerian Perspectives*, pp. 189–90.

49. Miller, *Way of Death*, pp. 40–139.

50. Few examples of such displays are known in inland areas, but Kea, *Settlements*, pp. 314–15, tells of the African merchant and chief revenue collector on the Cape Coast known as Jantie Snees, who put on an unusually lavish display there on April 6, 1667. Snees appeared accompanied by an entourage of musicians, wives, and slaves. He and his wives were clothed in fine imported silks and linens and bedecked with locally produced gold jewelry. He distributed rich gifts to those in attendance.

51. Anthony Hopkins, *An Economic History of West Africa* (New York: Columbia University Press, 1973), pp. 119–20; Eltis, "Precolonial Western Africa," pp. 103–110, quote p. 103; Thomas Fowell Buxton, *The African Slave Trade and Its Remedy* (London:

John Murray, 1840), pp. 304–8, compared the entire African trade unfavorably to the trade into Britain in eggs from France or pigs from Ireland.

52. Rodney, *How Europe*, p. 108.

53. By Robert S. Smith, *Warfare and Diplomacy in Pre-Colonial West Africa* (London: Methuen and Company 1976), pp. 91, 116, citing Jack Goody, *Technology, Tradition, and the State in Africa* (London: 1971), pp. 28, 52.

54. De Marees, *Description . . . of the Gold Kingdom*, pp. 85, 92; R. A. Kea, "Firearms and Warfare on the Gold and Slave Coasts from the Sixteenth to the Nineteenth Centuries," *Journal of African History* 12 (1971): 205; Mungo Park, *Travels in the Interior Districts of Africa: Performed in the Years 1795, 1796, and 1797* (London: John Murray, 1816), I:114–15.

55. Kea, "Firearms," p. 206; Martin Legassick, "Firearms, Horses and Samorian Army Organization, 1870–1898," *Journal of African History* 7.1 (1966): 95–115. See Buxton, *African Slave Trade*, pp. 479–80, for other examples of Africans repairing firearms, manufacturing all the parts of a musket except the flintlock, and making gunpowder.

Suggested Readings

Akyeampong, Emmanuel. *Drink, Power and Cultural Chanage: A Social History of Alcohol in Ghana, c. 1800 to Recent Times*. Portsmouth, NH: Heinemann, 1996.

Austen, Ralph. *African Economic History*. London: James Currey, 1987.

Curtin, Philip D. *Economic Change in Precolonial Africa*. Madison: University of Wisconsin Press, 1975.

Hopkins, Anthony. *An Economic History of West Africa*. New York: Columbia University Press, 1973.

Kea, Ray A. *Settlements, Trade, and Politics in the Seventeenth-Century Gold Coast*. Baltimore: John Hopkins University Press, 1982.

Law, Robin. *The Slave Coast of West Africa 1550–1750: The Impact of the Atlantic Slave Trade on an African Society*. Oxford: Clarendon Press, 1991.

Miller, Joseph C. *Way of Death: Merchant Capitalism and the Angolan Slave Trade, 1730–1830*. Madison: University of Wisconsin Press, 1988.

Northrup, David. *Trade without Rulers; Pre-Colonial Economic Development in South-Eastern Nigeria*. Oxford: Clarendon Press, 1978.

PASSAGES IN SLAVERY

Early in the year 1821, a youth in his early teens named Ajayi was "enjoying the comforts of father and mother, and the affectionate love of brothers and sisters," when his town of Osogun in the war-torn Oyo Empire was attacked by an army of some 20,000. As he tried to flee, Ajayi was captured along with his mother, two younger sisters, and a cousin. Other relatives young and old were also captured and soon led off in different directions as trophies of war, tied neck to neck with ropes. Within "the space of twenty-four hours," Ajayi later wrote, "I was made the property of three different persons," the last time in exchange for a horse. After two months with that owner, he was swapped back for the same horse and joyously reunited with his mother and baby sister. One evening three months later he was marched off to a market-town to be sold again. Ajayi passed the night weeping, "thinking of my doleful situation" and what would surely be a final separation from his mother. In the morning he was led away with many others all chained at the neck, to the market-town, where a woman speaking his own dialect of Yoruba bought him and took him to a distant town to the south, where he lived for some three months in comparative freedom as the companion of her son. He often thought of trying to escape, but the distance to his home was far and he feared the local spirits, whose shrines lined the roads out of town.

In his misery he tried suicide. Failing to strangle himself, he resolved that the next time they were crossing a river, he would leap out of the canoe and drown himself. When his owner divined his intentions, she sold him to an African trader, who sold him to another nearer the coast in exchange for tobacco, rum, and other articles that came from the Atlantic trade. Two months later he was taken to a slave market on the bank of a large river opposite Eko, the important eastern Slave Coast port that the Portuguese had called Lagos (the lake) because of its large lagoon. There he was sold for the seventh time, but as he crossed the great river in the bottom of a canoe, he was too sick and frozen with fear to carry out his suicide plan. Ajayi spent three months in Lagos, scarcely ever seeing a white face, until the day he was sold to a Portuguese ship. His mind was unnaturally calm that day: "Being a veteran in slavery, if I may be allowed the expression, and having no more hope of ever going to my country again, I patiently took what came; although it was not without great fear that I received, for the first time, the touch of a White Man, who examined me [to determine] whether I was sound or not."

For a time he lived chained by the neck with other boys and men, the boys suffering great bruises and near strangulation when the men yanked the heavy chains, especially at night when they slept confined in a windowless room, until, at last, "we boys had the happiness to be separated from the men," whose numbers had increased to the point that there were no more chains to spare for youths who didn't really need such heavy restraining. Ajayi and the other boys were tied with ropes but otherwise allowed more freedom than the adults during the four months their owners waited for an opportunity to evade the British patrols that were then trying to suppress the slave trade from Lagos.

On the morning of April 6, 1822, more than a year after his initial capture, Ajayi was one of 187 slaves loaded aboard the Brazilian schooner *Esperanza Felix*. He suffered his first dose of seasickness, but before the day was out, their slave ship was seized by a British patrol enforcing the five-year-old treaty with Portugal that made trading in slaves illegal north of the equator. At first fearful about this new turn of events and these new people, Ajayi and his five young comrades soon found themselves on one of the British naval vessels, where they were clothed, fed, and put to work aiding the crew. After seven and a half weeks, when other ships that had escaped the patrols would have been reaching their American destinations, Ajayi and his mates were landed in Freetown, Sierra Leone, quickly freed, and settled among other "recaptives" rescued by the British. In his new village Ajayi was placed under the care of British Church Missionary Society (CMS) missionaries and soon discovered many other Yoruba speakers from his locale, although no one from his own family or former acquaintants.[1]

The vivid details of Ajayi's very full account of his enslavement bring to life four important themes that are developed in this chapter. First, he takes us beyond the stereotypes of the slave trade and inside the thoughts and intense emotions that anguished captive Africans experienced. His detailed account brings to life his frightening experience of war and capture, his painful separation from home and relatives, his growing despair of ever escaping, and the successive waves of suicidal depression, apathy, and resignation that were in some form common to other captives. Second, he reminds us that slave experiences were not all the same—boys and adult men had very different experiences and, by implication, so did women. Third, he tell us of the bonding that gradually took place among those friendless, kinless souls, which gave them the strength to endure. He and his fellow orphans, Ajayi tells us, had become "one family, . . . six . . . friends in affliction," who kept together after their rescue so this new family would not be torn apart as their original families had been.

Finally, he suggests other ways in which African captives, recaptives, and slaves began to build new cultural identities and acquire new cultural skills, both African and European. Although he was reunited with none of his family members or townsmen in Sierra Leone (of the latter he could not find a dozen in all of the colony), he records his immediate "pleasure of meeting many of our country people," meaning simply people who spoke the same language. Those Yoruba whose dialects, shrines, and other ways had seemed so strange to him as he passed through their districts appeared less alien in this distant place. But his transformation was just beginning. In six months' time, under the missionaries' instruction the bright teenager "was able to read the New Testament with some degree of freedom" (apparently in English). Three years later he accepted baptism, embracing a new Christian community and receiving a new name, Samuel Crowther, the name of a CMS benefactor. After four more years, he married a woman rescued from slavery, like himself an Oyo and, he emphasizes, a Christian.

New communities and new languages, new names, and altered identities were common to nearly all Africans transplanted by the slave trade; the incidence of literacy and Christianity varied much more. We can use Samuel Ajayi Crowther no further as a model of larger experiences for, as the next chapter will chronicle, his life took quite exceptional turns that led to his becoming a famous Anglican bishop. In that he was unique, although it is worth noting that one of his close shipmates, Joseph Bartholomew, also became a CMS missionary. It is also unlikely that many other captives of the slave trade would have joined with Crowther in proclaiming the "unhappy day" of his capture was also a "blessed day" because it brought him to "the service of Christ." Crowther's assessment is his own and must be respected. Although other victims of the slave trade surely found less fulfillment and more sorrow in their new situations, all came to see their relationship to other Africans and to European culture from new perspectives.[2]

This chapter examines the external and internal passages of Africans in the Atlantic slave trade. It shows that the geographical passage across the Atlantic, the so-called "Middle Passage," was also a cultural passage. Because these external and internal passages often began long before Africans' first encounters with Europeans, the chapter begins with an overview of some additional African experiences of capture and enslavement. It probes the mental and emotional states of the trade's victims in order to bring to light experiences that are often hidden in accounts that consider only the physical sufferings of the Middle Passage. Finally, it examines how people torn from their homes and families created new identities, both as Africans and as members of new hybrid communities dominated by Europeans.

It is impossible not to be moved by the tremendous sufferings of those millions of African men, women, and children who encountered Europeans as victims of the Atlantic slave trade, but it is also important not to assume that the only role an enslaved African could play in those brutal circumstances was one of victim. Despite the sadness and dejection in which they boarded a European ship, individuals and groups sought to reshape their lives through resistance and accommodation. Stripped of their clothing, personal adornments, and dignity before embarking on a slave vessel, enslaved Africans still drew upon their personal strengths and their cultural baggage to build new lives, new communities, and new identities.

CAPTURE IN AFRICA

Personal accounts like Ajayi's are tremendously helpful in grasping the emotions individuals felt as they were separated from their homes and relatives and—over periods of weeks, months, or even years—journeyed toward the coast. However, for a broader perspective, one needs to match individual experiences with larger patterns of how Africans became enslaved and reacted to that experience. To keep these issues within manageable limits this chapter focuses on the peak period of the Atlantic slave trade, from the middle of the eighteenth century through the first part of the nineteenth century. A particularly large collection of personal narratives comes from people rescued from the slave trade by British patrols in the nineteenth century and, like Ajayi, resettled in the West African colony of Sierra Leone. There in 1850 a missionary named S. W. Koelle recorded brief tales of capture from over a hundred liberated Africans who were his informants for his compilation of African languages. Although one cannot see into every dark corner of the slave trade, such sources reveal many of its broad patterns and individual variations.

A high proportion of those who ended up in the Atlantic slave trade were enslaved in the course of wars among different African states, often at some distance from the coast.[3] Many of the captives were fighters in the wars, but others were women and children, like Ajayi, seized in the course of an attack, while fleeing the battle, or rounded up as part of the booty of war. As an earlier chapter has argued, Africans fought wars for many reasons, but slaves were usually the by-product of such conflicts, not their cause. A great many accounts of enslavement come from a series of loosely connected nineteenth-century wars fought in what is now northern Nigeria and Cameroon. The conflicts began in 1804 when a Muslim teacher from the Fulbe people proclaimed a *jihad* (holy war) against the nominally Muslim rulers of the Hausa states who continued to tolerate the non-Muslim practices of their rural subjects. The *jihad* spread rapidly across a vast area as Fulbe and Hausa Muslims raised armies that consolidated rule over a new Sokoto Caliphate, by 1810 the largest state in western Africa. Warfare continued for decades against the "pagan" villagers within or adjacent to this Muslim state, resulting in many prisoners. This was perhaps the fate of Yapanda, a man in his thirties from the Tiv town of Mukuwa on the southern edge of the caliphate, who told Koelle he was captured in a local war while on a trading tour in the 1820s. He was sold to Hausa traders, to Igala traders, and to others who carried him down the Niger River (probably through the market system mentioned in Chapter 4) to a coastal port that fed the Atlantic trade.[4]

Warfare also spread eastward against the Muslim-ruled state of Kanem-

Bornu, leading to many battles as well as a stinging exchange of theological arguments over the legitimacy of the *jihad*. In about 1812 a Kanuri resident of Bornu named Ali Eisami was captured by some Fulbe and passed along the well-established trade routes through the Caliphate into Yorubaland where he remained five years before being sold into the Atlantic trade. He and some two hundred fellow Kanuri were eventually freed in Sierra Leone, but thousands of others endured slavery in the Americas. To the southeast, Fulbe armies overran villages in a vast area called Adamawa, enslaving tens of thousands of people from the Cameroon Highlands. Some were kept as slaves locally, and others were exported into the Atlantic slave trade. Several from among Koelle's informants there were captured in raids by Muslim armies of Fulbe between 1819 and 1831 and sold through Old Calabar or other coastal ports in the Bight of Biafra. One of these was Mbepe, who told Koelle he was born and lived in the Nwala village of Ndob "till about his eighteenth year, when the Tipala [Fulbe] came to his country and burnt all the towns, so that the people had to flee for safety in every direction." During his flight Mbepe was captured and made a slave in a town that was itself soon attacked by the Fulbe. He fled again, was recaptured, reenslaved, and taken to Old Calabar, where he remained for three years before being sold into the Atlantic trade.[5]

As Ajayi's account reveals, to the southwest of the caliphate Fulbe armies invited in by Oyo Muslims to bolster their position in the internal politics of that disintegrating kingdom pillaged and enslaved, setting off a series of wars among different Yoruba groups that poured vast numbers of men, women, and children into the Atlantic trade. Many Yoruba speakers ended up in Cuba and Brazil, but thousands were rescued by the British patrol and freed in Sierra Leone. One of the latter was Joseph Wright, who, like Ajayi, was taken prisoner as a youth with other relatives in the 1820s and passed from hand to hand before being sold in a slave market. He too was kept roped with other youths at Lagos and experienced great sadness at the prospect of being sold away as well as the great fear hinted at by Ajayi that the Europeans would eat them. He tells more about the arrangements of the slaves on his ship: "[T]hey stowed all the men under the deck; the boys and women were left on the deck."[6]

Wars large and small elsewhere in Africa also fed the trade. From what is now Gabon comes a rare account by a woman, also named Yapanda, who was born and grew up in the Ndaza town of Peme. In about 1838, when her first child was just beginning to walk, Yapanda was taken prisoner in a local war. Her brief account does not say what became of that child, but it seems obvious that it was lost to her either at the capture or in the course of the next year as she passed from hand to hand over a distance of some five hundred miles to the coastal port where she was sold into the Atlantic slave trade. Judging by the name by which she was known in Sierra Leone, Mother Pratt, she must have remarried and had more children. She was the sole representative of her people in the colony.[7]

As important as wars and raids were in securing a supply of slaves, a nearly equal share of those sent into the Atlantic trade lost their freedom by being kidnapped, whether by strangers or false friends. Two youths who suffered this fate in the 1740s eventually escaped from slavery in the Americas and told their stories. One was Ukawsaw Gronniosaw, a child of the royal family of Bornu, whose vivid imagination was captivated by tales of white people and their ships ("houses with wings [that] walk upon the water") that were told by a visiting trader from the Gold Coast. He begged his family's permission to accompany the trader on his long journey home, but when Ukawsaw got there he became convinced that the Gold Coast king was going to behead him for being a spy. However, the boy was able to charm the king into agreeing to his being sold as a slave.[8] Some distance to the south of Bornu, an Igbo-speaking youth, Olaudah Equiano, and his sister were kidnapped from their home by two men and a woman while their parents were away in the fields. In his famous autobiography Equiano tells of his passage through a series of African masters toward the coast, his separation from his sister, and his eventual sale to Europeans at a port in the Niger Delta. Another Igbo speaker, William Pratt, told a Parliamentary committee of his enslavement as a boy in the early 1820s in these simple but haunting words: "I and a friend went out to set traps for rice birds and other birds in the field, and then I was kidnapped." Three of Koelle's five Igbo informants were also enslaved by kidnappers, two as children and one "by a treacherous friend" as an adult.[9]

Still others were sold by relatives for debt or other reasons or were sold by local authorities after being found guilty of adultery, witchcraft, or other crimes. Telling their stories years later, Koelle's informants who had been sold for adultery did not deny their guilt, but two cases he recorded illustrate the injustice of some sales. Edia of the Kossi people of Cameroon had prospered enough as a young man to have seven wives in the 1810s "when he was sold by his countrymen out of jealousy of his ability and influence." Bembi of the Ovimbundu people of southern Angola "was sold in about his twenty-eighth year in 1832 because his family had been accused of having occasioned the king's death by means of witchcraft." Although Bembi was transported across the Atlantic, he later emigrated to Sierra Leone.[10]

It is likely that the different ways in which people were enslaved affected their frames of mind when they reached the coast, even if those effects cannot be traced with precision. Those taken in war or kidnapped are likely to have seethed at the injustice of their enslavement more than those condemned for a crime they had actually committed, but all felt the agony of alienation from home and family. Hausa captives and Yoruba like Ajayi and Wright came from good-sized towns and language groups whose speakers numbered in the hundreds of thousands, most of Koelle's informants came from very small communities, and some came from very small language groups. All must have suffered from a deep sense of homesickness, but more painful than the loss of place was the loss of the kinship network that defined who they were. It was not simply the separation from mother, father, siblings, and grandparents that Ajayi so poignantly described, but the fact that for adults one's identity, position in society, and even one's occupation were tied to membership in a kinship-defined lineage or clan. Many of those from smaller languages would not have found any "country people" in their new homes. Such alienation was the occasion of extreme suffering, but, as will be examined in a later section, it also led to the development of substitute communities based on different geographical and associational ties.

Besides their origin and circumstances of enslavement, captives were also affected by the differences in their age and sex. Of Koelle's informants enslaved during the first half of the nineteenth century, about a quarter were under twenty years of age, half were in their twenties, and a quarter were over thirty; only a few were older than forty. Other records suggest that in this period the proportion of children actually entering the Atlantic trade was closer to 40 percent. The proportion of females of all ages averaged about a third.[11] Some studies suggest that because females in Africa were trained from childhood to accept a subordinate position in society, they accepted the circumstances of slavery more passively than males, who were raised to dominate and to fight. As Ajayi's narrative shows, youths could develop deep depressions in reaction to their enslavement, but their age also gave them great resilience and capacity for change. These differences had important implications during the ocean passage and what followed.

THE MIDDLE PASSAGE

First-person accounts by Africans of their passage to the Americas are precious, but many are frustratingly brief. Ottobah Cugoano, a slave who became an important abolitionist, wrote only this of his own experiences: "But it would be needless to give a description of all the horrible scenes which we saw, and the base treatment which we met with in this dreadful captive situation, as the similar cases of thousands, which suffer by this traffic, are well known." Female accounts are so scarce that one can only feel disappointment in discovering that an African woman named Try Norman who testified in 1848 to a British Parliamentary committee could only report that she was too young to remember her time on a slave ship before it was intercepted by a British vessel.[12] One must try to fill in these missing witnesses with the voices of those who left fuller descriptions.

The account of a West African Muslim, Mahommad Baquaqua, is more explicit than that of Cugoano about the great physical sufferings he endured on a voyage to Brazil in the 1840s:

> We were thrust into the hold of the vessel in a state of nudity, the males being crammed on one side, and the females on the other; the hold was so low that we could not stand up, but were obliged to crouch upon the floor or sit down; day and night were the same to us, sleep being denied us from the confined position of our bodies, and we became desperate through suffering and fatigue.

> Oh! the loathsomeness and filth of that horrible place will never be effaced
> from my memory; nay, as long as memory holds her seat in this distracted
> brain, I will remember that. My heart even at this day, sickens at the thought
> of it. . . .
>   The only food we had during the voyage was corn soaked and boiled. . . .
> We suffered very much for want of water, but was [sic] denied all we needed.
> A pint a day was allowed, and no more; and a great many slaves died upon
> the passage. . . .
>   When any of us became refractory, his flesh was cut with a knife, and pep-
> per and vinegar was [sic] rubbed in to make him peaceable (!) I suffered, and
> so did the rest of us, very much from sea sickness at first, but that did not
> cause our brutal owners any trouble. . . . Only twice during the voyage were
> we allowed to go on deck to wash ourselves—once whilst at sea and again
> just before going into port.[13]

A youth named Augustino, who was brought to Brazil in 1830, likewise
emphasized the disagreeable physical circumstances of the voyage in his
testimony to a Select Committee of the British Parliament in 1849. Because
of his youth he was not chained and was allowed on deck, but he witnessed
the misery of the naked adults below deck, the diet of boiled meal, the heat,
the inadequacy of the water rations, and the large number of deaths. He
believed most deaths were due to dehydration, but noted that some slaves
who were allowed on deck "jumped overboard, for fear they were being
fattened to be eaten."[14]

These two accounts are from late in the trade and may reflect some circumstances peculiar to the illegal trade to Brazil. Their concern with de-
tailing the physical sufferings of slaves is in line with the British abolitionist
campaign to stop the traffic in human beings by bringing such horrors to
light. Indeed, the two accounts derive from anti–slave trade efforts: Baquaqua told his story to an abolitionist publisher in New York, and Augustino
was responding to questions of a Parliamentary committee with an abolitionist mandate. The reality of these sufferings is beyond dispute, but there
are hints that Ajayi's emphasis on his mental anguish at this point in his
captivity was true here, too. Baquaqua acknowledges his deep inner pain
in a single sentence: "Our sufferings were our own, we had no one to share
our troubles, none to care for us, or even speak a word of comfort to us."
Augustino hints at the terrors that drove some to suicide.

Other narratives emphasize how the emotional strains and fears experienced en route to the sea continued to dominate many captives' minds in
their encounters with their first Europeans and the slave ships. Equiano's
well-known description of his passage in the mid-eighteenth century put
great emphasis on his emotional anguish. He recounted his "astonishment"
at the slave ship and his "terror" at the sight of the strange "red" men who
examined him. Here, too, his abolitionist views may have influenced his
portrait, but the sentiments resonate with those expressed by others and
are tied to fundamental African beliefs. Just a few pages earlier in his *Narrative* Equiano had recounted how "magicians" in his homeland were re-

vered for curing people of evil curses and discovering the perpetrators of evil magic. It is in the context of this belief in witchcraft that one needs to interpret his statement that on the slave ship he became convinced that he "had gotten into a world of bad spirits" who would feed on his flesh, just as Augustino's shipmates had feared. The idea already in his head was confirmed by the large copper cooking pot he saw on deck and by the dejected looks on the faces of the black people in chains all around him. All this pushed him into an emotional abyss at least the equal of the physical sufferings others endured. "Indeed," he writes, "such were the horrors of my views and fears at the moment, that, if ten thousand worlds had been my own, I would have freely parted with them all to have exchanged my condition with that of the meanest slave in my own country." Overcome by these emotions, Equiano fainted. When he regained consciousness, some of those Africans who had sold him tried to steady his nerves with a glass of alcoholic spirits and assurances that he was not to be eaten, but it had no good effect. Already "abandoned to despair," he was moved below deck where the loathsome stench added to his miseries and drove him still deeper into despair that he lost all desire for food and "wished for the last friend, Death, to relieve me."[15]

Many other accounts attest that fears of Europeans being evil spirits who feasted on human flesh had long been widespread and did not diminish during the century after Equiano's own enslavement. As Chapter 1 recounted, the Portuguese first heard such accusations on the Gambia in 1455. A French account in the late seventeenth century attributed the melancholy of slaves to the fact that "many of the slaves ... are prepossessed with the opinion, that they are carried like sheep to the slaughter, and that Europeans are fond of their flesh." A century later, an English observer in Jamaica, who had questioned his slaves about this as soon as they learned enough English, got a similar but fuller account of what was in their minds during the Middle Passage: "[s]ome of these poor wretches believe that they are bought in order to be fattened, and eaten. Others suppose, that the Europeans buy them to make gunpowder of their bones." An experienced British slave captain in the 1770s and 1780s reported that slaves usually showed fears of being eaten, "which it is the business of the traders to remove." In the 1820s, Joseph Wright similarly testified that he and his companions were driven to despair by the rumor "that the Portuguese were going to eat us," while the Portuguese, in turn, warned them that the British anti–slave trade patrol would eat them if they were caught. An allied belief was that the French made their red wine from the blood of slaves.[16]

These accounts suggest that the mental states of African captives on a slave ship may provide deeper insight into some aspects of the Middle Passage than do the familiar details of the physical accommodations. At different ends of the emotional spectrum, both suicide and mutiny were expressions of how slaves' depression, fear, and anger displaced their natural impulse for self-preservation. As both Ajayi and Equiano testify, they often thought of ending their miserable lives. It was so common for enslaved Africans on the Middle Passage to suffer from the state of depression that contemporary Europeans called "fixed melancholy" that the slavers took special steps to deal with it. Equiano states he was severely flogged for not eating, despite his tender years. Others had food forced down their throats by means of special devices the ships carried. A French slaver, who believed himself compassionate by nature, reported that the necessity he felt in forcing reluctant slaves to eat had sometimes resulted in breaking their teeth in order to insert a metal feeding device into their mouths.[17] Because the tedium of the voyage and overcrowding of the ships added to the slaves' depressed state, slavers enforced dancing and singing, knowing that activity would help break the melancholy. Perhaps it had a therapeutic effect, but one account reported the songs were all sad ones of "sickness, fear of being beaten, their hunger, and the memory of their country." When slaves on another ship began to cry out in a most melancholy and anguished way, they told the female slave interpreter sent to investigate that the reason was because they had been dreaming they were in their homes and, when they awakened, found themselves in the hold of the slave ship.[18]

Depression and misery drove many to contemplate suicide by more immediate means than self-starvation. Slave ships had to erect netting around the upper deck to prevent the slaves from leaping into the sea. Equiano says he would have done that himself if the netting had not prevented him and tells of two Igbo men on his ship who, despite being chained together, managed to get through the netting into the deep. Another "quite dejected fellow" quickly followed them and more would have followed had not the crew rushed to stop them. The first two drowned but the third was rescued and "flogged . . . unmercifully, for thus attempting to prefer death to slavery."[19]

Investors in the slave trade could suffer financial loss if crews failed to prevent individual suicides, but crews had greater reason to take precautions against another expression of slaves' disregard of their lives—slave rebellions, often termed "mutinies." To meet this threat, crews on slave ships were twice as numerous as on other vessels and were well armed. Although the chance of rebellious slaves successfully gaining control of a ship or escaping to shore were slim, this did not seem to discourage attempts. Modern research has uncovered evidence of slave rebellions on 383 ships, of which in only twenty-three cases did a slave succeed in making it to shore. In most cases the crew managed to put down the rebellion, although often at the cost of many slaves' lives. Captured ringleaders were often executed with extreme cruelty to intimidate the others. Mutinies resulted in the deaths of an average of fifty-seven slaves per revolt on ships from Senegambia, although the figure is lower for other coasts.[20]

Although there are many stirring accounts by captains and crew of suppressing revolts, African views were rarely recorded. Many seem to be desperate acts in which death was an acceptable alternative to enslavement or to the worse fates many feared. We get a clearer African perspective from the last recorded revolt, a successful one that killed many of the crew on the French vessel *Regina Coeli* off Liberia in 1858. It was not the conditions on the ship (nor perhaps the distant destination of the voyage) that drove them to rebel, but the injustice they felt at their African masters selling them away from their homeland. As domestic slaves born in slavery in this land, they believed their masters had no right to sell them away. Some rebels later asserted that had their masters been on board they would gladly have killed them along with the Europeans. Fleeing to Liberia, the rebels sought to escape the control of these unjust masters as well as to remain in Africa.[21]

The success of the rebellion on the *Regina Coeli* owed much to the fact that the slaves' common origin gave them a high degree of unity. More often slaves bought at a single port came from a number of different places, spoke different languages, and pursued different strategies. A slave revolt on the English ship *Brome* in 1693 was led by "Jolloffes" (i.e., Wolof speakers from Senegal), the captain reported, but the Bambara speakers from further inland "sided with the Master." Why the Bambara acted in this manner can only be guessed at, but the implication is that they feared if the Jolof were successful they might be worse off than they were in the hands of the Europeans. It is possible that religious differences lay behind this ethnic division: The Jolof were Muslim; the Bambara at this time were not and would have been sold to the English by Muslim traders.[22] One wonders how Ajayi might have reacted to a revolt led by the Oyo Muslims who had enslaved him.

If the mental states of the slaves deserve serious attention, this does not mean that the physical conditions and pain associated with them should be ignored. Although some authors give the impression that the arrangements on a slave ship were chaotic, that the slavers just jammed as many Africans into the hold as they could and sailed off, the slave trade was in fact a highly organized business driven by a very specific goal: to get the costly cargo of slaves across the ocean with as few losses as possible. Otherwise, profit was impossible, as not a few investors seeking a quick return discovered. As the abolitionists recorded, outrageous lapses could and did occur, but the rational purposes are evident in the statistical regularities that modern scholars have compiled.

During the peak decades of the trade, the ships themselves were specially built or adapted for slave cargoes. Special platforms between decks provided additional space to stow the slaves during the weeks of the passage. The maximum capacity was calculated carefully and sometimes diagrammed on charts, generally permitting each adult slave just enough room to lie down (although sometimes only on one's side or not at full length). Some ships failed to get the full cargo they desired; other captains could not resist packing extras in, but the averages were remarkably similar overall.

Slavers took great care to prevent disorder. All but the smallest vessels segregated the women, girls, and young children from the stronger and more aggressive men. Some vessels also kept older boys by themselves, just as Ajayi had experienced on shore, or allowed them greater freedom of movement above deck, since they posed no physical threat. On ships from Angola, the men were placed below decks, while women, infants, and small children were kept in the cabins. A common British design of the 1780s had strong partitions to divide the cargo hold into three chambers: "[T]he men are cooped up in the fore part of the ship, the boys in the middle, and the women and girls in the aft part of the vessel." Once ships were out of sight of land slaves were less inclined to revolt, as they lost hope and resigned themselves to their fates. One British slaver testified that women, youths, and children were always at liberty and the men's chains would gradually be taken off, "if they appeared reconciled to their condition," but another had a different emphasis: "[T]he females and boys soon recover their spirits—the men seldom; they remain gloomy a great while."[23]

Keeping a slave vessel clean was a nearly impossible task, not only because of the large numbers of people crammed into a small space but also because a high percentage of the slaves suffered from diarrhea and dysentery. Inevitably the sleeping platforms became fouled with the blood and excrement of those too weak to reach the tubs for public evacuation in the holds. Efforts at cleanliness varied from ship to ship and by nationality and century. Miller says the Portuguese only belatedly took up bathing slaves and describes their efforts to cleanse the ship as consisting "mostly of mopping up the mess, scrubbing down all parts of the ship at least once a day," and trying "persistently but vainly to clear the air below decks" with a variety of products from vinegar and tar to whitewash, whose efficacy he doubts. Stein, on the other hand, states that the French were quite fastidious, bathing slaves at least twice a week, washing the whole ship daily and scraping it down every two or three days in good weather, and doing a good job of ventilating and deodorizing the vessel. A contemporary Dutch source said that "the French, Portuguese, and English slave-ships are always foul and stinking," compared to the Dutch ships, which were "for the most part clean and neat." A British slaver, proud of his own record, reported that on his ships the slaves were "comfortably lodged" and their quarters were washed and fumigated every day. He believed the French were not so concerned with cleanliness as the Dutch.[24]

Although conditions varied greatly from ship to ship, over time improvements in food, water, ventilation, and sanitation led to a decline in the death rates on slave ships. To ensure their profits captains took great precautions to secure enough water and food to last the voyage, most carrying a substantial surplus to guard against emergencies. Nevertheless, as the testimonies of Baquaqua and Augustino confirm, shortages could occur. Overall, the efforts to reduce losses of life succeeded. Modern studies reveal that losses averaged 20 percent before 1600, but fell to 12 percent during the second half of the eighteenth century. However, such averages hide the fact that mortality varied widely from ship to ship. While a distressing number of ships lost a third or more of their slaves, the greatest number of ships recorded slave deaths below 5 percent. In the early nineteenth century death rates fell below one in ten per voyage, but as pressures on the illegal trade mounted from British patrols, evasive maneuvers and longer voyages from unpatrolled ports in southeastern Africa pushed losses back up in the last decades of the trade. Because so much of the trade was conducted during the period with the lowest losses, the average loss per voyage during the entire period of the Atlantic slave trade was 12.4 percent, one slave in every eight. Only in comparison to still worse cases can such numbers be seen as anything but horrific.[25]

The decline in mortality was the result more of a desire to increase profits than of a greater humanity among the slave traders, but the character of the slave traders is worth further exploration. It suited the abolitionists' propaganda efforts to stress slave traders' moral depravity, and they did not want for examples. The nature of the trade and the risks to life and limb did not attract the sea's finest. Already in the seventeenth century, Barbot had argued that most of the agents and employees the trading companies stationed in Africa were men driven by poverty who were not likely to be deterred in their pursuit of wealth by any moral scruples: "men of no education or principles, void of forethought, careless, prodigal, addicted to strong liquors, [and] some, perhaps no small number, are over fond of the black women."[26] A youthful crewman familiar with the peak years of the Liverpool slave trade lamented the officers' stinting on provisions for the crew and other forms of "rascality."[27] However, many of the abolitionists' most valuable recruits were ex–slave traders, especially ship doctors, whose firsthand testimony so vividly captured the horrors of the passage. Some of these had undergone a religious conversion, but their sensitivity and efforts to alleviate the misery of the slaves, even if for the sake of profit, make it clear that not all slavers were from the bottom of the barrel. As the author of one esteemed recent history of the trade puts it, "Brutality was neither normal nor inevitable."[28] No owner would knowingly place a valuable ship and cargo in the hands of a drunkard or psychopath. Ships' officers and doctors were well paid to complete the voyage expeditiously and with as few losses of life as possible. Moreover, captains were themselves often investors in the voyages and well understood the role of order and discipline in producing profits.

It is against this background that one must consider the differences in Africans' encounters with European slavers. A distressing number of Africans, of course, died during the Middle Passage. Some slaves took their own lives, finding in death, as Equiano put it, "the last friend" to rescue them from physical discomfort and mental anguish. Others died in rebellions or from whippings and other cruel punishments afterwards. But it has long been clear that the principal cause of death was disease. The journal of the English ship *Arthur* in March and April 1678 recorded the all-too-familiar experience. The slavers had chosen their slaves with utmost care, "as likely negroes as a man should see," treated them humanely, and fed them "as much provisions as they can make use of," yet some became sick. The sick were tended with "the greatest care we could" and given brandy and red pepper to revive them. Some recovered, yet by ones and twos others died.[29] Unlike most slavers in the peak decades of the trade, the *Arthur* carried no doctor and the curative powers of pepper and alcohol are small, but it is unlikely that a doctor with a full medicine chest would have produced much better results. There were no cures in these centuries for the diseases most likely to cause death. Despite careful selection of slaves to exclude anyone showing signs of disease, epidemics of smallpox often broke out, striking down those Africans and crew who had not acquired immunity from a previous infection. Even under the best conditions, it was easy in the crowded and unsanitary ships for bacterial infections to spread in food and water, causing diarrhea and dysentery. The dehydration that followed claimed many lives.

Among the survivors, experiences varied by age and sex. Many detailed accounts are by Africans who were boys at the time of their voyages and whose experiences were often notably different from those of adult slaves. Because they posed no threat to the slavers, boys' treatment was sometimes free of the harsh measures slave traders used to keep older males in check. Like Ajayi, these bright and clever lads were quick to make friends with other young captives and often charmed the crew as well. At the slave market in Rio de Janeiro in 1828, a British clergyman observed "some young boys, who seemed to have formed a society together" that was distinguished by mutual aid and affection.[30] Other boys developed close relationships with the European officers, becoming their "pets" or surrogate sons. Of course, the boys were quick to see the practical advantages of better food and treatment that this status afforded, but some may have found in these older men the father figure they had lost at captivity. The image is most obvious in Ukawsaw Gronniosaw's relationship with the Dutch captain whose ship carried him to the Americas. He narrates that he embraced the captain at first sight, crying "father, save me," begging to be rescued from a possible death at the hands of his African captors. As the voyage progressed, the devotion was reciprocated, "My master grew very fond of me," Gronniosaw recalled, "and I loved him exceedingly.... [M]y only pleasure was to serve him well." It was with some reluctance, Gronniosaw says, that at the crossing's end the captain sold him for fifty dollars to a gentleman from New York, who also treated him well.

Equiano recounts having a similar relationship with Captain Thomas Farmer, who worked for his master in Monserrat. "The captain liked me very much," Equiano wrote, and often persuaded Equiano's owner to let the youth accompany him on different trips between islands and to the mainland. With his master's consent, Equiano finally became a sailor on Farmer's ship, which pleased the youth very much: "I did all I could to deserve his favour, and in return received better treatment from him than any other [slave] ever met with in the West Indies." During the voyages Equiano was able to engage in trade on his own and eventually accumulated enough money to buy his freedom.[31] One may argue that Equiano was simply exploiting Farmer's affection for him to obtain better treatment. Even though that was a part of his intention, there is no reason to think he did not sincerely return the captain's friendship.

Another clear example of a youth's devotion to his captors occurred during a slave revolt on the ship *Eagle Galley* in 1704. Seeing that one of the rebels was about to club the captain, who had treated him well, the unnamed lad of about seventeen placed himself between them and took a heavy blow that fractured his arm. During an unsuccessful slave revolt on another English ship in 1787 a boy named Bristol, whom one of the officers was taking to England to give to his mother, helped the Europeans to persuade the slaves to submit and later gave warning of another plot to seize control. On the same ship the African cook played a leading role in putting down the first revolt. Lest it seem that such devotion can be only a sign of unusual subservience, consider the case of an African boy named Telemaque, who became the pet of Captain Joseph Vesey. Vesey sold the boy at the end of the trip but agreed to take him back when the boy began having seizures, faked, it would seem, to regain his former relationship. In any event it worked and Telemaque served Captain Vesey for two years on his slave ship, even taking the captain's name, before he was sold again. We do not know what Telemaque was thinking but in later life he played a different role in a slave revolt than the *Eagle Galley* lad. In 1822, Denmark Vesey (as he was then known) led the largest and best planned slave rebellion in the history of the United States.[32]

Female voices are so rare that their experiences must be sketched from other sources. Because it was believed that there was little chance of their starting a rebellion, females were less likely to be shackled and more likely to be allowed above deck, which certainly alleviated them of some of the horrors of the voyage. On the other hand, historian Joseph Miller suggests, women's freedom made them more "accessible for sexual abuse without requiring the crew to offend their senses or risk assault by the males by venturing below." There are no ways to measure either the frequency or the consequences of sexual abuse, but most accounts believe it was common. One reported instance, one hopes worse than most, involved the second captain on a French ship in the 1770s. Philippe Liot first raped a very pretty African woman, whose resistance is suggested in the fact that she sustained two broken teeth. Then he entered the hold and removed a little girl of eight to ten years, covering her mouth so that his fellow officers would not hear her protests. Three nights running he brutally raped her before being discovered. The physical and emotional damage to both slaves reduced their sale price in Saint Domingue, which is why the incident came to be reported.[33]

Women were capable of being much more than victims. A case of a woman who had the trusted role of interpreter has already been mentioned. Women also did some of the work of food preparation on ships. Despite stereotypes of their passivity, some also were rebels. A powerful woman on the Liverpool ship *Hudibras* out of Old Calabar in 1786, for example, was put in charge of the female slaves and used her position to plot with the men to try to take over the ship. After a slave revolt on the *Kentucky*, an American slaver trading from Mozambique to southern Brazil in 1844, a woman was among the forty-six rebels put to death.[34]

Adult men were usually the largest group of slaves, and in some ways their experiences may have been the least varied. However, as we have seen, there could be sharp differences among them along ethnic and religious lines. During part of the slave trade some male slaves helped the Europeans maintain order on the ships. The practice may have arisen from the castle slaves, or *grommetos*, who were brought from elsewhere in West Africa to serve European trading companies on the Gold Coast. As foreigners, these were loyal to their European owners and were useful in warning of impending rebellions among the slaves being readied for shipment. In the seventeenth century trading companies also employed African "guardians" from the Gold Coast on vessels carrying slaves from the Slave Coast. According to one report, these guardians were given whips and placed among the other slaves "to keep them from quarrelling" and to enable them to report any plotting before it could produce a revolt. Even though the guardians were themselves sold along with the rest of the slaves when the ship reached the Americas, the practice worked very successfully. The practice of African guardians on slave ships disappeared along with the trading companies themselves in the early eighteenth century. As Eltis notes, in the absence of guardians, the frequency of slave revolts rose.[35]

NEW IDENTITIES

Toward the end of the seventeenth century a West African woman had the great misfortune to be sold to a French slaver and the extraordinary luck to discover on his ship her husband and their four children from whom she had been separated after their capture. She was also lucky that the French captain was so struck by their rare good fortune that he decided to permit the family to stay together on board and even insisted on selling them as a family unit to a Martinique planter who promised to keep them together.[36] How fascinating it would be to follow the subsequent life of the family, if only the records existed! But it would be a very exceptional story. Families almost never made it to the New World intact. Indeed, it was unusual for even a married couple to be sold and transported together, although siblings sometimes were. With rare exceptions, enslaved Africans entered a world where they had no kinfolk, no old friends, and no fellow villagers. Some might pass years without speaking to a single person who knew their mother tongue. In such trying circumstances Africans were forced to build new social networks and new identities.

Several excellent new surveys explore the tribulations and survival strategies of Africans and their descendants in slavery comparatively or in various regions of the Americas.[37] To maintain this study's focus on persons born in Africa and on the lives of particular individuals, this section examines the fates of the 94,000 men, women, and children from all over Africa who were rescued from slave ships by British naval patrols and resettled in Sierra Leone between 1815 and 1850. Even if they never crossed the Atlantic, these "liberated Africans" evolved new lives in new communities that closely paralleled the social and cultural changes taking place in slave societies in the Atlantic world. The settlers in Sierra Leone are particularly enlightening as a case study of change in the African diaspora because their experiences are well documented both from within the African community and by outsiders.

The fact that they were freed from their captivity soon after landing means that Sierra Leonean settlers escaped the harsh circumstances of slavery in the Americas, but their lives illustrate how people torn from their homelands and mixed together in new surroundings went about reconstructing their cultural and social identities. Because they had greater freedom, liberated Africans in Sierra Leone were able to rebuild their lives more rapidly, but their choices were remarkably close to those observed in slave societies in the Americas. This similarity stems from three circumstances Africans liberated from slave ships in Sierra Leone shared with communities of Africans transported to the Americas. The first was that they were a diverse group drawn from many different parts of Africa, but with a predominant central core of people drawn from a single African region, just as was usually the case in the Americas. Three-fourths of the slaves liberated in Freetown came from the adjacent coasts of the Bights of Benin and Biafra in the Gulf of Guinea. Second, they found themselves in a colony run by Europeans who were more benevolent than those in plantation colonies but with similar expectations of the directions in which cultural change should proceed. Not surprisingly, these expectations included European values and institutions. Finally, liberated Africans took up residence in a colony with an existing non-European population of both indigenous people and earlier settlers whose presence shaped the direction of change. Freetown had originally been colonized in the 1790s by people of African descent from Britain, North America, and the West Indies seeking to build new lives. Although this experiment had not been very successful and these earlier settlers would be overwhelmed by the flood of newly liberated Africans from the slave ships, as in much of the Americas the trajectory of cultural change would be shaped in subtle ways by indigenous and settler populations.

The differences among Africans in Sierra Leone and the need to rebuild lives shattered by enslavement and the harsh experiences of the Middle Passage pushed cultural change in two different but complementary directions that have their clear counterparts in the Americas. Their first task was to learn how to speak, act, and live in their new setting. This process of acculturation is commonly called "creolization" in the Americas, meaning the acculturation of people of African descent to a non-African cultural environment. Strictly speaking, creolization was a long complex process, and only people born and raised in a creole society were deemed to be creoles. Thus, liberated Africans were not creoles, but their ways of living were being reshaped under the strong influences of European authorities and the African diaspora creoles who had first settled the colony. Their acculturation in Sierra Leone involved becoming familiar with English, the dominant language of the colony, as well as with other cultural norms, such as types of dress, decorum, and religion. Because the language, religion, and other cultural practices were of European origin, the process could be called "Europeanization," but creolization is preferred because it conveys the important fact that identities and cultures in colonial societies were derived only partly from Europe and partly from the large non-European population. In the Americas, the process might be called "Americanization" were it not for the widespread use of this term to describe the process of cultural amalgamation and innovation taking place just within the boundaries of the United States, especially the acculturation of large numbers of European immigrants between the 1840s and 1910s.

The other side of the cultural transformation taking place among newly arrived Africans in Sierra Leone and the New World lacks a common name. Indeed, it was once common to argue that Africans descending from slave ships brought no culture with them, that the traumatic experience of captivity and transport had made them into a kind of blank page on which a new creole culture could be imprinted. Recent historians have rediscovered the rich cultural baggage captives brought from their homelands and traced how it survived even under the harshest slavery. The most insightful of these historians have seen that this was not a static "survival" of pieces of old Africa but a dynamic part of the process by which Africans reconstructed their shattered lives and identities. Some have called this process of *ethnogenesis* (ethnicity formation) "Africanization," which seems a useful descriptive term. Although it may seem odd from an outsider's perspective that people from Africa could be Africanized, for those who descended from the slave ships that process was just as meaningful as creolization. Alienated from the rural villages of their homelands, they began to reidentify themselves with the broader population whose fate they shared. Just as the African coastal elite interacting with Europeans had been doing for centuries, the masses on slave ships were rediscovering themselves as part of a vast continent of dark-skinned people and repositioning themselves as members of newly defined cultural nations within Africa.

The processes of creolization and Africanization will be examined separately, but it is important to realize that they progressed simultaneously, if at separate paces. Some immigrants clung tenaciously to older ways, while many others made substantial changes in their lives. Young immigrants were the most open to change and in Sierra Leone's church-run and public schools some liberated Africans creolized themselves rapidly, becoming important agents of cultural transformation and occupying important positions in the churches, schools, and the colonial government. The conditions of slavery prevented such high achievements in the Americas, where it took more time and more freedom to produce a Westernized African elite. In parts of the Americas where the majority of slaves continued to be African-born well into the nineteenth century (notably in Brazil and the West Indies) Africanization remained a vibrant process that left a deep imprint on entire colonies. However, to describe all the different variations of acculturation and ethnogenesis in the Americas would require a much longer study. Let us return to the case study of Sierra Leone.

CREOLIZATION

In Sierra Leone as in the Americas those who descended from the slave ships had to adjust to a world in which Europeans dominated politically and European speech and culture were paramount. For some the process of creolization had begun before their arrival. As earlier chapters have shown, many coastal Africans were conversant in one or more European languages or pidgins. Inland Africans who spent much more than a brief time in coastal shipping ports might acquire some knowledge of a European language. Several men in a slave cargo taken from Old Calabar in 1786 had a good command of English, which they had learned while living in Old Calabar and its vicinity—whether as slaves or as free people is not clear. Others began learning a new language during the Middle Passage. Mahommad Baquaqua related, "I had contrived whilst on my passage in the slave ship, to gather up a little knowledge of the Portuguese language," which was sufficient, he found on arrival in Brazil, to understand what his new master wanted of him.[38] In surviving the harsh experience of enslavement new African and European languages would be important, as would new identities.

In many ways the spread of English in Sierra Leone mirrored the New World experience of slaves, but no one has ever suggested that enslaved Africans lost all memory of their mother tongues. Koelle had little trouble collecting vocabulary lists from Africans who had lived in the colony for decades, even in some cases with few occasions to use their language. His informant for the Karekare language of Northern Nigeria, for example, had spent twenty-six years in the colony without another countryman to talk to until one arrived four years earlier. Another man, forty years away from home with hardly any other speakers, still had a fine command of his mother tongue. However, Koelle did encounter some individuals who had lost fluency in their mother tongues.[39]

Of course, none of those whose first language had grown rusty were without a language, and the experience of most in Sierra Leone included learning one or more new languages. This might be the dominant African language in their settlement or another language they had brought from home. But for most the new language was English. A liberated African named George Crowley Nicol testified to a British Parliamentary committee in 1849 that all recaptives freed in Sierra Leone picked up English soon after their arrival since it was essential for communication with the authorities and with Africans speaking different languages. Even at home, he reported, married couples like his own recaptive parents spoke nothing but English when they had no African language in common.[40] Bright young-sters, such as Ajayi Crowther, might have been exceptional in the speed with which they mastered both spoken and written English, but even older people learned quickly. Koelle met a man of fifty, only three years in the colony, who spoke passable English. Another man, a Fulbe from Kano, only three years in the colony, spoke English "surprisingly well." This was of course similar to the New World experience of slaves, as another man of the Fulbe Koelle interviewed could attest. His good English had been ac-quired during the forty years he spent in Jamaica, where a slave ship had landed him in his late teens, before he came to Sierra Leone.[41]

A more complex cultural transformation came in religion. As Chapter 2 recounted, Christianity had also been spreading since the 1480s in parts of coastal Africa, so some enslaved Africans were likely to have brought Chris-tian beliefs and practices along with them. However, Muslims were far more numerous than Christians among enslaved Africans. Some like Ayuba persevered in their practices; others blended Islam with Christianity. The parents of Thomas Maxwell of Sierra Leone had both been raised Muslims in Bornu, but in Sierra Leone, while his father remained devoted to Islam, his mother became a Christian.[42]

The speed with which large numbers of Africans in Sierra Leone vol-untarily became Christians is an interesting complement to the situation in some New World colonies where plantation masters imposed Christian practices on their slaves because it suggests that many Africans in distress-ing new surroundings profoundly desired the consolations of a new reli-gion. In his great history of Sierra Leone, Christopher Fyfe summarizes the mental and spiritual transformations Africans underwent in vivid biblical images:

> Amid the Babel of tongues English became not only a lingua franca but a Pentecostal interpreter, speaking a message many were ready to hear. For abandoned by their own gods who had failed to protect them in their home-land, they came up from the hold of the slave ship like Jonah from the whale, cut off from their own life, ready to be re-born into a new.[43]

Those who had been torn from their families and communities and had experienced the traumas of the Middle Passage certainly found themselves in need of spiritual consolation and, in the absence of the rituals of their ancestors, were as open to new religious practices as they were to new languages.

In Sierra Leone recaptives were generally put into the care of Anglican, Methodist, or Baptist missionary societies, whose dedicated missionaries had much success in creating new Christian communities in short order. But it would be a great oversimplification to imagine Africans passively allowing themselves to be indoctrinated by Europeans. For one thing, the preachers were not all Europeans. Given the extraordinarily high mortality among European missionaries and their small numbers, much of the process of instruction and leadership was in the hands of Africans. Some were African-American settlers and their descendants, but both Anglicans and Methodists also employed newly converted liberated Africans. These lay leaders or "helpers" organized classes in which newly arrived Africans were given religious instruction in their own languages. Although under the pastor's supervision, the helpers' authority and influence in the congregations were often greater than that of the Europeans. In time, a number of Africans became teachers and catechists for the missionary societies. Some were ordained ministers, including Ajayi Crowther's shipmate, Joseph Bartholomew; an Igbo receptive, Charles Knight; and a Yoruba speaker, Joseph Wright. After two years of training in London, the latter two were named assistant missionaries in 1844 and, following their ordination as full ministers in 1848, the pair had precedence over more junior missionaries in the colony, much to the chagrin of some of the subordinate Europeans.[44]

In addition, African recaptives' response to this evangelization was far from passive. Their traumas of enslavement and forced relocation, as Fyfe suggests, made them very receptive to the message of salvation that missionaries and catechists preached. Nor did it take long for new congregations to gain significant control over their churches, sometimes by switching from one denomination to another. Others built their own churches and hired (and fired) their own ministers. As Chapter 2 has suggested, Africans were also quick to infuse European forms of Christianity with African religious sentiments. Many gravitated to the Methodists because they were more open than the Anglicans to appeals to the spirit. The process of conversion was demonstrated by "seeking and finding," encountering salvation through outward signs, such as visions and convulsions, rather than by passive acceptance of the preacher's message. Hymn singing was infused with distinctly African musical forms accompanied by hand clapping and dancing.[45]

Additional information on the process of ethnogenesis in Sierra Leone comes from an official report at mid-century. In it the acting governor estimated that there were some twenty-one thousand African Christians in the colony, along with two thousand Muslims and at least twelve thousand "Pagans," according even these traditionalists the courtesy of a capital letter. Some of the Muslims were indigenous to the region, but many were liberated Africans, especially Yoruba, who had adopted Islam before their entry into the Atlantic slave trade. The so-called "Pagans" similarly continued to follow religious traditions they remembered from their homelands, the very numerous Yoruba being conspicuous in following the worship of Shango, the god of thunder and other deities of the Yoruba pantheon. The acting governor believed that many inhabitants professing Christianity also continued to believe in the powers of traditional magic and witchcraft of their homelands. While conceding that decades of efforts had failed to convert many recaptives, he preferred to emphasize how much had been done.[46]

Especially for young Africans, the schools of Sierra Leone were an important agent of acculturation. Education was actively promoted by the missionaries and colonial officials, but it is impossible to ignore the very real enthusiasm with which liberated Africans embraced formal education in Western subjects. The schools had their beginnings among the colony's original black settlers from England and North America. Teachers, including some of African descent as well as European merchants and an occasional stranded sailor, were enlisted to meet the demand for schooling among both children and adults. Schools soon became an essential part of the settlements of liberated Africans. For a time schools were entirely in the hands of the missions, which spent great sums to keep up with the demand. Government subsidies helped, and even when the missions imposed modest fees in the 1830s to keep up with the costs, school enrollment continued growing in the prospering colony. In Fyfe's analysis, "Lack of schooling became a moral stigma: Europeans found their servants too busy writing to do housework. Schools overflowed; children had to be turned away; new schools opened." By 1840 there were over eight thousand children in Sierra Leone's schools (a fifth of the colony's population), and the colony's literacy rate was higher than in many parts of Europe. In 1845 a grammar school was opened, and shortly afterwards the old seminary that Ajayi had attended in the late 1820s at Fourah Bay was revitalized and again became an important center for African education.[47]

James Beale "Africanus" Horton, the son of Igbo recaptives, was one of the early graduates of Fourah Bay College and went on to study medicine at Edinburgh University. Horton had to study extra hard to make up for the shortcomings in his premedical studies, but his efforts were rewarded with certificates of honor in several medical exams and the prize in surgery. Horton completed his M.D. in 1859 with a thesis later published as *The Medical Topography of the West Coast of Africa*. Dr. Horton then served as a British Army physician for two decades, authoring many books and retiring at the rank of surgeon-major. A strong believer in the power of education, he left money in his will to endow a secondary school in the sciences. In 1863 he wrote: "The improvement of the West Coast of Africa . . . can never be properly accomplished except by the educated native portion of the community. . . . [T]he more the educated portion of the inhabitants is increased, the more will the rise of the other portion be made evident."[48] Generations of twentieth-century Africans strongly confirmed Dr. Horton's enthusiasm for Western education.

While Sierra Leone's freedom and schools have no counterparts in the slave systems of the New World, the process of creolization taking place on both sides of the Atlantic has many suggestive parallels. Language acquisition was a necessity. Religious change was an option that many found highly appealing. New skills were acquired in formal and informal contexts. Such similar outcomes suggest that the element of coercion by slave owners and managers needs to be balanced by sufficient attention to how much enslaved Africans were themselves agents in the process of creolization, responding to new circumstances in ways that reflected their fundamental needs, both material and spiritual. But as important as the adoption of elements of European culture was, it was only one side of the larger acculturation process that was taking place.

AFRICANIZATION

The second cultural transformation at work in Sierra Leone, Africanization, had two distinct components. As has already been suggested, the slave trade that tore Africans from their homelands made them aware of their common identity with strangers from other parts of the continent with whom they were enslaved and transported as well as of the divide that separated them from Europeans in appearance, culture, and authority. However, "African" was not a primary identity for most first-generation emigrants. Interestingly, such identification with the entire African continent was most common among those who immersed themselves most deeply in European culture, some of whom, like Dr. Horton in Sierra Leone and others in Europe (see Chapter 6), added "Africanus" or "the African" to their names as a badge of black identity. However, for most the pan-African category was merely the context in which they created and recreated identities at a subcontinental level. Just as people in Europe at this time rarely thought of themselves as Europeans (unless they happened to be in Africa or some other non-European place), most Africans away from their homelands redefined themselves in terms of group identities that were much broader than what they had conceived of at home but more meaningful than a generic African identity.

What to call this new level of identity is a problem. Following the European model, it has become common to speak of African *nations*, which is one of the terms contemporaries also used. Although legitimate, the term has led to two conceptual problems. The first, on which there is a large literature mostly dealing with Europe, is whether nations are natural or artificial. In its simplest formulation the romantic tradition and its followers have seen a nation (and nation-state) evolving on the basis of a common language, culture, and historical experience. Other historians have pointed out that nations were artificial creations of a particular moment out of fairly diverse populations and cultures, which only developed standardized language and cultures once political boundaries and centralized governments were imposed. Because these romantic and dynamic conceptions of nation have such different assumptions the use of the term can be very ambivalent in its implications.

Students of African subnational identities, often called ethnic or tribal identities, have also adopted romantic and dynamic positions. Many twentieth-century African nationalists, like their nineteenth-century counterparts in Europe, saw modern ethnic identities as having existed for centuries, or even millennia. However, this idea has been challenged by historians who argue that modern tribal or ethnic identities were largely created during the colonial era as the result of missionary education in newly standardized African language, by colonial policies seeking to govern Africans in homogenized units, by migrations out of local communities that gave Africans a greater awareness of themselves as members of larger cultural communities, and by the politics of anti-colonial African elites. While many scholars of the African diaspora have avoided the pitfalls of the romantic nationalist position, a number of recent scholars have tended to conflate the "national" identities of the diaspora with ethnic/tribal identities of twentieth-century African states, suggesting a static transfer of cultural practices from Africa rather than the dynamic process by which African customs were not simply blended or borrowed but actually reshaped and redefined in new settings.[49]

The activities and statements of liberated Africans in Sierra Leone provide a way to explore the development of these two levels of Africanization and to address, if not entirely resolve, some of the larger issues. The actions and identities of Africans in that colony strongly support the position that African "national" identities (for want of a better term) were new creations, often blending elements of several homeland cultures as they struggled to build meaningful communities in new circumstances.

The process of Africanization, like the process of creolization, for many had begun before the Middle Passage was over. Chapter 4 has shown that the expansion of internal trade promoted the use of some African trading languages (such as Hausa, Mande, and Efik) beyond their homelands. The lives of some captives recounted earlier in this chapter illustrate how enslavement and the Middle Passage also spread some languages. Ajayi became familiar with three new Yoruba dialects during his travels and formed close friendships with other Yoruba-speaking youths while awaiting the ship that would carry them away. Ali Eisami of Bornu would have learned Yoruba during his five-year residence among them, and Mbepe of Nwala would have learned Efik during his three years in Old Calabar. The only native Duala speaker in Sierra Leone told Koelle that many others in the colony could speak his language, having learned it as slaves of the Duala or while awaiting shipment into the Atlantic trade from the coastal town of the same name.[50] Speaking the same language did not inevitably lead people to form common bonds, but it was an important building block of a new identity.

The need to construct larger African identities grew after the voyages were over. Although Koelle collected vocabularies in Sierra Leone from 160 different languages, some with several distinct dialects, the Sierra Leone partial census of 1848 lumped the speakers of almost all of them into just nineteen "tribes" or "nations." Rather than being identity groups transported from elsewhere in Africa, most of these "nations" were creations of the diaspora, and many of the "nations" named in the Sierra Leone census were also widely used in the Americas (although their membership might be differently constructed).

Some particular examples will make the process of identity development clearer. The largest of the African "nations" in Sierra Leone had a linguistic base. The census identified over a third of those counted as "Akoo," or Aku. These were Ajayi's people, like him victims of the wars that ravaged what is now southwestern Nigeria in the nineteenth century. Today most speakers of this language would identify themselves as Yoruba, but in this period that name was common only for residents of the northern kingdom of Oyo, although missionaries had begun using it for other dialects as well. Koelle was against using "Yoruba" as the name for all of the dozen dialects he catalogued, preferring "Aku," the name by which they were called in Sierra Leone. As he knew, the fact of the matter was the speakers of these dialects had no common name for themselves in their homeland because they had no common identity. "Aku" was simply a word that occurred in a greeting common to them all.

Next most numerous in Sierra Leone were the Igbo, or "Eboo," as the census spelled the name. At home the Igbo speakers inhabited hundreds of autonomous villages and village groups spread over a large area. Their political disunity and geographical dispersal, as Koelle discovered, had fostered linguistic and cultural fragmentation. He collected examples of five dialects of Igbo and listed a total of fifteen "countries" whose people were called Igbo in Sierra Leone, but stressed that, like the Yoruba, Igbo speakers in their homeland shared no national name and knew "only the names of their respective districts or countries." "In speaking to some of them regarding this name [Igbo]," Koelle wrote, "I learned that they never had heard it till they came to Sierra Leone." The Niger explorer William Baikie also emphasized the great dialectical and cultural differences "between different parts of this extensive country" and pointed out how such diverse homeland roots produced a common identity only in the diaspora: "In Igbo each person hails, as a sailor would say, from the particular district where he was born, but when away from home all are Igbos."[51]

Some other "nations" in Sierra Leone shared a common language. Speakers of the various dialects of Efik ("Calabar" in Sierra Leone), Hausa, Fulbe, Akan ("Kromantee") of the Gold Coast, or Wolof came to use language as a way of distinguishing themselves from other Africans in Sierra Leone, even though no such national consciousness or political unity existed in their homelands. However, several other "nations" in Sierra Leone had neither political unity in their homelands nor a common language in the diaspora. The third largest group in the 1848 census were the "Paupah" (or "Popo") from the hinterland of the western Slave Coast—people whom Koelle reported spoke five different languages. Other such polyglot nations were the Mandingo (five Mande or Mandinka languages), the Bini (the Edo of the kingdom of Benin, plus speakers of six or seven neighboring languages), the "Moko" of Cameroon (sixteen different languages), the "Kongo" (eighteen distinct languages scattered over a vast area of West Central Africa), and the "Mozambique" of southeastern Africa (six languages). John Thornton has tried to argue that such regional clusters already possessed a large measure of cultural unity. The evidence is really too thin to prove or disprove such an assertion. Thornton's assumption that language is a surrogate for culture is akin to the circular reasoning of romantic nationalists, but it may well duplicate the thoughts of the members of these nations-in-formation. However, as a careful reading of the events leading to the creation of Germany and Italy in the nineteenth century makes evident, the territories and peoples who were included in each new state were not preordained. The fact that African "nations" developed out of different memberships in the diaspora further directs one's attention to the dynamics of the particular events, not to static assumptions of national destiny.[52]

In Sierra Leone, it is clear that these new African "nations" were jointly created by the British authorities overseeing the resettlement of the tens of thousands of recaptives rescued from the Atlantic slave trade and by the recaptives themselves. At first officials encouraged the formation of villages on an ethnic or linguistic basis, as linguistic names like Kissy Town, Bussa Town, and Congo Town suggest. Like early neighborhoods of "Irish" or "Italian" immigrants in eastern American cities, these appeared more homogeneous to outsiders than to the disparate individuals who inhabited them. Some of these early villages show clearly how slender ties could become the basis of new unity. The liberated Africans' Pa Demba's Town in 1813 had in common only a knowledge of Portuguese. The Vai, Mandinka, Wolof, and Susu (Mende) settlers who founded the village of Hogbrook shared only a loose regional connection. In the face of growing numbers of recaptives arriving in the 1820s, Sierra Leone authorities abandoned efforts to create settlements defined by language or region. Instead, Africans liberated about the same time from ships captured on different parts of the coast might be settled together, despite the fact that they spoke dozens of mutually unintelligible languages. Newly arrived Africans were still put under the care of residents who spoke their own language or something close to it, but to communicate with their neighbors they needed English or another common language.[53]

Within these artificial communities African settlers regularly took steps to create their own solidarity by forming beneficial societies, often called "companies," whose fellow members accorded each other the kinds of mutual aid customary in kinship-based villages elsewhere in Africa. Many of these companies had a common linguistic core (to which some outsiders attached themselves), but others were based on different principles. One Sierra Leonean (himself descended from African Americans from Nova Scotia) reported that soon after a new shipload of people "of different tribes or nations" was settled in a village they formed a club "including the whole of their shipmates, without distinction of nation, for the purpose of mutual assistance." This club of all shipmates, he indicated, was called the *Big Company*, which he distinguished from the *Little Company*, a separate ethnically based club that, in addition to other activities, helped preserve the festivals, dances, music, and other customs of their homelands. Inevitably, these transplanted "traditional" cultural events were composites of the more varied versions in the homeland communities with new features or understandings added based on life in Sierra Leone. As might be expected, the largest ethnic companies in the villages were formed by Yoruba speakers, who even had a "king" to whom Yoruba from villages all over Sierra Leone pledged allegiance. Perhaps in imitation of the numerous and well-organized Yoruba, other "national" groups, such as the Nupe, Igbo, Mandinka, and Susu, also chose kings and other officers, although none of them achieved the Aku's degree of solidarity. However, it is instructive that this solidarity did not persist among the many Yoruba who left Sierra Leone and returned to their homeland, where decades of civil warfare had led to the formation of several new kingdoms. As Fyfe puts it, "only in Sierra Leone were all the children of Odudua, the Yoruba ancestor-god, united." Nor were companies all dedicated to preserving homeland customs. Some Sierra Leoneans formed multiethnic Christian companies dedicated to warding off the attraction of "pagan" practices among their members. Other Christian congregations developed a strong ethnic base.[54]

These new "nations" drew upon shared languages and customs, but they were formed in Sierra Leone under circumstances conceivable only outside their homelands. They not only made use of institutions, such as written constitutions (in English), that had no counterpart in their homelands, but they also borrowed freely from the other emerging nations around them. Sometimes members showed their awareness of the new structures that held them together, as "when a group of Bassa described themselves as of the Bassa Society, not nation." Finally, national identities were not ethnically homogeneous. One reigning "king" of the Aku in Sierra Leone, who went by the name John Macaulay, was apparently Hausa in origin. The members of numerous languages in Sierra Leone with a dozen or fewer native speakers had little choice but to affiliate with larger groups that did not represent their actual origins.[55]

To be sure, these new nations were not created out of nothing. In their struggle to rebuild their lives and communities, Africans naturally drew upon everything they knew and loved from home, but they also adapted old ways to new circumstances, adopted new customs and beliefs, and enlarged the circle of their contacts and understandings. The most important point is the dynamic nature of what was happening, not the static "survival" of bits and pieces from home. To focus on the relics (the survivals) rather than on the dynamics by which African individuals and communities survived by reinventing themselves is to miss the point. To use a scriptural image Sierra Leonean recaptives would have understood, they were pouring old wine into new wineskins as well as new wine into old skins. Sierra Leone showed a marvelous blend of creolization and Africanization, sometimes existing in harmony, sometimes in conflict, and sometimes running along parallel lines of development.

The same capacity for inventing new "national" identities in Sierra Leone also manifested itself in the development of inter-"national" organizations and alliances. In the village of Waterloo, for example, the leaders of the major ethnic groups organized a sort of United Nations of Africa to mediate disputes. Known as the "Seventeen Nations," it represented the village's seventeen largest ethnic groups, as they had evolved in the colony. The Seventeen Nations had been formed to settle interethnic disputes following a "war" involving three of the nations during Christmas week in 1843. The "war" was reportedly set off by the unauthorized bathing practice of a "Calabar" woman, which offended "Aku" sensibilities. However, in the conflict the vastly outnumbered "Calabar" were joined by the "Igbo" people, perhaps out of some sense of common regional origins, but just as likely growing out of "Igbo" rivalry with the numerically dominant Yoruba speakers. Such rivalry prefigures the ethnic politics of twentieth-century Nigeria, but in precolonial times the Yoruba and Igbo homelands were too isolated from each other for rivalry to have taken place. Such rivalries and identities were first born in the diaspora.[56]

Recaptives in Sierra Leone obviously had much greater freedom than Africans who became slaves in the Americas, yet the process of Africanization proceeded along remarkably similar lines. At greater remove from their homelands and with less freedom of movement, the development of a pan-African identity probably proceeded faster among what historian Ira Berlin has called the "plantation generations" in the Americas than it did in Sierra Leone. The development of African "nations" with a linguistic or regional core also paralleled what happened in Sierra Leone. As Berlin puts it, "rather than transporting a primordial nationality or ethnicity to the New World, . . . Igbos or Angolans who searched out their countrymen in the Americas may have made more of those connections in the New World than they did in the Old precisely because of their violent separation from their homeland." Not only were such national identities greatly enhanced, but they were also highly diverse in membership, especially as they transcended the first generation. Historian Philip Morgan has pointed out that music, dance, and other aspects of African-American culture regularly blended styles from various places in Africa under the name of a single African nation and that individuals regularly adopted the identity of a nation to which they had no historic claim. The product might be a blend or a synthesis or something entirely new. Customs from one part of Africa might be adopted by people from another part, as in Jamaica, where Angolan immigrants used personal names originally from the Gold Coast.[57]

If, as Ira Berlin puts it, "identity was more a garment that might be worn or discarded, rather than a skin which never changed its spots," the names of African nations in the Americas could also be quite plastic. Thus the same cluster of Yoruba-speaking people called Aku in Sierra Leone were known as Lucumi in Jamaica and Cuba and as Nagó in Brazil and Saint Domingue. The names Calabar and Moko became confused in the Americas, where Moko was sometimes used for all Efik speakers and Calabar might be employed to include all who passed through Old Calabar on their way to the sea. In the Americas Igbo was also often used in a broader sense, in some places including Efik speakers, just as Calabar sometimes included Igbo speakers. Koelle's informants included a dozen individuals who stated they were sold from Calabar, not a single one of which was a native speaker of Efik or any Igbo dialect. Each of the twelve spoke a distinct language, and Koelle assigned these languages to four different language families.[58]

CONCLUSION

How much did the Africans who encountered Europe as victims of the slave trade have in common with the princes, kings, and merchants who dealt with Europeans as equals? Subordination and sufferings, abuse and alienation from homelands set the captive exiles apart, but when the enslaved Africans' inner experiences are considered, one can discern some remarkable parallels. Even though the process of enslavement, alienation from home, and transportation across the ocean was a traumatic one, African exiles showed great capacity for adjusting to new situations and learning new skills. Like their elite brothers and sisters of the coastal ports, they mastered new languages, internalized new religions, acquired new skills, and created new social networks. The process in the Americas took place over generations, but change was most rapid in the first generation. As Herbert Klein points out: "In all slave societies where statistics on origins are available, it appears that Africans were represented in the skilled occupations in numbers equal to their share of the population. They became carpenters, stonemasons, blacksmiths, and even artists in as equal a ratio to their numbers as did the creole slaves."[59]

Both creolization and Africanization were faster and deeper among the Africans whom Europeans estranged from their homelands than among those who encountered Europeans coming to their coasts to trade. Enslaved Africans brought some occupational skills, such as blacksmithing and farming, with them to the Americas, just as they brought cultural skills and traditions. In the mix of Africans from various places and African Americans in slave societies in the Americas, particular languages, religions, and folkways did not long survive unchanged, but influenced speech patterns, belief systems, and musical, grooming, and eating patterns in the Americas. Rather than isolated "survivals" of a particular part of Africa, one sees a dynamic process of reinventing African cultural norms and identities. In the absence of close kinship networks and village ties of the homelands, "national" identities assumed an importance they did not have in Africa and acquired a membership that was often at variance with actual origins. For Africans, as for other immigrants, the Americas were not a museum in which to display ancestral traditions, but a canvas on which identities might be blended and reinvented. The past did not tyrannize the present; the living breathed new life into forms from the past.

Such "nations" might endure for decades or fade away, but they existed and were meaningful only in the context of a larger and even newer identity. The forced immigrants discovered themselves as Africans in the Americas and their children as African Americans. Under less brutal and often quite comfortable circumstances, African immigrants and visitors were experiencing similar transformations of culture and identity in Europe. As we will see in the next chapter, there too the discovery of the foreign involved a rediscovery of self.

Notes

1. "The Narrative of Samuel Ajayi Crowther [1837]," edited with an introduction by J. F. Ade Ajayi, in *Africa Remembered: Narratives by West Africans from the Era of the Slave Trade*, ed. Philip D. Curtin (Madison: University of Wisconsin Press, 1967), pp. 298–316, quotations pp. 299, 304–5, 310, 311, 313.

2. Ibid., pp. 311–16. The formation of modern Yoruba identity and the case of Crowther are explored at length in J. D. Y. Peel, *Religious Encounter and the Making of the Yoruba* (Bloomington: Indiana University Press, 2001), especially pp. 278–309.

3. Analyses of how people were initially enslaved comes from Mungo Park, *Travels in the Interior Districts of Africa: Performed in the Years 1795, 1796, and 1797* (London: John Murray, 1816), pp. 280–90; P. E. H. Hair, "The Enslavement of Koelle's Informants," *Journal of African History* 6 (1965): 193–203; and my own recalculation of the statements in S. W. Koelle, *Polyglotta Africana, or A Comparative Vocabulary of Nearly 300 Words and Phrases in more than 100 Distinct African Languages* (London: Church Missionary House, 1854), "Introductory Remarks," pp. 1–20. For the geographical distribution of Koelle's informants, see Philip D. Curtin and Jan Vansina, "Sources of the Nineteenth Century Atlantic Slave Trade," *Journal of African History* 5 (1964): 185–208

4. Koelle, *Polyglotta*, p. 20.

5. Ibid., pp. 10, 12.

6. "The Narrative of Joseph Wright," in Curtin, ed., *Africa Remembered*, p. 331.

7. Koelle, *Polyglotta*, p. 19.

8. "A Narrative of the Most Remarkable Particulars in the Life of James Albert Ukawsaw Gronniosaw, an African Prince, as Related by Himself," in *Pioneers of the Black Atlantic: Five Slave Narratives from the Enlightenment, 1772–1815*, ed. Henry Louis Gates, Jr., and William L. Andrews (Washington, DC: Civitas, 1998), pp. 31–40, quotations pp. 37 and 40. The original *Narrative* was published in 1770, but most readers will find this reprint more accessible. Some parts of Gronniosaw's story are so improbable that it might make more sense if he had misunderstood what was told him in an unfamiliar language and was simply the victim of a merchant turned kidnapper. However, his fears were real enough and convinced him that it would be better to live as a slave than risk being "treated very ill, or, possibly, murdered."

9. Olaudah Equiano, *The Interesting Narrative and Other Writings*, ed. Vincent Carretta (New York: Penguin Books, 1995), pp. 46–55; Great Britain, *Parliamentary Papers* [hereafter PP] 1847–1848, xxii (536), Third Report from the Select Committee on the Slave Trade, testimony of William Henry Pratt, 4 July 1848, p. 185; Koelle, *Polyglotta*, p. 8.

10. Koelle, *Polyglotta*, pp. 13, 15.

11. Hair, "Enslavement," pp. 194–95; David Eltis, *Economic Growth and the Ending of the Transatlantic Slave Trade* (New York: Oxford University Press, 1987), pp. 256–57.

12. Ottobah Cogoano, *Thoughts and Sentiments on the Evil and Wicked Traffic of the Slavery and Commerce of the Human Species* (1787) in Gates and Andrews, eds., *Pioneers*, pp. 94–95; PP 1847–1848, xxii (272), First Report from the Select Committee on Slave Trade, pp. 62–65.

13. *Biography of Mahommad G. Baquaqua, a Native of Zoogoo, in the Interior of Africa. . . . Written and Revised from His Own Words, by Samuel Moore* (1854), in *Children of God's Fire: A Documentary History of Black Slavery in Brazil*, ed. Robert Edgar Conrad (Princeton, NJ: Princeton University Press, 1983), p. 27.

14. PP 1850, ix (53), Report from the Select Committee of the House of Lords, on the African Slave Trade, pp. 162–63.

15. Equiano, *Narrative*, pp. 42–43, 55–56. Equiano's account may incorporate details from voyages other than his own, since he may have been no more than six at the time of his passage.

16. Jean Barbot, *Description of the Coasts of North and South Guinea*, in Elizabeth Donnan, *Documents Illustrative of the History of the Slave Trade to America* (Washington, DC: Carnegie Endowment, 1930), I:289; Edward Long, *The History of Jamaica* (London: Lowndes, 1774), II:397; PP 1789 (4132), Report of the Lords of the Committee of Council . . . Part II, View of Evidence concerning the Manner of Carrying Slaves to the West Indies, p. 117, testimony of James Penny; "Narrative of Joseph Wright," p. 331.

17. Barbot, *Description*, in Donnan, *Documents*, I:290.

18. Daniel P. Mannix and Malcolm Cowley, *Black Cargoes: A History of the Atlantic Slave Trade* (New York: Viking Press, 1965), p. 114 (quoting Dr. Ecroide Claxton) and pp. 115–16 (quoting Dr. Thomas Trotter).

19. Equiano, *Narrative*, pp. 56, 59.

20. David Eltis, *The Rise of African Slavery in the Americas* (New York: Cambridge University Press, 2000), pp. 171–73, 229–33.

21. PP 1859, xxxiv [2569], enclosure in no. 147, Commander Hunt to Commodore Wise, 6 November 1858, p. 205, citing the testimony of knowledgeable headmen. Technically, the *Regina Coeli* was not recruiting slaves but rather indentured laborers for the Indian Ocean colony of Réunion, but, because it obtained such recruits by purchasing them from their African owners and then declaring them free, most observers have seen this as a continuation of the slave trade in disguise.

22. Quoted in Eltis, *Rise of African Slavery*, p. 229. Jolof was a state, but the term was also used as an ethnic designation; Jolof were Wolof speaking. For the meaning to Barbara in this period, see Philip D. Curtin, *Economic Change in Precolonial Africa: Senegambia in the Era of the Slave Trade* (Madison: University of Wisconsin Press, 1975), pp. 178–80.

23. William Butterworth, *Three Years Adventures of a Minor in England, Africa, the West Indies, South Carolina and Georgia* (Leeds: Thomas Inchbold, 1831), p. 39; Miller, *Way of Death*, p. 412; PP 1789 (4132), Report of the Lords . . . Part II, testimonies of James Penny and John Newton, pp. 117–18.

24. Miller, *Way of Death*, pp. 411–12; Robert Louis Stein, *The French Slave Trade in the Eighteenth Century: An Old Regime Business* (Madison: University of Wisconsin Press, 1979), p. 102; William Bosman, *A New and Accurate Description of the Coast of Guinea*, 2d ed. (London: J. Knapton, 1721), p. 342; PP 1789 (4132), Report of the Lords . . . Part II, testimony of James Penny, p. 117.

25. Miller, *Way of Death*, pp. 413–24; Herbert S. Klein, *The Atlantic Slave Trade* (New York: Cambridge University Press, 1999), pp. 136–39.

26. Jean Barbot, *Barbot on Guinea: The Writings of Jean Barbot on West Africa 1678–1712*, ed. P. E. H. Hair, Adam Jones, and Robin Law (London: The Hakluyt Society, 1992), II:394, 397.

27. Butterworth, *Three Years Adventures*, p. 40.

28. Hugh Thomas, *The Slave Trade: The Story of the Atlantic Slave Trade, 1440–1870* (New York: Simon & Schuster, 1997), p. 417.

29. "Journal of the *Arthur*, December 5, 1677–May 25, 1678," in Donnan, *Documents*, I:228–31.

30. Conrad, ed., *Children of God's Fire*, pp. 51–52.

31. Gronniosaw, *Narrative*, in Gates and Andrews, eds., *Pioneers*, p. 40; Equiano, *Narrative*, pp. 114–37, quotation p. 116.

32. William Snelgrave, *A New Account of Some Parts of Guinea, and the Slave Trade* (London: Knapton, 1734), pp. 166–67; Butterworth, *Three Years Adventures*, pp. 106–9, 117; David Robertson, *Denmark Vesey: The Buried History of America's Largest Slave Rebellion and the Man Who Led It* (New York: Knopf, 2000), pp. 29–31.

33. Miller, *Way of Death*, p. 412; Stein, *French Slave Trade*, p. 101.

34. Butterworth, *Three Years Adventures*, pp. 122–23; Conrad, *Children of God's Fire*, p. 41.

35. Eltis, *Rise of African Slavery*, pp. 226–32, quotations pp. 226, 229.

36. Barbot, *Description*, in Donnan, *Documents*, I:289.

37. Ira Berlin, *Many Thousands Gone: The First Two Centuries of Slavery in North America* (Cambridge, MA: Harvard University Press, 1998); Michael A. Gomez, *Exchanging Our Country Marks: The Transformation of African Identities in the Colonial and Antebellum South* (Chapel Hill: University of North Carolina Press, 1998); Philip D. Morgan, *Slave Counterpoint: Black Culture in the Eighteenth Century Chesapeake and Lowcountry* (Chapel Hill: University of North Carolina Press, 1998); Michael Mullin, *Africa in America: Slave Acculturation in the American South and the British Caribbean, 1736–1831* (Urbana: University of Illinois Press, 1994).

38. Butterworth, *Three Years Adventures*, p. 96; *Biography of Mahommad G. Baquaqua, a Native of Zoogao, in the Interior of Africa* (1854), in *The African in Latin America*, ed. Ann M. Pescatello (New York: Alfred A. Knopf, 1975), p. 188.

39. Koelle, *Polyglotta*, pp. 8, 10.

40. PP 1850, ix (53), Report . . . on the African Slave Trade, pp. 98–99.

41. Koelle, *Polyglotta*, pp. 9, 17–18.

42. PP 1850, ix (53), Report . . . on the African Slave Trade, p. 102, testimony of Thomas Maxwell, 14 May 1849; for another Muslim convert to Christianity, see "Autobiography of Omar ibn Seid, Slave in North Carolina, 1831," *American Historical Review* 30 (1925): 791–95.

43. Christopher Fyfe, *A History of Sierra Leone* (Oxford: Clarendon Press, 1962), pp. 127–28.

44. Ibid., p. 254.

45. Ibid., p. 201.

46. Great Britain, Colonial Office, CO267/204, Acting-Governor [Benjamin] Pine's Annual Report on the Colony of Sierra Leone for 1847, in Christopher Fyfe, ed., *Sierra Leone Inheritance* (London: Oxford University Press, 1964), pp. 151–53.

47. Fyfe, *History*, pp. 55, 69, 77, 172, 213 (quote), 236–37. Fourah Bay College later became the University of Sierra Leone.

48. Christopher Fyfe, *Africanus Horton, 1835–1883: West African Scientist and Patriot* (New York: Oxford University Press, 1972), pp. 19–36; Robert July, *The Origins of Modern African Thought* (New York: Frederick A. Praeger, 1967), pp. 112–22, quote p. 120.

49. An excellent introduction to this debate is Leroy Vail, ed., *The Creation of Tribalism in Southern Africa* (Berkeley: University of California Press, 1989). For its application to diaspora studies, see David Northrup, "Igbo and Myth Igbo: Culture and Ethnicity in the Atlantic World, 1600–1850," *Slavery and Abolition* 21 (2000), 1–20.

50. Koelle, *Polyglotta*, p. 11. See Ralph Austen and Jonathan Derrick, *Middlemen of the Cameroons Rover: The Duala and Their Hinterland, c. 1600–c. 1960* (Cambridge: Cambridge University Press, 1999).

51. Koelle, *Polyglotta*, pp. 8–9; W. B. Baikie, *Narrative of an Exploring Voyage Up the Rivers Kwóra and Bínue in 1854* (London: John Murray, 1856), pp. 307–8.

52. John Thornton, *Africa and Africans in the Making of the Atlantic World, 1400–1800*, 2d ed. (New York: Cambridge University Press, 1998), pp. 183–91; for a fuller critique, see Northrup, "Igbo and Myth Igbo."

53. Fyfe, *History*, pp. 119–20, 127, 138.

54. Jacob Boston Henzeley in Fyfe, ed., *Inheritance*, p. 143; Fyfe, *History*, pp. 170–72, 233–35, 292–94, quotation p. 292.

55. Fyfe, *History*, pp. 233–34. Fyfe also points out that Hausa often exercised great influence over Yoruba speakers in the Americas; see also Robin Law and Paul Lovejoy, "The Changing Dimensions of African History: Reappropriating the Diaspora," in *Rethinking African History*, ed. Simon McGrath et al. (Edinburgh: Centre for African Studies, University of Edinburgh, 1997), p. 191.

56. Fyfe, *History*, pp. 233–34.

57. Berlin, *Many Thousands*, pp. 61–62, 95–108, quotation p. 105; Morgan, *Slave Counterpoint*, p. 586, and "The Cultural Implications of the Atlantic Slave Trade: African Regional Origins, American Destinations, and New World Developments," *Slavery and Abolition* 18 (1997): 134–42; Klein, *Atlantic Slave Trade*, p. 174. For a related discussion, see Peter Caron, " 'Of a Nation Which the Others Do Not Understand': Bambara Slaves and African Ethnicity in Colonial Louisiana, 1718–60," *Slavery and Abolition* 18 (1997): 98–121.

58. Berlin, *Many Thousands*, p. 105; Robin Law, "Lucumi and Nago," *History in Africa* 24 (1997): 1–16; Northrup, "Igbo and Myth Igbo." Cf. David Geggus, "Sex Ratio, Age and Ethnicity in the Atlantic Slave Trade: Data from French Shipping and Plantation Records," *Journal of African History* 30 (1989): p. 32, and Stanley Stein, *Vassouras: A Brazilian Coffee County, 1850–1900* (Princeton, NJ: Princeton University Press, 1985), pp. 76–77.

59. Klein, *Atlantic Slave Trade*, p. 179.

Suggested Readings

Curtin, Philip D. Editor. *Africa Remembered: Narratives by West Africans from the Era of the Slave Trade*. Madison: University of Wisconsin Press, 1967.

Eltis, David. *The Rise of African Slavery in the Americas*. New York: Cambridge University Press, 2000.

Fyfe, Christopher. *A History of Sierra Leone*. Oxford: Clarendon Press, 1962.

Klein, Herbert S. *The Atlantic Slave Trade*. New York: Cambridge University Press, 1999.

Northrup, David. Editor. *The Atlantic Slave Trade*. Second Edition. Boston: Houghton Mifflin, 2002.

Africans in Europe,

1650–1850

A short and unusual autobiography, *A Narrative of the Most Remarkable Particulars in the Life of James Albert Ukawsaw Gronniosaw, an African Prince, as Related by Himself*, was published circa 1770 in the English city of Bath. It quickly went through several more editions. James Albert (the former Prince Ukawsaw Gronniosaw) had told his life's story to an Englishwoman of Leominster, who arranged for its publication. In the first part Gronniosaw tells of his childhood in the kingdom of Bornu, his enslavement by a false companion and transport to Barbados, his life as a servant in New York City, his religious conversion, and his military service in the West Indies. The second part records his adventures in Europe, where he moved from the West Indies. Although his first experience in Europe was to be defrauded of his savings by an English landlady, most of his recollections are of aid and kindness from good people. After working for a year as a butler in Amsterdam, Gronniosaw returned to England to marry a poor English weaver named Betty, whose debts he paid off. The happy couple had children, losing one to smallpox, and, like the majority of English people at the time, lived near the edge of poverty.

Two themes in Gronniosaw's life may surprise modern readers. The first is his positive view of race relations. Some people who treated him badly may have had prejudice in their hearts, but not once does Gronniosaw suggest that his color or place of origin was at the root of his misfortunes. In contrast, he often tells of Europeans who treated him well: his Dutch master in New York who "was very good to me" and whose wife sent him to school, the "gracious worthy Gentleman" who employed him in Amsterdam and was also "very good to me," the "agreeable young woman" in that Dutch city whose savings and hand in marriage he refused in order to marry the indebted English widow Betty (his "blessed partner"), the Quaker gentleman (his "worthy friend") who rescued him from acute poverty and helped him find regular work—even the Dutch sea captain who bought him in Africa (thus, Gronniosaw believed, rescuing him from being killed). Indeed, it seems probable that several of the white people who became his benefactors were good to him because of his being black. It is surely unlikely that his life would have been recorded at all were he not African born, although the circumstance of his being a prince added an intriguing detail to his account.[1]

The second theme Gronniosaw emphasizes about his encounter with the West was the importance for him of Christianity. The Dutch captain had encouraged him to take up Christian practices and read the Scriptures, and so had his master and teachers in New York, but the turning point in his commitment followed a profound inner religious experience. So compelling was his new commitment, by his account, that thirty-eight Calvinist ministers eagerly met with him every Thursday for seven weeks in Amsterdam to hear him tell his life's story and religion's role in it. Out of this reflective recounting of his life, it would seem, came the narrative he later told to the good lady of Leominster. Gronniosaw summarizes the amazing story of his life in these words:

> I cannot but admire the footsteps of providence; astonished that I should be so wonderfully preserved! Though the Grandson of a King, I have wanted bread, and should have been glad of the hardest crust I ever saw. I who, at home, was surrounded and guarded by slaves . . . and clothed with gold, have been inhumanly threatened with death; and frequently wanted clothing to defend me from the inclemency of the weather; yet I never murmured, nor was I discontent. I am willing, and even desirous to be counted as nothing, a stranger in the world, and a pilgrim here; for "*I know that my* Redeemer *liveth*," and I'm thankful for every trial and trouble that I've met with, as I am not without hope that they have been all sanctified to me.

Gronniosaw returns to this theme in the concluding paragraph of his *Narrative*:

> As Pilgrims, and very poor Pilgrims, we [he and Betty] are traveling through many difficulties toward our Heavenly Home, and wanting patiently for his gracious call, when the Lord shall deliver us out of the evils of this present world and bring us to the Everlasting Glories of the world to come. To Him be Praise for Ever and Ever, Amen.[2]

It might be argued that these two themes tell us more about the *Narrative*'s intended readers than its author: that Gronniosaw (or his transcriber) was telling pious white people what they wanted to hear. As one modern study points out, "one cannot be sure of the extent to which Gronniosaw's oilier pieties might have been interpolations of the hand of the young Lady of Leominster, [but] some anecdotes are told with a revealing plainness that looks thoroughly authentic."[3] One needs to read such texts critically as well as sympathetically, but one must avoid picking and choosing according to the dictates of modern tastes. Unless there is a convincing case for a passage being inauthentic, it seems better to risk including distortions of an African voice than to block out what it is saying. Since proof of falsehood is rare, this chapter adopts the strategy of joining Gronniosaw's voice and those of other African narratives in a chorus of African voices. A single false note will not spoil the melody. Each life has its own unique qualities. Each biography presents its special problems of interpretation. We can never recapture the past completely and perfectly, but in the patterns of many varied experiences lies an authentic picture.

Set against the chorus of these experiences Gronniosaw's *Narrative* exhibits eccentricities and shares common features with the swelling numbers of Africans making their own discoveries of Europe between 1650 and 1850. In four ways Gronniosaw was exceptional among blacks in Europe in this era: He was African born, he was of aristocratic birth, the slavery he experienced was mild, and he came to Europe by choice and at his own expense. Most blacks in Europe had been born into slavery in the Americas, knew well its harshness, and had been brought to Europe by their owners. Because this study is devoted to the experiences of persons born in Africa, it cannot pay much attention to this black majority, whose lives, especially in Britain, have been amply studied elsewhere.[4] Even those born in Africa whose lives the chapter considers were mostly brought to Europe by others, if not actually as slaves, then as children under the control of European masters. As we will see most blacks from both continents experienced some amelioration in their position after coming to Europe.

Gronniosaw was typical of blacks in Europe in his poverty. Indeed, Gronniosaw's life had much in common with members of the European working class in this era. However, as a struggling worker, he stands apart from the other Africans in this chapter, who more often are found in the courts, academies, and salons of Europe's elite. That circumstance is unavoidable, for those Africans whose European experiences are knowable from surviving records tend to be those who traveled among the literate elite, not those who toiled among the unlettered masses.

How representative are Gronniosaw's two larger themes? There is much debate among modern scholars about European racism and how it varied by class, region, and century. One study offers the judgment that a mixed marriage such as James and Betty Gronniosaw's "tended not to be seen as problematic to the English of that era because they primarily occurred among the lower working classes" and "that race was secondary, to the working class at least, is also clear from Gronniosaw's story."[5] That judgment of the English working class as a whole may be valid, but the implication that racism was more widespread at higher levels of society is questionable. Gronniosaw tells often of kindness he received from middle-class Europeans, both Dutch and English. Nor can one blame racism on aristocrats as a group, whose individual kindness to Africans features prominently in many accounts in this chapter. Class did make a difference, but it was the class of the African that may have been more influential. As Gronniosaw was not alone in knowing, it was better to be an African prince fallen on hard times than a poor soul born on a slave plantation. For this reason it is likely that not all who claimed African birth and/or royal (or noble) birth were speaking the truth, even if we cannot separate out the impostors from the true princes.

Racism was surely present in Europe during the two centuries between 1650 and 1850 covered by this chapter, and it was increasing, although the greatest increase would come after 1850. Yet it remains difficult to be precise about its intensity in different places. Slave owners regularly brought the harsh racial stereotypes typical of plantation societies in the Americas into Britain and France along with the slaves who accompanied them as servants. The planters' prejudices spread and blended with older European ideas of social hierarchies based on ethnicity, nationality, and birth. Racism could also be ignited in any class that felt its self-interest threatened, although only in parts of Britain were free blacks numerous enough for poor whites to fear competition for jobs or for the middle class to feel threatened by the crimes that they associated with unemployed blacks. As criticism of slavery and the slave trade rose, the planters and their allies were also quick to use stereotypes of black inferiority in defense of their incomes. Even members of the British royal family defended slavery as essential to the nation's economic welfare. But, while most Europeans would have found Africans strange and exotic (and therefore not really their equals), they were not inclined to see in such differences a proof of general inferiority. As many examples in this chapter attest, those Africans who achieved distinction in European academic learning, music, languages, piety, or other endeavors greatly reduced or eliminated the cultural divide that seems to have been at the base of most Europeans' prejudices. Gronniosaw was not alone in realizing that being a Christian in a Christian land opened many doors (although, as we will see, a Muslim prince from Africa could also be lionized).

The mention of religion brings us to Gronniosaw's second theme, whose African and European contexts need to be examined. As Gronniosaw is at pains to stress in the account of his own life, his devotion to religion began in Africa: He had been an avid seeker of religious understanding as a child long before he became a "pilgrim" in the sense Calvinists prized. As many examples here and in earlier chapters testify, such receptivity to Christianity was common among Africans encountering the European world. In the two centuries after 1650 African religious experiences in Europe differed in some aspects from those considered in Chapter 2. For one thing, most Africans were in the Protestant lands of northern Europe instead of in Catholic southern Europe. Although the most severe sectarian conflicts of the Reformation era had waned, passion for religion had hardly cooled. In the movements for Christian piety and missionary activity some Africans would play a notable role, as they did in more secular intellectual pursuits and in the debates over the legitimacy of slavery.

AFRICAN DELEGATES AND STUDENTS

Most Africans reached Europe through European agency, but, as in earlier times, some Africans still came to Europe in pursuit of their own ends. The growing trade with Europe along the West African coast in the seventeenth century prompted a resurgence of African trade delegations. As in the earlier centuries, some of these were received at royal courts, while others negotiated with the African trading companies that were proliferating in Europe. Such commercial contacts between Africa and Europe also had their cultural and educational sides. Numbers of young Africans were dispatched to Europe at the instigation of their parents to improve their grasp of European languages and cultures so as to improve business contacts. Other African youths were brought to Europe by European mentors to perfect their Christian education. In many cases the lines between delegate and learner and between African and European sponsorship are fuzzy, so these different individuals will be examined together in chronological and geographical groups.

The kings of the small state of Allada on the Slave Coast seem to have been particularly eager to expand European contacts. Allada's first envoy was sent to Spain in 1657 in search of missionaries. Baptized as Don Phelipe Zapata, he returned in 1660 with some Catholic priests and as their interpreter, "an Allada man . . . who had resided in Spain for forty-four years and married there." A more elaborate embassy from Allada went to France in 1670–1671. After a voyage via the French Antilles, Don Mattéo Lopez (as the ambassador styled himself) arrived in France accompanied by three wives, three sons, a trumpeter, and four servants. Reflecting the eagerness of the French to expand their share of the African trade, Don Mattéo was soon received by King Louis XIV at his Tuileries Palace in Paris on December 3, 1670, and was lodged in splendor at the Hôtel de Luynes. Over the next several months, a trade agreement was worked out and a notable French artist was commissioned to draw the ambassador's portrait. Even though the agreement was never fully implemented, Don Matheo's reception is Paris was a notable example of African-European diplomatic relations.[6]

Africans also undertook different sorts of trading pacts. One decidedly African act by the king of Asini on the Ivory Coast was the giving of hostages as pawns to seal a trading pact. The king sent two young servants from his household to France in the custody of French Dominicans in 1687–1688. Once the one named Banga had picked up enough French, he persuaded his captors that he and his companion Aniaba were important members of the royal family of Asini, correctly perceiving that this would greatly enhance their standing. Through the intervention of the influential Mme. de Maintenon, the two were presented at the court of Louis XIV; entrusted to the royal advisor Bishop Bossuet, the bishop of Paris, for instruction in Catholicism; and made officers in the king's own regiment. In 1701, Aniaba returned to the Ivory Coast with a French delegation to promote both evangelization and trade. Banga, who had come home six years earlier, served as the Frenchmen's interpreter. Other African delegations visited France during the eighteenth century, the visit serving as a sort of finishing school for future coastal rulers. In 1787 one African ruler sent his fourteen-year-old daughter, named Quircana, to France for her education, as is known from the favorable mention the young princess attracted in the French press.[7]

Other seventeenth-century African delegations included Gold Coast embassies to the Netherlands and the Elector of Brandenburg and Kongolese embassies to the Dutch in Brazil. One early traveler from the Gold Coast was Tom Osiat, born at Cape Coast in about 1670, who traveled to Ireland as a youth with his master, who placed him in the care of the landlady of a tavern. The basic education that Osiat acquired may have been rough about the edges, but it was sufficient for him to become a wealthy intermediary with the British at Cape Coast in later life. Another Cape Coaster, Edward Barter, who was brought to England and educated there by his English father about the same time, also went on to a successful career as a commercial middleman back home. In 1727 the Royal African Company began sending batches of African youths for study in England, so that they might master English and become literate employees of the company. Africans from the Bight of Biafra were also common in eighteenth-century England. In 1701, for example, the ruler of Bonny sent a nephew to London, apparently to promote that Niger Delta port's trade. Students and visiting traders from Old Calabar became common later in the century.[8]

Gold Coast delegates and students continued to go to various parts of Europe during the eighteenth and nineteenth centuries. Frederick Noi Dowunnah, son of a Ga chief, spent several years in Copenhagen as a youth in the 1820s "to get to know Danish civilization." While in Europe he gained a good command of Danish, become a Christian, and promoted the study of the Ga language in Denmark and Switzerland. After his return he worked with both Danish and British traders. A decade after Dowunnah's stay, two delegations arrived in Europe from the Asante kingdom. In 1836, two young princes of the Asante kingdom came to Britain for further education: Owusu Ansa and Owusu Nkwantabisa had been handed as hostages to the British governor of the Gold Coast as a pledge for peace after a long period of conflict. They were accompanied by a Fante teacher named Joseph Smith, who had been educated at Quaque's Gold Coast school and who served as their companion and translator. The next year two other Asante princes, Kwame Poku and Kwasi Boakye, arrived in the Netherlands for studies under the sponsorship of the Dutch Colonial Ministry. All four princes became Christians. Their fates suggest something of the range of African responses to such European experiences. The two in the Netherlands seem to have been more thoroughly Europeanized but adjusted to it in different ways. Kwame Poku returned to the Gold Coast from the Netherlands in 1847 but made a poor readjustment. During his stay in Europe he apparently had forgotten most of his native language and refused to relearn it. He committed suicide in 1850. Kwasi Boakye never returned home from the Netherlands, making a very successful career as a mining engineer and serving as the Director of Mines for Java in the Dutch East Indies.

Smith and the two princes in his charge in Britain made a better adjustment to life in Africa. The two princes returned to their families in 1841 with generous pensions from the British government of £100 a year each. Owusu Nkwantabisa lost his pension after being convicted by an Asante court of adultery, but he later served for a time as the official British representative in the Asante capital. Smith worked with the coastal Fante, who had evolved a close relationship with British interests in fear of Asante power, and with British officials who administered the Gold Coast as a crown colony beginning in 1850. Smith was the colony's collector of customs and justice of the peace for a time before turning his talents to the service of the African population as a lay preacher and politician. The other prince, Owusu Ansa, saw himself in a similar role as mediator of Christianity and modernization for his Asante kingdom. He briefly became a lay missionary to Asante in 1850 for the Wesleyan Methodists, taught for a time at a Cape Coast school, and worked for the British on various missions trying to promote peace between Asante and the British Protectorate at the coast. From 1867 Owusu Ansa held influential positions in the Asante foreign affairs department, handling delicate negotiations with both British and the Dutch in a time of growing tensions.[9]

Another place where Western education developed deep roots in some families was Sierra Leone. The Temne king who reigned as Philip II (1665–1680) had received a Jesuit education in Portugal, as did his successor, Naimbana, as well as Naimbana's brother and rival for the Temne throne, Serenkombo.[10] Dealing with altered circumstances in the later part of the eighteenth century, a Sierra Leone chief sent one of his sons to Lancaster in 1769 to study with the English Christians and another inland to study with the Muslims of Futa Jalon at a time when West African Islam was going through a tremendous period of reform and expansion. In the 1790s, the prominent Sierra Leone chief also known as Naimbana went him one better by having one son educated locally as a Muslim and sending two others to Europe. Having recently ceded Gambia Island to the French, this Naimbana dispatched his son Pedro (later known as Bartholomew) to France. To balance his connections he sent the third son, John Frederic (later baptized Henry Granville), to London. This was a strategic move, for Naimbana had also ceded some land in 1788 to British investors in the Sierra Leone Company for a small settlement of blacks from Britain. After a rocky early history, that colony became a major center of European influences and connections, as the previous chapter related.

We know most about the experiences of the third son. Dressed for the departure in white satin breeches and a black velvet coat, surmounted by a blue cloak decorated with gold lace, the twenty-four-year-old John Frederic showed himself as mentally alert once in Britain as he was fashionable. He mastered the intricacies of reading English in eighteen months and was entrusted to the care of two English clergymen as tutors. Over the next two years, he made great educational progress and became a sincere Christian. He was pleased to discover that the English among whom he lived were not such drunkards as the English traders on the Gold Coast. Although generally courteous and humble in his dealings with others, John Frederic was quick to take offense at anyone impugning his homeland. On one occasion, having attended a debate about the slave trade in Parliament, he threatened to kill one member, who had made disparaging remarks about Africans while defending the institution. When his English companions tried to urge Christian forgiveness on him, John Frederic declared that while he could forgive someone who robbed him, shot at him, or even sold him into slavery, he could not forgive someone who made racist and disparaging remarks about Africans, for "if anyone takes away the character of black people, that man injures black people all over the world" by laying the justification of enslaving and abusing people because of the color of their skin.

Unfortunately John Frederic became ill and died just before a ship returning him to Sierra Leone landed in Freetown. Perhaps reflecting distrust of Europeans generally or of the British particularly, the French-educated Bartholomew charged that his brother had been poisoned to keep him from revealing secrets he had learned in Europe. Although this rumor was believed by many Temne, it did not prevent other Temne chiefs from sending their sons for schooling in England.[11]

Another Upper Guinea family carrying on a tradition of education in Europe was the Afro-English Clevelands of the Banana Islands south of Freetown. A slave trader from a respected English family, William Cleveland, sent two sons by his African wife, John and James, to Liverpool for education in the later eighteenth century. John, in turn, sent his two sons to be English educated. Their uncle James, an important trader, was described as living "as nearly conformable to the European Custom, as Circumstances will admit," but he was also a member of the influential African secret society known as Poro. Like so many in his circumstances he was a man of two worlds: "With a White Man he is a White Man, with a Black Man a Black Man."[12]

Interest in European education grew rapidly with the establishment of a British colony in Sierra Leone first as a resettlement area for free blacks from London and the British colonies in the Americas and then, more successfully, as a depot for "recaptives," Africans rescued from the Atlantic slave trade. The British governor of the Sierra Leone colony, Zachary Macaulay, brought twenty-four African children to England in 1799: The twenty boys were enrolled at the "African Academy" in the abolitionist center of Clapham, and four girls studied with a female tutor. After their studies several worked in the Sierra Leone colony, one as an pharmacist, another as a printer, and others as clerks. The academy closed a few years later in favor of more aggressive educational efforts in Africa by missionaries once the British made the slave trade illegal. Some of the children of the recaptives began to imitate the creole practice of sending their children to school in England. The Thomas Carews, prosperous but illiterate liberated Africans, sent two of their children to England in about 1837.[13]

As was explained in Chapter 5, the Sierra Leone colony also sent many students to Britain for more advanced education, at first for clerical careers and later for other professions. The first Sierra Leonean to enter a British university was John Thorpe, the son of a Maroon trader and mason, who in 1832 enrolled in the newly founded University College, London, as a student of physics and law. After practicing law in Sierra Leone for a time, he returned to Britain and entered the Inner Temple in 1846 and "was called to the bar" in 1850. Many Sierra Leoneans followed Thorpe's footsteps, the most notable of whom in the nineteenth century was Sir Samuel Lewis; the child of a leading Yoruba recaptive in Freetown sent to study law in London in 1866, he became acting chief justice of the colony in 1886 and received his knighthood in 1896.[14]

SERVANTS HIGH AND LOW
IN CONTINENTAL EUROPE

As Europe extended its connections to distant lands, it became fashionable to have black musicians and black servants, especially page boys. The craze seems to have started in southern Europe and then spread through military units and aristocratic courts in the north. Although the sharply defined status differences between masters and servants resemble racial hierarchies, there is little evidence that black servants were more often mistreated than their European counterparts, although Africans must have suffered more from loneliness and exposure to unaccustomed climates and diseases. Blacks were treated more like rare or exotic pets and as ways of displaying their owners' wealth. Despite its negative aspects, this status brought substantial advantages. The black servants of the rich were well fed and housed, elegantly clothed, and sometimes educated. Moreover, the more talented among them often earned elevated social, economic, or intellectual status.

As Chapter 1 recounted, African musicians became a feature of court entertainments and especially in military bands in southern Europe from the sixteenth century. After 1650, many parts of northern Europe cultivated black musicians both because of their musical accomplishment and because of their exotic appearance. Spreading both from the Islamic East and from the Americas, this musical fashion reached a peak in late eighteenth-century Europe. The Eastern influence is seen in the craze for "Turkish" military bands that originated in imitation of janissary musical groups in the Ottoman Empire. These units were distinguished by their Oriental dress and distinctive music, produced on special instruments, including kettle drums, cymbals, triangles, tambourines, and a belled pole called *chaghána* in Turkish, which came into English as a "jingling johnny." Turkish musicians were soon replaced with blacks clothed in outlandish uniforms and the music evolved along its own lines. When the Prussian King Frederick the Great of Prussia had his Turkish band play for the Turkish ambassador in the mid-eighteenth century, the ambassador was heard to remark: "That's not Turkish." Whatever it was, the distinctive rhythms of Turkish band music spread to the concert halls in compositions by Mozart and Beethoven.

The fashion for black military musicians was also being fed from across the Atlantic. British and French military units in the West Indies recruited black musicians as well as black soldiers from the colonies' large African populations. Following the introduction of West Indian military bands into the British Isles in the 1760s, a steady flow of black musicians crossed the Atlantic as British military units eagerly competed for their talents. After the War of the American Revolution, Hessian troops fighting for the British brought a hundred black musicians back to different German lands and other musicians may have returned with troops to Britain. No expense was spared on the instruments these black musicians played and on their elaborate uniforms, which were usually of a "Turkish" design with turbans, broad sashes, and scimitars. Crowds flocked to see them parade and perform, but most of all to hear their lively music.[15]

It is impossible to discover exactly how many of these black musicians were African born, but many certainly were. Prussian officials recruited youths directly from West Africa in the early eighteenth century and trained them for military bands. A century later the Worcestershire Regiment in Britain was doing exactly the same thing. Those recruited in the Americas would have reflected the percentage of African-born persons in their overall population: high in the West Indies, low in North America.[16]

Africans were also in high demand for noble and royal courts, where European aristocrats continued the ancient custom of displaying their wealth in exotic people as much as in pomp and palaces. As in the case of African musicians, the craze for court Africans spread into Europe from plantation colonies in the Americas, directly from Africa, and from Asia, where for hundreds of years African servants had been in demand in the Islamic Middle East and even in far away China.

The Russian court of Tsar Peter the Great had several court Africans. As part of his larger campaign to make Russia the equal of its neighbors, the Russian emperor introduced the custom of African court pages, which had separately evolved in the Ottoman capital to the south and in the courts of Western Europe. At the end of a visit to the Netherlands in 1697, Peter brought three black men back to Russia with him: a servant given to him by the Dutch East India company, a sailor, and a painter. He must also have embellished his court with black servants, for one peers over his shoulder in an engraving by Adriaan Schoonebeeck.

One of Peter's Africans became considerably more than a decorative novelty. Ibrahim (or Abram) Hannibal claimed aristocratic origins in Ethiopia but by some mischance had been enslaved as a young child and carried to Istanbul, capital of the Ottoman Empire, where he was purchased by the Russian ambassador. The ambassador brought the boy of about seven to Moscow and presented him to Tsar Peter about 1705. Tsar Peter adopted the youth as his godson and provided him a festive home and a good education. For his part, Ibrahim had the wit and determination to make the most of the tutoring he received and of the practical details of warfare and statecraft he learned at Peter's side during his first decade in Europe. "To follow the thoughts of a great man is a wonderful school," the famous Russian author Alexander Pushkin later wrote regarding this period in the life of Ibrahim Hannibal, who was his great-grandfather. From 1717 to 1723 Ibrahim studied in military engineering in France and gained practical bat-tlefield experience during a French campaign in Spain, during which he was wounded. According to family legend, Tsar Peter left the capital to greet his godson on his return from France. Ibrahim had also returned with a fine library of four hundred volumes. Although he was out of favor dur-ing the years after Peter's death in 1725, Ibrahim was eventually promoted to the rank of general in the Russian army and in 1741 made governor of Reval (now Tallinn), an important port for Russia's Baltic fleet. From 1752 until his retirement in 1762 Major-General Hannibal distinguished himself as the head of military engineering in Russia and the first great military engineer in Russia. For all his Russian success, he never forgot his origins, and a brother is said to have brought him news of the family in Ethiopia at the time of his father's death.[17]

German interest in exotic Africans went back at least to 1680, when Fred-erick William, the Great Elector of Brandenburg, had promoted the estab-lishment of a Prussian outpost on the Gold Coast of West Africa so that he might obtain a few "handsome and well-built" African men to adorn his court. Such *Hofmohren* ("court Moors," that is, Africans) show up regularly in Prussian paintings. His grandson, Frederick William I, even before be-coming king of Prussia in 1713 had asked the Brandenburg African com-pany to supply him with "several black boys aged between 13 and 15, all well shaped" to be trained as musicians for his military regiments. When the Brandenburg company sold its African holdings to the Dutch West India Company in 1718–1720 part of the payment included a dozen African men, while another provision required the Dutch to furnish Prussia with a reg-ular supply of carefully chosen youths, many of whom wound up as ser-vants in entourages of German notables. The most famous *Hofmohr* was Anton Wilhelm Amo, whose career as an academic philosopher is discussed later in this chapter. Under Prussian law, these Africans could not be slaves, even though their military or court service left them almost completely dependent on their patrons.[18]

Another notable African who graced a powerful European court was Angelo Soliman (ca. 1721–1796). Bought, it would seem, in a Mediterranean slave market and passed from hand to noble hand, Soliman became a court pet at the Habsburg court in Vienna at the age of twelve. Soliman's origins in Africa are obscure. He reported his African name as Mmadi-Make, but the place names he remembered cannot be assigned with any certainty to a particular part of the continent, although the details of his early life sup-port an origin somewhere just south of the Sahara. Soliman served as aide-de-camp to his master, General Johann Christian Lobkowitz, until the

Angelo Soliman, shown here in the orientalized "Moorish" dress favored for court Africans in Habsburg Vienna. Historisches Museum der Stadt Wien: Vienna, Austria.

latter's death in 1755, when he was acquired by another high-ranking member of the court, Prince Wenzel Liechtenstein. It was his attachment to the prince, who employed Soliman as his chamberlain, that gained him the pretentious title of Chief Princely Moor (*Hochfürstlicher Mohr*). As a member of so well placed a household, Soliman was well fed and splendidly dressed in the Oriental fashion favored for court Africans.

However, Soliman was no mere decoration. He took advantage of the opportunities for education in the court, mastering several languages, and was well known for his knowledge of many subjects. As a result, he was employed on various diplomatic missions and served as tutor to the emperor's son. An ambiguous measure of Soliman's social standing is the fact that his marriage to a recently widowed Viennese noblewoman, Magdalena Christiana Kellerman, was kept secret. It seems that the secrecy was due less to his color than to the custom of servants not being married lest they compromise their total devotion to their masters. A clearer measure of Soliman's high status is the fact that he was admitted to membership in the Masonic lodge in Vienna that included the capital's prominent scholars, artists, and writers. One of Soliman's lodge brothers was the famous composer Wolfgang Amadeus Mozart. Some believe that Soliman was the model for the African character Monostatos in Mozart's opera "The Magic Flute," although others find this unlikely, since the character of Monostatos resembles Soliman not at all.

For all that, there was a cruel irony at Soliman's death in 1796 that echoes Monostatos's charge that he is treated differently because of his blackness. Over his daughter's protests, the emperor ordered Soliman's mortal remains to be given to the medical faculty for experiments. Soliman's skin was removed from his body and stitched onto a specially made wooden frame. This gruesome effigy remained on display in the local museum, dressed in a fanciful costume of beads and a feathered crown and waist cloth, along with three other skinned African "representatives of mankind" until they were destroyed by a bombardment in the revolutionary year 1848.[19]

Soliman's fate was not unique. One is reminded of the statue of a female African still displayed prominently in the Musée de l'Homme in Paris. This is a plaster cast made of Saartjie Baartman, a Khoisan woman from southern Africa, whose living form—characterized by steatophrygia, dense fat deposits that greatly enlarged her hips and thighs—was exhibited in England as the "Hottentot Venus" in 1810. At a legal inquiry sought by abolitionists she testified that she was an orphan and had come voluntarily to England to exhibit herself (clothed) in return for half of the profits. Her keepers later took her to France, where, on one occasion at least in 1815, she consented to be exhibited and painted in the nude. After she died in France, her body was subject to medical investigations similar to those done on Soliman's remains. Another southern African who was being displayed at a fair in Germany was rescued by missionaries in 1826.[20]

With its considerable connections in Africa and the West Indies, the Netherlands was also home to a significant black servant population. As in the period before 1650, a number of servants attending to their masters and mistresses are strikingly portrayed in works of art of later centuries, although, despite diligent investigations by Allison Blakely, little else is known about them.[21]

In France, the number of people of African descent was also increasing, in tandem with that nation's involvement in the trans-Atlantic trade. Several graced the court of King Louis XIV (1643–1715), including one African boy presented as a gift to Queen Marie Thérèse in 1663 and another boy who was baptized at the Fountainbleau Palace with the queen acting as his godmother in 1681. We have already recounted the story of two other African boys from Asini on the Ivory Coast, Banga and Aniaba, who were favorites of King Louis and his court.

The French government paid the travel expenses of another supposed African prince from Alexandria to Marseilles in 1701. A handsome young man in his mid-twenties, he was said to have a "mature and refined" mind and "a desire to learn." Ironically, the passion for court Africans seems to have expanded during the last quarter of the eighteenth century just as the Atlantic slave trade reached a peak, deflecting to comfortable lives in French aristocratic courts a few young Africans who would otherwise have ended up as plantation slaves in the French West Indies. From the small French colony of Senegal, Chevalier Stanislas de Boufflers, the governor, regularly fed royal and noble courts in France with *négrillions familiers* (a phrase that might be rendered into English as "pet pickaninnies"), along with other "living souvenirs" of Africa, such as parrots and ostriches. Ourika, a teenage Senegalese girl he brought to France in 1788, was adopted by the Marshal de Beauvau. Although Ourika survived for only a few years before dying of a mysterious disease at the age of sixteen, she managed to win the hearts of her adoptive family by her "charm, beauty, sweet temper, taste, reticence, [and] spirit" and made such a positive impression on other guests of the Beauvau family that one made her the heroine of a novel bearing her name. Jean Almicar, a boy Boufflers brought from Senegal and presented to Queen Marie-Antoinette in 1787, also died young, but he left his mark on that revolutionary era. During the revolutionary Terror of 1792–1793 his resourcefulness in taking care of the man in whose care he was placed gained him recognition by the leaders of the revolution.

A bit more is known of the views of another African lad, Zamoré, who lived longer and had more defined political opinions. A French prince brought the African-born Zamoré to France from India in about 1750 and presented him as a pet to Madame du Barry, King Louis XV's mistress. When the revolution began in 1789, Zamoré betrayed his patron to the revolutionary Committee of Public Safety—whether out of resentment against his own mistreatment at her hands or out of revolutionary zeal against the old order is not known. After a peremptory trial Madame du Barry was decapitated in early December 1793 (eight weeks after the queen). Like many other participants in the revolution, Zamoré ultimately became one of its victims: He was guillotined a few weeks later.[22]

ANGLO-AFRICANS

Although their numbers cannot be known with precision, it is likely that more people of African descent resided in Britain in the latter part of the eighteenth century than in all the rest of Europe combined. Unlike France, British law did not impose special restrictions on their term of residence nor on their freedom to marry, but there was some vociferous opposition to their presence on racist and pro-slavery grounds. A letter to the *Gentleman's Magazine* in 1764 noted "the main objection to their importation is that they cease to consider themselves as slaves in this free country, nor will they put up with an inequality of treatment."[23] Two decades later, the influx into Britain of "Loyal Blacks," freed by British troops in the course of the war of the American Revolution, raised concern among both those who wanted to help them and those discomforted by their presence.

As in France, the experiences of persons of African birth has to be seen in the context of this larger black population and of attitudes that were developing toward blacks in general, even though many Africans in Britain lived more cordial and comfortable circumstances than the refugees from slavery. The lives of so many Africans in Britain are known to us from their own surprisingly abundant writings or from the notice they attracted that they merit more detailed treatment than is possible for the rest of Europe.

We have already considered the extraordinary life of Ottobah Gronniosaw at the beginning of the chapter. Hardly less bizarre a tale of triumph over adverse circumstances is the life of another African of the same era, Joseph Emidy (Emidee, Emedy). Born in West Africa and sold into the Atlantic slave trade, Emidy acquired such proficiency in playing the violin while a slave in Brazil that, when his owner brought him to Lisbon, he became second violin in the opera house. Peter Fryer recounts the next turn in this extraordinary life:

> In the summer of 1795 he was kidnapped, violin and all, by British seamen on the instructions of Sir Edward Pellew (afterwards Admiral Viscount Exmouth), commander of the *Indefatigable*, who wanted a good fiddler to entertain his frigate's crew with jigs, reels, and hornpipes, admired Emidy's energetic playing, and coolly decided to have him "impressed" [forcibly recruited]. The young musician was for several years not allowed to go ashore, lest he escape. He was the only black man on board, and had to take his meals alone.

When Pellew was transferred to another vessel in 1799, Joseph was put ashore at Falmouth, England, where he made his home and supported himself by playing at parties, giving music lessons, and performing in concerts. According to Fryer, "He became leader of the Falmouth Harmonic Society and wrote many chamber works and symphonies, which were played at local concerts and much admired."[24]

The talent and fulfillment that shaped Emidy's life were shared by some other Afro-Britons whose transition from slavery to celebrity were free of the gross exploitation Emidy endured for many years. One of these was Charles Ignatius Sancho, who was conceived in Africa but born on a slave ship in 1729. The soon-orphaned baby was baptized Ignatio in Cartagena (Colombia), and was brought to England at the age of two and placed in the care of three sisters who named him Sancho after the fictional servant in the novel *Don Quixote*. By good fortune the youth's great intelligence was recognized by John, the second duke of Montagu, who encouraged him to read. After the duke's death in 1749, Sancho served as butler to the duchess of Montagu, who provided for him in her will. Like many other young men with new wealth, Sancho soon squandered his legacy, but he found new employment as valet to the new duke of Montagu, who in 1768 had his prized servant's portrait painted by the famous artist Thomas Gainsborough. After leaving the Montagus' service in 1774, Sancho ran a successful grocery in central London with considerable help from his wife, Anne, a black woman whom he had married in 1758. Yet he retained his high-born connections in his new career and through his wit cultivated new ones, including the novelist Lawrence Sterne, to whom he had written in 1766, "the early part of my life was rather unlucky," more, as Sancho relates it, because he was deprived of books than because he was a slave.[25]

In the course of his life Sancho overcame his early misfortunes, writing many works that no longer survive, including poems, a book *The Theory of Music*, two plays, and many essays in newspapers. However, he is best remembered for the two-volume collection of his letters that was published shortly after his death, when his fame was well established. As the latest editor of these letters, Vincent Carretta, points out, Sancho was "the first African to be given an obituary in the British press," a subject of literary commentary by Thomas Jefferson, and the only eighteenth-century Afro-Briton whose life was subsequently found worthy of entry in the British *Dictionary of National Biography*. The first edition of the letters was a great financial success for his widow, selling out in a year to readers "ranging from fellow servants to aristocrats." The letters are a selection, mostly from the last years of Sancho's life, and do not include the full range of Sancho's friends and correspondents. There is only one (misdated) letter of several he wrote to Sterne, but included in the collection are letters to the literary booksellers John Ireland and John Wingrave, letters to newspapers, and letters to his many friends. The largest number are to John Meheux, an aspiring young writer and artist whom Sancho counseled—the first black patron of a white English artist, Carretta points out.[26]

Modern readers may not find the letters quite as enchanting as did contemporaries. Sancho's warm, breezy prose reflects the tastes and interests of a different era and some letters are more notable for the fame of Sancho's correspondents than for the depth of his thinking. He writes of sermons,

Ignatius Sancho, a London grocer, was also the friend and correspondent of members of the British literary and artistic elite in the eighteenth century. Astor, Lenox, and Tildens Foundation, New York Public Library, Schomburg Center for Research in Black Culture.

ideas, and plays; gossips about mutual acquaintances; and comments on the politics of the day in the free and informal manner of his time, filling his letters with clever word plays, witty remarks, poetry, warmth, and charm. For our purposes, it is most important to note that Sancho wrote to successful Englishmen as a friend and equal and that his letters record how he thought of himself and of his extraordinary position in British society. Sancho's awareness of his dark complexion and African origins is never far below the surface. In some letters Sancho engages in gentle mockery of himself and his race. He described himself to Lawrence Sterne as "one of those people whom the vulgar and illiberal call 'Negurs,' " styling himself "only a poor, thick-lipped son of Afric" and describing a violent mob (that included a number of blacks) as displaying "worse than Negro barbarity." Thus conscious of his position as an outsider who can be the object of prejudice, Sancho also used his position as an outsider to champion opinions, in letters to the press often signing himself "Africanus," a name that both identified his origins and associated him with a learned and classical past.[27]

However humble he was in asserting it, Sancho had no doubt of his own equality. Yet just as he rejected the "vulgar" prejudice against all blacks, he is careful not to claim equality merely on the basis of a common humanity. Rather, he argues, equality must be earned by talent and morality. In a letter of October 11, 1772, to Julius Soubise, a fellow Afro-Briton, Sancho speaks frankly of "the miserable fate of almost all of our unfortunate colour—superadded to ignorance,—see slavery, and the contempt of those very wretches who roll in affluence from our labours superadded to this woeful catalogue—hear the ill-bred and the heart-racking abuse of the foolish vulgar." After a sea captain had brought Soubise to Britain at a young age from the West Indies, he had been taken into tutelage by the eccentric and well placed Catherine Hyde, the Duchess of Queensbury, who had raised him as she might have raised a privileged and spoiled son. Through her patronage Soubise became an accomplished horseman and an elegant, if foppish, London gentleman, who sometimes passed himself off as an African prince. Sancho raised this image of black exploitation in his letter to Soubise precisely in contrast to their own extraordinary good fortune to be well-bred, educated, and able to travel in the highest reaches of English society. He counseled Soubise to persevere in his resolve to resume the high road of virtue and respectability after a series of notorious excesses of wine, women, and extravagance. Reform came hard to Soubise, who in July 1777 was sent into exile in India to avoid prosecution for sexual assault. It was there that Sancho wrote him in November 1778, thanking Soubise for his own good letters, advising him of the deaths of both the duchess and the Duke of Queensbury, and counseling him to pay his debts and continue the reform of his life. Sancho's words reflect his own values: "improve your mind with good reading—converse with men of sense, rather than fools of fashion and riches—be humble to the rich—affable, open, and good-natured to your equals—and compassionately kind to the poor."[28]

As Gretchen Gerzina points out, while Soubise became "something of a staple metaphoric figure for eighteenth-century folly in prints and engrav-ings," especially appealing to some English tastes because he showed the folly of trying to uplift an African, Sancho was the proof of the "alternate portrait of a black man wholly at home in England and English society, while at the same time amusedly aware of his position as both an insider and outsider."[29] Not that Sancho was a saint—as a young men he too had indulged himself in the pleasures and perils of easy sex and gambling, but had married, reformed, and become a successful grocer, while keeping up a notable correspondence and social life.

This is a good place to mention another literary African, Phillis Wheatley (ca. 1753–1784) of Boston, even though her stay in Britain was a scant forty days in the summer of 1773. Only a dozen years earlier this self-described young woman "of Afric's sable race" while "young in life, by seeming cruel fate/was snatched from Afric's fancy'ed happy seat," transported by slav-ers to Boston, where her native intelligence so impressed her benevolent mistress that she had her educated. From private tutors Wheatley received, in Vincent Carretta's judgment, "an extraordinary education for a woman of the time, and an unprecedented one for a female slave." Not only did she quickly master spoken English, but in a few short years she became famous for her skills in a range of poetic forms. Wheatley's journey to London had a triple mission: to improve her health, to visit the countess of Huntingdon (to whom Gronniosaw dedicated his *Narrative*) who had agreed to sponsor the publication of a collection of her poems, and to see the volume through the press. Circumstances thwarted her plans, but her presence in England, where just a year earlier Justice Mansfield had ruled no enslaved person such as herself might legally be forced back to a slave-holding colony, enabled her to extract a promise of manumission from her Boston owners in return for her promising to return to care for her mistress. Wheatley's book *Poems on Various Subjects, Religious and Moral* received fa-vorable reviews. Sancho wrote that her "poems do credit to nature—and put art—merely as art—to the blush" and referred to her as "a genius . . . in bondage."[30]

The Interesting Narrative of Olaudah Equiano provides another special op-portunity for encountering eighteenth-century Britain through African eyes. This substantial autobiography, first published in 1789, reached a wide readership in the several editions published in Equiano's own lifetime and has reached a large modern audience in anthologies and new editions. Equi-ano recounts being kidnapped in about 1756 from his home among the Igbo of southeastern Nigeria, his sale into the Atlantic slave trade, his subsequent experiences as a slave in Barbados and Virginia, how he gained his freedom, and his many experiences as a free person in England, including his im-portant roles in the abolitionist movement. But the *Narrative* is much more than a chronicle of an unusual life. Artfully blended with this seemingly candid and naive narration of events is Equiano's analysis of how, in the course of his discovering and understanding Europeans and their world, he discovered himself as an African.

Vincent Carretta, who has produced the most thorough modern edi-

Despite servile origins, Phillis Wheatley was celebrated for her considerable poetic talents during her visit to London in 1773. The legend reads, "Phyllis Wheatley, Negro Servant to Mr. John Wheatley of Boston." From Poems on Various Subjects, Religious and Moral *(London, 1773).* Library of Congress.

tion of the *Narrative*, documents the remarkable accuracy of Equiano's account of his adult life, but suggests that he may have altered or invented parts of his early life. Carretta finds evidence that Equiano may have left Africa earlier than he says, and thus at a much younger age, between six and eight rather than the age of eleven suggested in the *Narrative*. If true, this by itself would diminish the credibility of Equiano's detailed account of his early life in Africa, but Carretta also finds evidence that brings into question whether Equiano was born in Africa at all. On two documents, a birth certificate and a ship's muster book, Equiano (or his patrons) listed his place of birth as the Carolinas. The evidence is not conclusive and, as another editor has noted, "slaves are often mistaken regarding their early history [for] memory is often colored by the emotions and imagination."[31]

Perhaps Equiano simplified the details of his birth in some records, or perhaps he invented an African childhood to erase the social stigma of being born a slave and add authority to his arguments against the slave trade. If so, he at least resisted the temptation to claim a princely birth, as Soubise and others did. For our purposes, the accuracy of the early part of the *Narrative* is less important than Equiano's view of himself as an African in Europe. It is a complex picture, whose scope is reflected in the names the author used for himself. Although modern accounts invariably call him by the African name he used in writing the *Narrative*, throughout his life outside Africa Equiano invariably identified himself as Gustavus Vassa, the name of the Swedish king given him by his English master. As Equiano he was an African in Europe, but as Vassa he was a Briton who took pride in his African ancestry. Like many other Africans in Europe Equiano was a man of two worlds, passionately tied to the value of Africa, his actual or ancestral continent of origin, and as passionately tied to the people and culture of Europe, his adopted continent.

In reconstructing his life story the mature Equiano was well aware of how his psychological identity shifted as he encountered Europe and Europeans and traces in the *Narrative* his passage from naive ignorance to well-rounded understanding of himself and his adopted country. As Equiano tells it, his discovery of Europe began early in 1757 when the unsophisticated twelve-year-old was taken to England by the sea captain who was then his master:

> I was very much struck with the buildings and the pavement of the streets in Falmouth, and, indeed, any object I saw filled me with new surprise. One morning when I got upon deck, I saw it covered all over with snow that fell over-night: as I had never seen anything of the kind before, I thought it was salt; so I immediately ran down to the mate and desired him, as well as I could, to come and see how somebody in the night had thrown salt all over the deck. . . . After this I went to church, and having never been at such a place before, I was again amazed at seeing and hearing the service. I asked all I could about it; and they gave me to understand it was worshipping God, who made us and all things. . . . I was astonished at the wisdom of white people in

Gustavus Vassa, born Olaudah Equiano, rose from slavery
to intellectual distinction in eighteenth-century Britain as
an abolitionist and autobiographer. *From his* Interesting
Narrative *(London 1789), Astor, Lenox, and Tildens Foundation,
New York Public Library, Schomburg Center for Research in Black
Culture.*

all things I saw; but was amazed at their not sacrificing or making any offer-
ings, and eating with unwashed hands, and touching the dead. I likewise
could not help remarking the particular slenderness of their women, which I
did not at first like; and I thought they were not so modest and shamefaced
as the African women.[32]

As the strangeness of these new places and people faded during the year,
Equiano's frame of reference began to shift. English customs that had once
been strange and fearful now seemed attractive and superior to those of
Africa. In one passage he observes that "from what I could understand . . .
of this God, and in seeing that these white people did not sell one another
as we did, I was much pleased; and in this I thought they were much
happier than we Africans."

Not only did he begin to admire English customs, but he grew to dislike
his own physical difference from the English people around him. A passage
concerning the sailors on his master's ship suggests his growing alienation
from his own people: "As I was now amongst a people who had not their
faces scarred, like some of the African nations where I have been, I was

very glad I did not let them ornament me in that manner when I was with them."³³ A few lines later there is an even more revealing passage. Having arrived at Guernsey, he was lodged with English friends of his master, in whose five- or six-year-old daughter Equiano took great delight:

> I had often observed that when her mother washed her face it looked rosy; but when she washed mine it did not look so; I therefore tried often times myself if I could not by washing make my face of the same colour as my little playmate (Mary), but it was all in vain; and I now began to be mortified at the difference in our complexions.³⁴

This growing awareness of his physical and cultural distance was balanced by Equiano's growing comfort in living among the British. After recounting his amazement at the men and weapons of a British war ship he was visiting, he remarked:

> However, my surprise began to diminish as my knowledge increased; and I ceased to feel those apprehensions and alarms which had taken such strong possession of me when I first came among the Europeans, and for some time after. I began now to pass to the opposite extreme; I was so far from being afraid of anything new which I saw that, after I had been some time in this ship, I even began to long for an engagement. My griefs too, which in young minds are not perpetual, were now wearing away, and I soon enjoyed myself pretty well and felt tolerably at ease in my present situation.

Considering himself "extremely well" treated by his seafaring master, for whom he developed a very great attachment, as the years passed Equiano ceased to be terrified by strange sights and became, he tells us, "in that respect at least, almost an Englishman." He became for a time a servant in a comfortable home in London, a city he enjoyed exploring. It was there in February 1759 that he took further steps in his acculturation, finally obtaining his master's permission to be baptized, the parish register recording on February 9, 1759, "Gustavus Vassa a Black born in Carolina 12 years old."³⁵

Along with its marine technology and Christianity, the aspect of Europe that fascinated Equiano most profoundly was literacy, a feature so unknown in his part of Africa that it took him some time to fathom what it consisted of. Echoing earlier accounts by other writers, he tells us of his first impression:

> I had often seen my master and Dick employed in reading; and I had a great curiosity to talk to the books, as I thought they did; and so to learn how all things had a beginning: for that purpose I have often taken up a book, and have talked to it, and then put my ears to it, when alone, in hopes it would answer me; and I have been very much concerned when I found it remained silent.³⁶

However, two or three years later his views of whites and of written language were more sophisticated:

> I could now speak English tolerably well, and perfectly understood everything that was said. I now not only felt myself quite easy with these new country-

men, but relished their society and manners. I no longer looked upon them as spirits, but as men superior to us; and therefore I had the stronger desire to resemble them; to imbibe their spirit and imitate their manners; I therefore embraced every occasion of improvement; and every new thing that I observed I treasured up in my memory. I had long wished to be able to read and write; and for this purpose I took every opportunity to gain instruction, but had made as yet very little progress. However, when I went to London with my master, I had soon an opportunity of improving myself, which I gladly embraced.[37]

In reading Equiano's account of what can only be described as his "Europeanization," the reader may wonder what had become of Equiano's understanding of his own otherness and of his fellow African people. He does not return to the subject explicitly in the *Narrative*, but he does provide the reader with many indications that as he matured he grew more comfortable with the African side of his person. He relates what was surely a key incident that occurred when he was still a youth early in 1761 on the Isle of Wight:

I was one day in a field belonging to a gentleman who had a black boy about my own size; this boy having observed me from his master's house was transported at the sight of one of his own countrymen, and ran to meet me with the utmost haste. I not knowing what he was about turned a little out of his way at first, but to no purpose; he soon came close to me, and caught hold of me in his arms as if I had been his brother, though we had never seen each other before. After we had talked together for some time, he took me to his master's house where I was treated very kindly. This benevolent boy and I were very happy in frequently seeing each other till about the month of March 1761, when our ship had orders to fit out again for another expedition.[38]

Although Equiano terms this encounter "a trifling incident," there is reason to think that in time his satisfaction with his own African features was becoming as great as the anonymous African youth's pleasure at seeing another black face on the Isle of Wight. Subsequent travels to the West Indies, to Pennsylvania and Georgia, as well is in the Mediterranean and Central America provided him with a more balanced understanding of the personal qualities of different peoples. On the one hand, his contact with both enslaved and free blacks in the Americas and their frequent kindness to him gave him a striking reminder that Africans had many virtues that balanced the faults he noted earlier. On the other hand, his highly positive views of white people were much tempered by the ill-treatment he received at the hands of many Europeans, who robbed and cheated him, attempted to reenslave him, broke their word, and in other ways gave him a more realistic view of the range of qualities the race possessed. More than once he compares Christian Europeans disparagingly with other groups. To one set of white villains he rejoined that "I had been twice amongst the Turks [who treated Greeks no better than West Indian planters treated their slaves], yet I had never seen any such usage with them, and much less

could I have expected any thing of this kind amongst Christians." Escaping
to the Miskito Indians of Belize, who received him hospitably, he comments,
"They acted towards me more like Christians than those whites I was
amongst last night, though they had been baptized."[39]

Despite the tone of these remarks, the mature Equiano never returned to
anything like the negative stereotypes he first formed of Europeans. What
his *Narrative* and his life showed was an awareness of the range of humane
and inhumane qualities among Europeans. He retained his appreciation of
the best qualities of European life. After exploring other religions and religious traditions, his devotion to Christianity was eventually confirmed,
and, as his best-selling autobiography shows, he mastered the English language to a very high standard. Yet he also became an ardent champion of
Africans and African rights, appending "the African" or "the Ethiopian" to
his signature almost as a title of nobility. He devoted his mature years to
the abolitionist cause and in 1787 planned to return to Africa with the black
settlers of the Sierra Leone Company, although he did not get further than
the port of Plymouth, where he was dismissed from his post as Commissary
for Stores, apparently for his zeal in resisting corrupt practices. He did not
abandon hope of returning to Africa, attempting unsuccessfully to volun-
teer as a missionary and then as an explorer for the African Association.

In April 1792 his life took a different turn when the successful author
married the much younger Englishwoman Susanna Cullen (1762–1796),
with whom he subsequently had two daughters, Anna Maria and Johanna.
Despite the responsibilities of domestic life, Equiano's commitment to Africa and to education remained strong. His will provided that funds set
aside for his daughters should go instead for the Sierra Leone Company
school should they die before their majority. In fact, Anna Maria died four
months after her father. The surviving daughter, Johanna, inherited the substantial sum of £950 from his estate when she attained her majority in
1816.[40]

Equiano's role as a prominent abolitionist in Britain was shared by his
fellow African, Ottobah Cugoano, born on the western Gold Coast to a
chiefly family. Cugoano had served a term in slavery in the West Indies,
where he received the name Steuart, to which he added the name John at
his baptism. In his abolitionist tract, *Thoughts and Sentiments on the Evils of
Slavery*, published in London in 1787, Cugoano tells that he chose to be
baptized after coming to England on the advice of some good people, so
"that I might not be carried away and sold again." While not strictly true,
it was widely believed at the time that a Christian could not be forced into
slavery. Despite the expediency of his motive in seeking baptism, Cugoano's profession of faith was not a sham, and his book (the composition
of which Equiano may have aided) uses Christian beliefs as well as secular
logic to refute the arguments of the pro-slavery forces. Ahead of his time
in advocating not just the ending of the slave trade from Africa and the
amelioration of the conditions of slavery, Cugoano proposed "a total abolition of slavery" and "a universal emancipation of slaves" along with a

naval patrol to enforce the ban on slave trading. He was also ahead of his time in predicting the possibility of a violent revolution by slaves to free themselves.[41]

SCHOLARS AND CHURCHMEN

A number of Africans besides Sancho and Equiano achieved intellectual distinction in Europe, continuing in the tradition described in Chapter 1. Some who had been educated in Africa helped stimulate European interest in African studies, while satisfying their own interests in Europe. More common were Africans schooled in Europe who achieved celebrity within European intellectual traditions. These included a professor of philosophy and a number of distinguished members of the Christian clergy.

The Ethiopian priest Abba Gregoryos was major contributor to European studies of Africa in the seventeenth century. Well trained in Ethiopian traditions of religious learning, he was named abbot of the Ethiopian monastery in Mechereca on an island in Lake Tana while still in his early twenties. Then he became intrigued by the larger ecclesiastical Christian world through his contacts with the Portuguese Jesuit missionaries. In pursuit of this ecumenical reconciliation between the Latin and Alexandrian churches, Gregoryos spent some years studying with the Jesuits in Ethiopia from 1625, accepted reordination as a Catholic priest, and became fluent in Portuguese. However, Gregoryos's knowledge went beyond religious studies. In a letter of 16 October 1650 he identified himself as a member of the Amharic nobility, "who are Governours of the Ethiopian people, princes, generals, and councillors of the King of Kings of Ethiopia," a circumstance that made him well familiar with the political and social activities of the Ethiopian ruling families.

The expulsion of the Catholics from Ethiopia in 1632 turned Gregoryos into a wanderer for some years, during the course of which he made favorable contacts with the Protestant Europeans through the Lutheran missionary Peter Heyling. No longer welcome in Ethiopia, Abba Gregoryos traveled in 1649 to Europe, where he remained for a decade. Initially he resided at the long-standing Ethiopian center of Saint Stephen in the Vatican from 1649 to 1652, learning Latin and Italian, but he was soon drawn into contact with the German scholar Job Ludolf, an avid student of Ethiopian studies. From 1652 Gregoryos continued his studies at the court of the Saxon Duke Ernest in Saxe-Gotha with Ludolf, whom he tutored in the Ethiopian languages of Ge'ez and Amharic.

So far as one can tell, Gregoryos's European experiences were highly positive, aside from the inevitable loneliness of being an exile and the difficulties of learning new languages in middle life. There is no record of his having experienced any harsh discrimination because of his origins or appearance. Indeed, being an Ethiopian religious scholar greatly enhanced his status for Ludolf and members of the Saxon court, who believed that the

Ethiopian literary and liturgical language Ge'ez was close to the primal human language and that Ethiopian practices continued a purer form of early Christianity than the Western churches. Gregoryos spent considerable time explaining to Ludolf and others the intricacies of Ethiopians' beliefs and lives. Even the Duke's eldest son Prince Johann Ernst, then eleven years of age, spent much of his time with the fascinating visitor to their castle.

Abba Gregoryos exhibited reciprocal interest in Europe. He was drawn to Ludolf, the German scholar who had found him in Rome and who already knew so much about Ethiopia and its literary languages that he could speak to Gregoryos in Ge'ez, although haltingly, as he had never heard the language spoken. When he went to meet Gregoryos at Nuremburg to escort him deeper into Germany, Ludolf relates, Gregoryos "fell into an ecstasie of joy, most affectionately embracing me, that he almost drew tears from me." Gregoryos also displayed enormous interest in the affairs of Europe, questioning his German hosts about the complex political structure of the Holy Roman Empire. He admired the Duke's efforts to beautify the city of Gotha but, not surprisingly, seems particularly taken by European scholarly activities. While, as was mentioned in the Introduction, he criticized the European "itch" to publish accounts of everything, whether well grounded in fact or not, he confided to Ludolf that when he first encountered printed libraries in Italy he regarded the printing press as a "sacred invention." Although initially suspicious of the reference works that the German scholars prized, he came to be delighted with the design of dictionaries and grammars of various languages and with the study of the etymology of words.

The cold of northern Europe, however, brought him no delights and he longed to return home with his new knowledge, but a first effort in 1653 failed. His death in a shipwreck on a second attempt in 1658 prevented Gregoryos's contribution to modern Ethiopian studies in Europe from being matched by his imparting European religious traditions and scholarship to his native land.[42]

European interest in Islamic West Africa was stimulated by the arrival in England, at the end of April 1733, of another educated African, a Muslim from the Gambia named Ayuba Suleiman Diallo, whose early life was recounted in Chapter 3. Ayuba had been rescued from slavery in Maryland through the intervention of James Oglethorpe, the founder of the colony of Georgia and recently retired as director of the Royal African Company. Brought to Britain by his rescuers, Ayuba found members of the English elite eager to learn of his homeland and unhappy adventures in slavery. Besides local gentry he met with scholars, translating Arabic inscriptions and three times writing out the entire Koran from memory. Dressed in specially made rich silk garments of his own design, he was presented to King George II and the rest of the royal family. Queen Caroline presented him with a gold watch. The Duke of Montagu, patron of the young Ignatius Sancho, and some other English nobles who spent time with Job Solomon (as the English rendered his name) presented him with a variety of English tools and other goods and money worth in excess of £500, to take with him on the RAC ship that returned him to his homeland.

The reasons Ayuba received this extraordinary treatment was that he was a literate and well-educated Muslim, of good family, and for those reasons a great novelty, but his personal friendliness and charming manners also delighted the English elite. Once he had mastered the rudiments of English (which he appears to have accomplished largely during his voyage from America to England), Ayuba was able to tell his hosts and their guests of his homeland, its customs, and Muslim beliefs, which he did with "a solid judgment, a ready memory, and a clear head." Ayuba's brief residence in Europe did not produce any extraordinary amount of scholarship, but the interest he aroused among the English elite added to the growing interest in Europe of discovering more about inner African life and geography.[43]

Another group of African scholars distinguished themselves within the Western intellectual traditions. They differed from Gregoryos and Ayuba in having been introduced to Europe at a young age and, by their native abilities, they continued their European educations beyond the level attained by other Africans and earned scholarly degrees that were still a rarity for Europeans. One was Anton Wilhelm Amo, who became a lecturer in philosophy at German universities. Born on the Gold Coast, Amo was brought to Amsterdam in 1707 as a child by a representative of the Dutch West India Company and presented to the Duke of Wolfenbüttel, who became his patron. At his baptism, Amo was christened Wilhelm, the name of the duke and the duke's eldest son. During the schooling his patron provided, Amo mastered Latin and Greek along with German. The brilliant young man went on to acquire a series of university degrees. In 1729, two years after entering the Faculty of Philosophy at the famous new University of Halle in Prussia, Amo defended his thesis *On the Law of the Moors in Europe (De jure Maurorum in Europa)*, and a year later he received an M.A. in philosophy from the historic University of Wittenberg. In 1734 he obtained his doctorate from the same university with a dissertation on *The Unfeelingness of the Human Mind (De humanae mentis apatheia)*, in which he sought to combine the medical and mathematical insights of the Enlightenment. He subsequently lectured at the University of Halle and the University of Jena.

Amo was a disciple of the rationalist philosopher Christian Thomas Wolff, who had been driven from his chair at the University of Halle in 1723 by the pietists, but who returned in triumph as chancellor twenty years later. Like his mentor Amo faced heated opposition in the polarized intellectual climate of the German Enlightenment. This poisoned atmosphere seems even to have undone Amo's love life; his German girlfriend jilted him and married his philosophical rival. It also led to his break with the Wolfenbüttels, a move that caused him much financial hardship. These factors, perhaps combined with the death of his new mentor and friend, led Amo to decide to return to his childhood home in about 1748, where he lived for some decades without, it seems, making any use of his philosophical education.[44]

Amo was unusual among Western-educated African scholars in his devotion to rationalist positions. Several others carried on the tradition begun in the early sixteenth century of becoming agents of Christian evangelization in their homelands. In contrast to the uniquely Catholic nature of this enterprise before 1650, the greater number were agents of the Protestant denominations. The most notable of these African clerical scholars was Jacobus E. J. Capitein (1717–1747), whose early life followed a familiar pattern. After becoming an orphan on the Gold Coast, the youth (whose original name may have been Asar) was sold to a Dutch resident of the Gold Coast forts. His Dutch owner, Jacob van Goch, brought his ten- or eleven-year-old charge to the Netherlands in 1728, a country that had outlawed slavery within its boundaries eighty years earlier. Van Goch sponsored the youngster's schooling in the Hague, "the place," Capitein later wrote, "where our sequestered youth was devoted to noble studies." From private tutors, he reports, he "learned the rudiments of the Dutch language [and] worked on the art of painting, in which I proved to be quite talented." He showed an equal bent for the catechism classes he attended. With the support of other Dutch burghers in 1731 Capitein entered the prestigious Latin School in the Hague, where he studied Latin, Greek, and Hebrew. Partway through these studies, he chose to be baptized a Christian, taking the names of his patron Jacob, Van Goch's sister Eliza, and his cousin's wife Johanna, who were his witnesses at the ceremony. Capitein saw this decision to become a Christian as continuing an ancient African tradition, as he later compared the event to the decision seventeen centuries earlier of a senior Ethiopian official to receive baptism from the hand of the Apostle Philip (Acts 8:27–40).

The depth of Capitein's commitment to a Christian mission is also reflected in the public lecture he gave "on the conversion of the heathen" at the end of his Hague studies in 1737, and by his next step, beginning the study of divinity at Leiden University in 1737 at which time he published a dissertation on the calling of the Gentiles to Christianity. He was ordained in 1742, after completing his studies and defending a dissertation arguing that "slavery was not contrary to Christian liberty" and soon went to be chaplain to the Dutch West India Company at Elmina.

Some matters of Capitein's intellectual and literary life deserve to be considered before taking up his life as a chaplain. The elegant Latin verse he wrote in keeping with the literary fashions of the day record some of his reactions to his European experiences. One poem praised the city of Middleburg, where he first resided in the Netherlands, as "the most agreeable place on earth," in part "because I began there to be acquainted with knowledge." He also wrote poems praising his patrons, teachers, and fellow students, some of the latter reciprocating in verse of their own. Some of their praise poems about him, along with his own poetry and his dissertation, were published and sold in pamphlet form.

His dissertation defending the compatibility of slavery with Christian

*Jacobus E. J. Capitein, age 25, on the occasion of the
publication of his dissertation on the theology of slavery in
1742. Leiden University Library.*

beliefs needs to be understood in both its historical and theological context.
Capitein directs his argument against those Christians who feared evangelization would undermine slavery, especially against the belief, gaining
strength in the Netherlands, that Christian "freedom cannot coexist with
servitude of the body." To modern ears the argument may sound contrived
and unconvincing, as it did to radical social critics of the early nineteenth
century such as Abbé Grégoire, who drew attention to the achievements of
Capitein and other Africans. It is worth remembering that Capitein's own
enslavement had been brief and benign, whereas his embrace of Christianity was a powerful force in his life. While not defending the institution
of slavery, he clearly believed that it was better to be a slave and a Christian
than not to be Christian at all. Capitein argued that under the Spanish and
Portuguese slavery became a means by which the Christian truth was
spread, and thus an example of the way in which God could use imperfect
human institutions to His higher purpose. He eruditely cited a long line of
Christian thinkers who argued that the freedom of the soul brought by
Christianity is more important than the freedom of the body. As he put it,
Christianity "demands only *spiritual* freedom in order that we can worship
God, not necessarily *external* freedom." Whether because of its unrevolu-
tionary message or its erudition, the dissertation, along with separate col-

lections of his sermons, enjoyed a wide circulation in Dutch translation and added to Capitein's growing fame.[45]

Capitein took up the office of chaplain at Elmina castle, ranking just below the Dutch governor. His duties were to minister to the needs of the Dutch community, but, like Philip Quaque (whose life was discussed in Chapter 3), he devoted considerable energy to evangelizing the African population in the vicinity. He reopened the local school, prepared a catechism in the local Fanti language, and attracted students even from the court of the powerful Asante ruler, Opoku Ware. One of the Asante youths ("Jacjé") was sent for study in the Netherlands. Like many missionaries, Capitein died at an early age in 1747, after having had only modest success as a missionary in Africa.[46]

Another future missionary was Philip Quaque (or Kwaku) (1741–1816), who as a youth had been sent to London for education along with two other boys by missionaries of the Society for the Propagation of the Gospel. All three boys came from elite Gold Coast families, so this venture must also have had their families' support. Unfortunately the other two youths died before they could return, one of consumption, the other as the result of a mental breakdown, but Quaque survived the experience. He received a good education, and, in light of his religious turn of mind and good character, his patrons decided to prepare him for the priesthood. In 1765 he became the first African ordained to the Anglican priesthood and the same year married Catherine Blunt, a young Englishwoman who had much less education. They went off to the Gold Coast early in 1766 to the British outpost of the Cape Coast Castle, where, like Capitein, Quaque took up the post of chaplain and undertook the evangelization and education of local youths. Debrunner says he forgot how to speak any African language.[47]

Another African missionary was David Boilat of Senegal—in this case a Roman Catholic priest. He too had been sent at a young and impressionable age from his Senegalese homeland to study in France, where from 1825 to 1840 he was trained along with several other Africans for a clerical career. Three years after his ordination as a priest in 1840, he returned to Senegal. Over the next decade there he devoted himself to the creation of a French-style secondary school for the African elite and to the study of his homeland, the latter resulting in a lengthy volume, *Esquisses Sénégalaises*, published in 1853. During the final years of his life he lived again in France as a parish priest.[48]

Like Capitein and Quaque, Boilat was an ardent champion of Western Christianity, language, and culture as the mechanism for transforming and saving Africa. His seminary education instilled in him an inflexible antipathy to Islam, which he saw as having undermined an older African intellectual tradition. Boilat's European education also gave him an immense appreciation for the subtlety and profundity of European languages—in his case French. Robert July tells a revealing story:

> When Boilat first returned to Senegal, he was struck by the excellent instruc-
> tion in French which the young girls were receiving in the schools of Goree
> and St. Louis and yet, despite the efforts of both teachers and pupils, these
> students somehow lacked "that gentle piety that characterized young persons
> in France." . . . Sorely puzzled, Boilat continued to search for some blemish in
> the apparently blameless lives of these students. At last he could find but one
> thing—the continuing habit of speaking Wolof outside the classroom.[49]

From his perspective, perfection in French was needed not only to master
the subtleties of the formal curriculum and for refinement of manners but
also to absorb the refinements of their spiritual training as well. He urged
the young women's parents to see "all the moral riches which your children
will gather from studying French." For all his devotion to French culture,
Boilat's goal was not to turn Africans into Europeans, but to use French
culture to modernize Africa:

> What a glorious future is in prospect for Senegal! With education you will see
> the flowering of commerce, science, art, religion, and above all, an improved
> morality. You will see the fall of those gross, if not dishonourable, ways known
> as *the custom of the country.* You will witness the disappearance of all those
> absurd superstitions born of that silly deplorable gullibility with which most
> of the population deludes itself.[50]

One finds in Boilat, not surprisingly, a man of his times informed by its
prevailing passions and prejudices, but passionately dedicated to the transformation of his homeland. The same characteristics are found in the famous African Anglican bishop, Samuel Ajayi Crowther, whose captivity
and liberation in Sierra Leone were recounted in Chapter 5. Crowther did
not spend much time in Britain, but his European experiences profoundly
affected his life. He first went to England in 1827 for a short stay and paid
a longer visit in 1842–1843 that culminated in his ordination as a priest. He
was back in 1851 and again in 1864, at which time he received a Doctor of
Divinity from Oxford University and was consecrated as a bishop by the
Anglican Church's primate, the Archbishop of Canterbury. In between he
was an active participant in British expeditions exploring the lower Niger
in 1841 and again in 1857, writing and publishing perceptive accounts of
African life with an eye to future missionary enterprises. Crowther also
translated parts of the Bible into Yoruba, although many of his collections
and translations were lost in a tragic fire in 1862. Like Boilat, Crowther
promoted Christianity as the key to reform and modernization in Africa.
Like his fellow British CMS missionaries, he saw the mission's goal as "introducing the Gospel and the Plough," that is, commercial agriculture, both
working "hand-in-hand—the Gospel primarily; Industry [i.e., agriculture]
as the handmaiden to the Gospel."[51] Crowther also made a clear distinction
between valuable parts of African cultures that were to be preserved and
the "degrading and superstitious defects" that were to be abolished. The
basis of this distinction was as much practical as anything else. He wrote
in 1869, "If judicious use be made of native ideas, their minds will be better

Bishop Samuel Ajayi Crowther in 1888, shown in English clerical dress. From Jesse Page, Samuel Crowther *(London, 1910).*

reached than by attempting to introduce new ones quite foreign to their way of thinking." He applied the same principle to the modernization of African institutions. It is noteworthy of the bishop's transformed self-identity that he writes of "their" ideas and institutions, not "our." As Robert July notes, Crowther became so committed to his British identity that in one place he even followed the British practice of calling England "home."[52]

Crowther shared Boilat's view of Islam as not only theologically at variance with Christianity but also as promoting benighted superstition, ignorance, slavery, and, of special importance in Crowther's view, the unjust and immoral subordination of women in society and in polygamous marriages. He shared with his fellow missionaries the view of Africa as a benighted continent, but he believed a good part of the blame lay with the European-directed slave trade, just coming to an end during his lifetime. Thus it was not surprising that Crowther saw Europeans as morally obliged to play a major part in the continent's redemption. In 1869 he expressed the view that "to claim Africa for Africans alone, is to claim for her the right of a continued ignorance to practice cruelty and acts of barbarity as her perpetual inheritance. For it is certain, unless help came from without, a nation can never rise much above its present state."[53]

Another African missionary of this era, Tiyo Soga (1829–1871), had his formative experiences in Scotland. His first visit was in 1846–1848, when in his teens. He had already had some elementary and secondary education at mission schools in his Xhosa homeland on the troubled eastern frontier of the Cape Colony when he was brought to Glasgow by a Scottish missionary who wanted to give the promising student the advantages of a good Scottish education. Tiyo soon found the support he needed. A local *laird*, John Henderson, agreed to pay his living and educational expenses, and the pastor and congregation of the John Street United Presbyterian Church adopted the young African. Tiyo's educational progress during these two years was slow, held back by his still imperfect command of English and a growing homesickness, surely not helped by the Scottish climate. However, his commitment to Christianity grew rapidly, and he later identified his decision to be baptized in the John Street Church in May 1848 as the highlight of his stay in Scotland.

Tiyo returned to Xhosaland in 1849 and was reconciled with his chiefly father, but another outbreak of frontier warfare soon had him back on a ship to Europe. From 1851 to 1857 he was again in Scotland, combining preaching with a strenuous program of studies in the Arts Faculty at the University of Glasgow and at the United Presbyterian Church seminary. At the end of five years of theological studies, he received his concluding testimonials, including an address signed by 186 students and a library of thirty-eight volumes of Christian literature. After passing his final exams and being ordained a minister in December 1856, he went on a strenuous preaching tour in Scotland that proved immensely popular. Then, in February 1857, he married Janet Burnside, the Scottish woman who had become the love of his life. The two returned as missionaries to South Africa in 1857, where they raised two daughters and four sons, all of the sons receiving Scottish educations.

Like the other African ministers, Tiyo was convinced of the truth of Christianity and the superior achievements of European civilization, a view reinforced in 1851 by his visit to the justly famous Crystal Palace exposition in London. Despite the discrimination he faced in the color-conscious Cape Colony because of his European wife and despite the destruction ongoing frontier wars were causing in his homeland, he remained a faithful British subject. Yet, in his way, he was also a faithful Xhosa. This man of two worlds labored to record and preserve his people's cultural traditions, while translating European mores to their needs and promoting a Xhosa

Tiyo Soga, educated in Scotland and a pioneer Presbyterian missionary among his Xhosa people. From the photograph reproduced in John Chalmers, Tiyo Soga *(Edinburgh, 1877).*

Christianity as free from European control as was possible under the circumstances.[54]

Viewed from the present, it can be all to difficult to accept these African missionaries on their own terms and all too easy to dismiss their impor-tance. Yet one must try to see them in their historical context. Even though their thinking was shaped and their lives circumscribed by European influ-ences, one must not fail to see how profoundly African priorities dominated their lives and careers. In a time of crisis and transformation they were determined to build a new and better Africa. If their identification with

Europe seems overly strong and their view of Africa overly critical and remote, it must not be forgotten that they were the founding generation of nationalists. Tiyo Soga's translations and collections of Xhosa lore reflected his vision of a reformed society that was still profoundly African and, as will be recounted in the next section, he raised his children to carry on his efforts. Bishop Crowther's grandson, Herbert Macaulay, is celebrated as the father of Nigerian nationalism. As missionaries and modernizers, these Africans were pioneers whose efforts deserve to be celebrated, for they were precursors of larger changes that would transform Africa.

CONCLUDING OBSERVATIONS

This chapter has examined the notable African presence in Europe during the two centuries before the continent was colonized. In the last part of the eighteenth century, Africans were found at every level of society: from the marginally employed and the humble domestic servants to the aides of the rich and powerful, from students to professors, pastors, musicians, and writers. They were involved in religion and philosophy, in war and revolution, in the arts and abolitionism. Their overall impact on Europe may have been small, but it was significant for the individuals themselves, and their collective experiences tell us some important things about Europe and about Africa.

One fact that readers will have noted is that the African presence in Europe was as predominantly male as was the European presence in Africa during this period. Not surprisingly, this imbalance also resulted in patterns of sexual relations that point to larger realities. Only a few African men in Europe married women of African descent. According to Vincent Carretta, Ignatius Sancho, who married a black West Indian named Anne in 1758, was "one of only two known all-Black marriages recorded [in Britain] during the century."[55] Some other African men, such as Africanus Horton, did not marry while in Europe. Shortly after returning to Sierra Leone in 1861 from his student years in Scotland, Horton married Fannie Mariette Pratt, who like her husband was European educated, the child of a recaptive, and an Igbo. Some years after her death, Horton married for the second time, to Selina Beatrice Elliott, granddaughter of one of the colony's original African-American settlers from Nova Scotia. Her father had been a rural magistrate, her mother the daughter of a prominent European trader and his country wife.[56]

These exceptions aside, the majority of African men chose their sexual partners from among their European hosts. In France, a 1777 decree decried the alleged facts that blacks "marry Europeans, the houses of prostitution are infected by them, the colors mix, the blood is changing." Writers in Britain expressed similar complaints, the disapproving Jamaican planter Edward Long fuming in 1772, "The lower order of women are remarkably fond of the blacks, for reasons too brutal to mention," which the thoroughly racist Long then went on to detail. Because such statements came from those opposed to a black presence, they may well exaggerate the ease of sexual mixing, but some commentators believe that opposition to inter-marriage was small. An older history of blacks in France argues, "There was no animus against them by the populace, and socially they might mix with the French, save that there was a class barrier among the French them-selves. . . . A few married—some to whites—and these generally remained in France." In a thoughtful recent essay, historian Seymour Drescher argues that in France, as in Britain in this era, there was "tolerance of many black people . . . as socially acceptable marriage partners" despite some vocal opposition.[57]

As far as one can judge, the many marriages of Africans in Europe seem generally to have been little bothered by expressions of prejudice from their neighbors and untroubled at a personal level by the different backgrounds of the spouses. Some examples reveal the variations. In his early student days in Glasgow Tiyo Soga became enamored of an African-American ab-olitionist speaker named Stella, but she died before the romance blossomed. It is interesting to speculate how his life might have been different had he married her, but it was not to be. His marriage in 1857 to Janet Burnside was a love match that may not have disturbed many in Scotland, but its reception was different in the Cape Colony, where prejudice against mixed marriages had greatly increased since the celebrated marriage of Eva and a Dutch company official in the early years of the colony recounted in Chapter 3. Although treated with respect by missionaries and senior gov-ernment officials, Tiyo Soga developed some bitterness at the color preju-dice he and Janet encountered from many European settlers and at the culture prejudice his European way of living evoked from many Africans. But he was adamant in his instructions to his children to accept their dual heritage and insist on their equality despite "the taunt of men, which you will sometimes feel":

> . . . [C]herish the memory of your mother as that of an upright, conscientious, thrifty, Christian Scotchwoman. . . . [B]e thankful for your connection by this tie to the white race. . . . [N]ever appear ashamed that your father was a Kafir [African], and that you inherit some African blood. It is every bit as good and as pure as that which flows in the veins of my fairer brethren.

Yet Soga's charge to his children also reflected his appreciation of where in that racially divided colonial society his sons would find their identity: "*take your place* in the world as *coloured*, not as *white* men; as *Kafirs*, not as Englishmen."[58]

Such prejudice, however, was not the norm in Europe nor in European outposts in West Africa. When Capitein, who had not married in Europe, applied to his religious superiors to marry one of his African students in his Gold Coast, they refused permission. Instead, they sent out to him a Dutch girl, Antonia Grinderdos, whom he apparently did not know, who became his wife in 1745. In this case the issue was religion. Capitein could not marry an unbaptized person and the Dutch churchmen did not feel it proper that he instruct the woman he would marry in the Christian faith. While cultural prejudice may have influenced their preference for a European woman, quite clearly they did not find it inappropriate for African and European Christians to marry.[59]

The views of Africans on intermarriage that is so evident in their deeds in Europe was given voice by Equiano in a letter of 1788:

> If the mind of a black man conceives the passion of love for a fair female, [it should not be that] he is to pine, languish, and even die, sooner than an intermarriage be allowed, merely because [of] foolish prejudice.... God looks with equal good-will on all his creatures, whether black or white—let neither, therefore, arrogantly condemn the other.[60]

Equiano acknowledged that prejudice existed but judged it unworthy of a "cultivated mind" and rightly pointed out that such sentiments were imported from the plantation colonies, where hypocritical white planters routinely exploited black women sexually. A close parallel of the color-blind free love Equiano advocated was the relations of African women and the Europeans resident in Africa considered in Chapter 3. There love matches and marriages took place with little overt disapproval. A further instructive parallel may be noted: Europeans in Africa adopted the African custom of polygamy, adding a "country wife" to a spouse many had left at home, while Africans in Europe abandoned the polygamous customs of their homelands and established only monogamous relationships. While practical expediency played a role in these decisions, one can also see in their marriage patterns in Europe Africans' voluntary cultural assimilation.

These diverse attitudes about interracial (and intercultural) marriage may be helpful in asking what these African experiences reveal about the larger state of racism in Europe. Much ink has been spilled on this subject. Researchers have sought to explain where the dreadful prejudices of the later nineteenth and twentieth centuries came from, but, perhaps because of their concern with finding racism's origins, they exaggerate the pervasiveness of race prejudice in Europe before 1850. In 1845, the great African-American abolitionist Frederick Douglass, who was born in slavery in Maryland, reported that, during four months in the British Isles (nearly all of it in Ireland), his experiences had been free of the ugly racism he had known all too well in the United States. "The truth is," he wrote, "the people here . . . measure and esteem men according to their moral and intellectual worth, and not according to the color of skin."[61] Like many of the Africans we have considered in Britain, Douglass's personal talents turned away prejudice and enabled him to move among those of "cultivated mind" who believed racism beneath them. But in another letter written a month later in Scotland Douglass also captured the fascination with which the British public regarded talented blacks: "It is quite an advantage to be a 'nigger' here. I am hardly black enough for the british taste, but by keeping my hair as wooly as possible—I make out to pass for at least half a negro at any rate."[62]

As hard as it may be to imagine Africans in Europe lionized for their color, that was as much a reality as was the simultaneous presence of color prejudice. The literary lion Ignatius Sancho had had warned Soubise seven decades earlier that only talent and respectability kept men like them from "the heart-racking abuse of the foolish vulgar" in Britain. Their contemporary in Vienna, Angelo Soliman, would know astonishing respect and privilege in life, but after death his person received much the same shameful treatment as Saartjie Baartman, the "Hottentot Venus," both in life and after death. In their cases one cannot blame the abuse on ignorance and vulgarity, for it was science that made them museum displays.

Attitudes, of course, were not static. As Equiano and Douglass both noted, the prejudices of the slave owners in the Americas were penetrating Europe. They were also introducing slaves into parts of Europe where the institution had not been seen in centuries. It is revealing that, for conservative theological reasons, Capitein had had to argue with great vigor against the widespread Dutch belief that slavery, already illegal in the Netherlands, must be morally wrong. In France and Britain the growing numbers of blacks from the Americas provoked responses that were both similar and divergent. There was growing prejudice, especially against poor, ill-educated blacks of servile origins. Longstanding prejudice against strangers played a part. As already seen, some raised objection to the mixing of the blood. But there was an interesting new objection in the 1760s and 1770s: slaves' assimilation of European ideas of freedom. A letter to a British magazine in 1764 argued against admitting new blacks because "they cease to consider themselves as slaves in this free country, not will they put up with an inequality of treatment." A French decree of 1777 similarly noted that when slaves who had for a time in France "return to America, [they] bring with them the spirit of freedom, independence, and equality, which they communicate to others."[63] The French state responded to domestic complaints with a decree in 1738 prohibiting slaves from marrying or remaining more than three years in the country. Similar French decrees in 1777 and 1778 renewed these restrictions and imposed more stringent ones. But in Britain, with ten times the black population as France, such views failed to gain sufficient Parliamentary support, an outcome Drescher suggests reflected not a difference in attitudes but merely the greater ease with which well-placed vocal minorities were able to influence French state policy. Moreover, in Britain slave owners suffered a serious blow when in 1772 Justice Mansfield ruled in the Somerset Case that English law did not recognize the right of slave owners "to take a Slave by force to be sold abroad." The abolitionist cause made progress in both countries during the next two decades.[64]

Focusing on the African presence in Europe forces us to confront the complexities of attitudes and events. It also requires us to reconsider such Africans' connections to Africa. For many Africans whose adult lives were spent entirely in Europe, Africa could be remote, a memory (if that), the continent of origin but not of cultural identity. But for many other Africans,

Europe was one pole of a personal and intellectual network whose long history this volume has charted. The great circuit that ran between Africa and Europe, and sometimes included the Americas as well, transported culture as readily as commerce. The cultural dialogue is obvious for those generations of African students who spent a few years in European schools and a lifetime interacting with Europeans in Africa. Grounded in Africa, their cultural world embraced European languages, customs, and beliefs. For these students, as for some other Africans, completing the circuit back to Africa was critical, although not all were successful. Abba Gregoryos and John Frederic Naimbana died trying to return. Equiano was frustrated from returning by the politics of the Sierra Leone colonization effort. Not all who returned advanced the dialogue: One looks in vain for ways in which someone like Anton Wilhelm Amo made use of his European philosophical training. As a group, African missionaries had the clearest agenda and the greatest impact, although in most parts of Africa before 1850 their impact was small. Capitein and Quaque on the Gold Coast, like Boilat in Senegal, did more to sustain an elite African tradition of biculturalism than spread it. Only toward the end of our period in the very different British colonies of Sierra Leone and the Cape Colony does one find an expanding cultural frontier.

In the careers of Ajayi Crowther, Africanus Horton, and Tiyo Soga are signs of the larger changes to come, but that story extends beyond 1850. As their lives demonstrate, there is nothing magical about that date. At most it marks a threshold in an accelerating process of African-European interaction, not an end point. This work has chosen to end there for a reason that is both pragmatic and purposeful. To continue would require one or more additional volumes, or the condensation of this volume's contents to a mere preamble to that larger period of interaction. One stops, hopefully, when one has said enough. One may also pause in 1850 because the patterns explored in this volume do not change substantially after that date except in scale. The age that followed was full of persons and events of importance in their own right, but the patterns of interaction had already been set. Consciously or not those who came later were repeating what had already taken place on a larger scale in these earlier centuries. For this reason Africa's discovery of Europe before 1850 is important as an incubator of the larger trends that would follow and important in its own right as well.

Notes

1. James Albert Ukawsaw Gronniosaw, *Narrative of the Most Remarkable Particulars in the Life of James Albert Ukawsaw Gronniosaw, an African Prince, as Related by Himself*, in *Pioneers of the Black Atlantic: Five Narratives from the Enlightenment, 1772–1815*, ed. Henry Louis Gates, Jr., and William L. Andrews (Washington, DC: Counterpoint, 1998), quotations on pp. 40, 41, 53, 54, 58.

2. Ibid., pp. 52–53, 59.

3. Paul Edwards and James Walvin, *Black Personalities of the Era of the Slave Trade* (Baton Rouge: Louisiana State University, 1983), p. 76.

4. Gretchen Holbrook Gerzina, *Black London: Life before Emancipation* (New Brunswick, NJ: Rutgers University Press, 1995); Peter Fryer, *Staying Power: The History of Black People in Britain* (London: Pluto Press, 1984); and Edwards and Walvin, *Black Personalities*, are particularly recommended.

5. Gerzina, *Black London*, pp. 21–22.

6. Robin Law and Kristan Mann, "West Africa and the Atlantic Community: The Case of the Slave Coast," *The William and Mary Quarterly* 3d series 56 (1999): 316; Hans Werner Debrunner, *Presence and Prestige: Africans in Europe: A History of Africans in Europe before 1918* (Basel: Basler Afrika Bibliographien, 1979), pp. 69–70. More in Edouard Dunglas, "Contributions à l'histoire du moyen Dahomey, chapt IX" in *Etudes Dahonéennes* 19 (1957): 115–118.

7. Debrunner, *Presence and Prestige*, pp. 70–71; John D. Hargreaves, ed., *France and West Africa: An Anthology of Historical Documents* (London: Macmillan, 1969), pp. 54–58; Selby T. McCloy, *The Negro in France* (Lexington: University of Kentucky Press, 1961), pp. 14–15, 37–38.

8. Debrunner, *Presence and Prestige*, pp. 66–67, 76–79; David Eltis, *The Rise of Slavery in the Americas* (New York: Cambridge University Press, 1999), p. 249n.

9. Ivor Wilks, *Asante in the Nineteenth Century* (Cambridge: Cambridge University Press, 1975), pp. 203–5, 596–608; Allison Blakely, *Blacks in the Dutch World: The Evolution of Racial Imagery in a Modern Society*. (Bloomington: Indiana University Press, 1993), pp. 256–59; Debrunner, *Presence and Prestige*, p. 183.

10. Debrunner, *Presence and Prestige*, p. 74.

11. Zachary Macaulay, *The African Prince* (1796), in Paul Edwards and James Walvin, *Black Personalities in the Era of the Slave Trade* (Baton Rouge: Louisiana State University Press, 1983), pp. 204–10; Christopher Fyfe, *A History of Sierra Leone* (London: Oxford University Press, 1962), pp. 11, 30, 54; Gerzina, *Black London*, pp. 174–78.

12. Fyfe, *History*, p. 10; Debrunner, *Presence and Prestige*, p. 75; quotations from *Report of the Privy Council . . . Concerning the Recent State of the Trade to Africa, and Particularly the Trade in Slaves . . .* , 1789, Part I, No. 5, excerpted in Christopher Fyfe, ed., *Sierra Leone Inheritance* (London: Oxford University Press, 1964), pp. 101–2.

13. Debrunner, *Presence and Prestige*, pp. 177–78; Fyfe, *History*, p. 205.

14. Fyfe, *History*, pp. 188–89, 214, 252, 254, 312; Fryer, *Staying Power*, pp. 436–37. The first lawyer from the Gold Coast was John Mensah Sarbah, who qualified as a barrister in 1887.

15. A myriad of details on British units can be found in Fryer, *Staying Power*, pp. 80–88, quotation p. 83; for information on the black musicians recruited by the Hessians I am indebted to Vera Lind, personal communication.

16. Fryer, *Staying Power*, p. 84; see also Roger Norman Buckley, *Slaves in Red Coats: The British West India Regiments, 1795–1815* (New Haven, CT: Yale University Press, 1979).

17. Richard Pankhurst, "Ibrahim Hannibal, Ancestor of Alex. Pushkin," appendix F in his *An Introduction to the Economic History of Ethiopia* (London: Lalibela House, 1961); Allison Blakely, *Russia and the Negro* (Washington, DC: Howard University Press, 1986), pp. 13–25. Ibrahim was his original name, which he kept despite the tsar's desire to christen him Peter. Hannibal was added later either in honor of the North African Punic general for his martial exploits or from an Ethiopian place name. See also Pushkin's fictionalized account, *The Negro of Peter the Great*.

18. Adam Jones, "Brandenburg-Prussia and the Slave Trade, 1680–1700," in *De la trait à l'esclavage: actes du Colloque international sur la traite des noirs, Nantes 1985*, ed. Serge Daget (Nantes: Centre de Recherche sur Histoire du Monde Atlantique, 1988), I:292–93; Debrunner, *Presence and Prestige*, pp. 94–95, 96–97.

19. Volkmar Braunbehrens, *Mozart in Vienna, 1781–1791*, trans. Timothy Bell (New York: Grove Weidenfeld, 1986), pp. 85–87; Debrunner, *Presence and Prestige*, pp. 112–14, 145.

20. Debrunner, *Presence and Prestige*, p. 221. Still another Khoi woman was exhibited in London in 1838 and gave rides to children perched on her posterior; Edwards and Walvin, *Black Personalities*, pp. 171–182.

21. Blakely, *Blacks in Dutch World*, pp. 103–25.

22. McCloy, *Negro in France*, pp. 15–16; Debrunner, *Presence and Prestige*, pp. 98–100.

23. Cited by Gerzina, *Black London*, p. 41.

24. Fryer, *Staying Power*, pp. 430–31.

25. Vincent Carretta, "Introduction," *Letters of the Late Ignatius Sancho, an African*, ed. Vincent Carretta (London: Penguin Books, 1998), pp. ix–xii, quotation p. 73.

26. Carretta, "Introduction [to Sancho]," pp. ix, xiv–xv.

27. Sancho, *Letters*, quotations at pp. 73, 216, 217.

28. Ibid., quotations at pp. 46, 149; see the profile of Soubise in Gerzina, *Black London*, pp. 54–59.

29. Gerzina, *Black London*, pp. 56–57, 61–62.

30. Phillis Wheatley, *Complete Works*, ed. Vincent Carretta (New York: Penguin Books, 2001), pp. xiii, xxii–xxvi, xxviii–xxix.

31. Vincent Carretta, "Olaudah Equiano or Gustavus Vassa? New Light on an Eighteenth-Century Question of Identity," *Slavery and Abolition* 20 (1999): 96–105; Valaurez B. Spratlin, *Juan Latino, Slave and Humanist* (New York: Spinner Press, 1938), p. 6.

32. Olaudah Equiano, *The Interesting Narrative and Other Writings*, ed. Vincent Carretta (New York: Penguin Books, 1995), pp. 67–68.

33. Ibid., pp. 68–69.

34. Ibid., p. 69.

35. Ibid., pp. 70, 77, 261 note 197. The baptismal registry entry is, of course, at variance with the *Narrative*'s claim that he was born in West Africa in 1745.

36. Ibid., p. 68. As editors have pointed out, this passage resembles the one in Gronniosaw's *Narrative* of 1772 and other African lives.

37. Ibid., pp. 77–78.

38. Ibid., p. 85.

39. Ibid., pp. 211, 213–14.

40. Ibid., pp. 353–55.

41. Ottobah Cugoano, *Thoughts and Sentiments on the Evil and Wicked Traffic of the Slavery and Commerce of the Human Species* (London, 1787), in Gates and Andrews, eds., *Pioneers of the Black Atlantic*, pp. 88, 163, 167, 169–70; Fryer, *Staying Power*, pp. 98–102.

42. Debrunner, *Presence and Prestige*, pp. 54–56; Job Ludolf, *A New History of Ethiopia: Being a Full and Accurate Description of Abessinia*, trans. J. P. Gent (London: Samuel Smith, 1684). All quotations are from Ludolf's unpaginated Preface. The later efforts to spread European studies in Ethiopia of another Jesuit-trained Ethiopian priest, Abba Antonio d'Andrada, likewise ended tragically in 1670 when he was executed by the Turks while trying to reach his mother's homeland; Debrunner, *Presence and Prestige*, p. 54.

43. Philip D. Curtin, "Ayuba Suleiman Diallo of Bondu," in *Africa Remembered: Narratives by West Africans from the Era of the Slave Trade*, ed. Philip D. Curtin (Madison: University of Wisconsin Press, 1967), pp. 17–59, quotation p. 52 excerpted from Thomas Bleutt, *Some Memoirs of the Life of Job, the Son of Solomon the High Priest of Boonda in Africa* (1734); Fryer, *Staying Power*, pp. 421–23.

44. Debrunner, *Presence and Prestige*, pp. 107–8: Grégoire, *Enquiry*, pp. 76–78.

45. J. E. J. Capitein, *The Agony of Asar: A Thesis on Slavery by the Former Slave, Jacobus Eliza Johannes Capitein, 1717–1747*, trans. Grant Parker (Princeton, NJ: Markus Wiener Publishers, 2001), quotations pp. 87, 93, 113, and from Debrunner, *Presence and Prestige*, p. 80. See also Kwesi Kwaa Prah, *Jacobus Eliza Johannes Capitein, 1717–1747: A Critical Study of an Eighteenth Century African* (Trenton, NJ: Africa World Press, Inc., 1992), pp. 37–54. The precise identity of those Capitein opposed is obscure, but anti-slavery had a long history in the Netherlands. It was Dutch immigrants in Pennsylvania who authored the first anti-slavery manifesto in the Americas, the Germantown Petition of 1688; see David Brion Davis, *The Problem of Slavery in Western Culture* (Ithaca, NY: Cornell University Press, 1966), pp. 308–11.

46. Debrunner, *Presence and Prestige*, pp. 80–81; Grégoire, *Enquiry*, pp. 85–90.

47. Debrunner, *Presence and Prestige*, pp. 81–82.

48. Ibid., pp. 186–87.

49. July, *Origins*, p. 159.

50. Ibid., p. 160, translating Père David Boilat, *Esquisses Sénégalaises* (Paris: P. Bertrand, 1853), pp. 9–18, 227–38, 477–79.

51. July, *Origins*, p. 185, quoting Crowther's 1866 memorandum to the clergy of the Niger Mission.

52. Ibid., pp. 187–91, quotation p. 187.

53. Ibid., pp. 188–93, quotation p. 193.

54. Donovan Williams, "Tiyo Soga, 1829–71," in *Black Leaders in Southern African History*, ed. Christopher Saunders (London: Heinemann, 1979), pp. 127–41; Hastings, *African Christianity*, pp. 368–71; Debrunner, *Presence and Prestige*, pp. 228–34.

55. Carretta, "Introduction [to Sancho]," p. xii.

56. Fyfe, *Africanus Horton*, pp. 49–50, 124–25; for the next generation's marriages, see pp. 152–53.

57. McCloy, *Negro in France*, p. 41; Long quoted in James Walvin, *Black and White: The Negro in English Society 1555–1945* (London: Allen Lane The Penguin Press, 1973), p. 52; Seymour Drescher, *From Slavery to Freedom: Comparative Studies in the Rise and Fall of Atlantic Slavery* (New York: New York University Press, 1999). pp. 283–84.

58. Quoted in Williams, "Tiyo Soga," p. 136.

59. Parker, "Introduction," pp. 6–7.

60. Equiano, *Narrative*, p. 329.

61. Frederick Douglass to William Lloyd Garrison, Belfast, 1 January 1846, in *Frederick Douglass: The Narrative and Selected Writings*, ed. Michael Meyer (New York: Random House, 1984), p. 236.

62. Quoted in William S. McFeely, *Frederick Douglass* (New York: Simon and Schuster, 1991), p. 131; for the details of Douglass's travels, see pp. 119–62.

63. Letter to the *Gentleman's Magazine*, quoted by Gerzina, *Black London*, p. 41; William B. Cohen, *The French Encounter with Africans: White Responses to Blacks, 1530–1880* (Bloomington: Indiana University Press, 1980), p. 111.

64. McCloy, *Negro in France*, pp. 5, 13–18, 27–33; Drescher, *From Slavery*, pp. 284ff; Gerzina, *Black London*, pp. 90–132, 165–204, Mansfield quoted p. 129.

Suggested Readings

Blakely, Allison. *Russia and the Negro: Blacks in Russian History and Thought*. Washington, DC: Howard University Press, 1986.

Blakely, Allison. *Blacks in the Dutch World: The Evolution of Racial Imagery in a Modern Society*. Bloomington: Indiana University Press, 1993.

Capitein, Jacobus Eliza Johannes. *The Agony of Asar: A Thesis on Slavery by the Former Slave, Jacobus Eliza Johannes Capitein, 1717–1747*. Translated with Commentary by Grant Parker. Princeton, NJ: Marcus Wiener, 2000.

Cohen, William B. *The French Encounter with Africans: White Responses to Blacks, 1530–1880*. Bloomington: Indiana University Press, 1980.

Debrunner, Hans Werner. *Presence and Prestige: Africans in Europe: A History of Africans in Europe before 1918*. Basel: Basler Afrika Bibliographien, 1979.

Equiano, Olaudah. *The Interesting Narrative and Other Writings*. Edited by Vincent Carretta. New York: Penguin Books, 1995.

Fryer, Peter. *Staying Power: Black People in Britain since 1504*. London and Boulder, CO: Pluto Press, 1984

Gates, Henry Lewis, Jr., and William L. Andrews. Editors. *Pioneers of the Black Atlantic: Five Slave Narratives from the Enlightenment, 1772–1815*. Washington, DC: Counterpoint, 1998.

Gerzina, Gretchen Holbrook. *Black London: Life before Emancipation*. New Brunswick, NJ: Rutgers University Press, 1995.

Grégoire, Henri. *An Enquiry Concerning the Intellectual and Moral Faculties, and Literature of Negroes* (1810). New edition edited by Graham Russell Hodges. Armonk, NY: M. E. Sharpe, 1977.

Sancho, Ignatius. *Letters of the Late Ignatius Sancho, an African.* Edited by Vincent Carretta. New York: Penguin Books, 1998.

Wheatley, Phillis. *Complete Writings.* Edited by Vincent Carretta. New York: Penguin Books, 2001.

Epilogue

Two unfamiliar theses stand out from the fascinating and complex relations of Africa with the West that this work has surveyed. In contrast to prevailing stereotypes of African incapacity and passivity in global relations, this work demonstrates on almost every page immense African curiosity and capacity for change in many and varied directions. Second, in counterpoint to the prevailing litanies of African misery at the hands of Europeans, this work is able to present a generally positive story of resilience and accomplishment. The latter does not cancel the former, but it does present a more balanced understanding.

This book recounts the adaptability and inventiveness of a comparatively small number of Africans up to 1850, but the patterns of accomplishment it chronicles were to be multiplied over the next 150 years and show no signs of slowing today. The encounters of Africa with Europe after 1850 accelerated and extended the impact: European colonial regimes were imposed, boundaries were drawn, the continent was drawn more deeply into the world economy, and European cultural influence grew more pervasive. Compared to colonial regimes in South and Southeast Asia and the Americas, European rule in most of Africa was brief, but it greatly intensified European contacts over most of inland Africa. Like the period before 1850, the period that followed had many harsh features, including forced labor, racist discrimination and abuse, and the alienation of land and resources, but it also continued many of the happier trends that this book has chronicled. The genuine but generally limited and transient interest Africans showed in Christianity before 1850 became widespread and deep during the twentieth century. Many parts of sub-Saharan Africa have become predominantly Christian and among the most dynamic and dedicated parts of Christendom. Islam also saw its most rapid spread in Africa during that century. European-style formal education has also spread from its small beginnings in coastal Africa and the small groups who went to learn in Europe. Literacy has become commonplace and literacy rates have risen from single digits to majorities in many places. African educational systems have grown from humble beginnings, and the small number of African students and scholars in Europe before 1850 became a flood that expanded to the Americas and Asia.

One of the most remarkable transformations since 1850 has come in the use of European languages. The practical and poetic attraction of European languages for a few before 1850 has become pervasive. Except for nations using Arabic or Swahili, the national languages that unite African peoples within their new borders and connect them with the rest of the world are European languages. These are the languages of education and politics. Local languages remain vibrant. Dozens of African countries have made English their national language; many others use French. Portuguese is the language of five African nations large and small, while Spanish is official in Equatorial Guinea. Beyond the practical utility of European languages for national unification and international communication, an astonishing number of modern Africans have continued in the literary footsteps of Sancho, Wheatley, and Equiano, writing prize-winning novels, poems, and autobiographies that have found an avid audience in their homelands and abroad.

Finally, the trend of identity formation and re-formation that the encounters with Europe began during the centuries before 1500 blossomed in the twentieth century. Africans have reinvented older ethnic identities and embraced new national identities that, if sometimes fragile, are more often proving remarkably resilient. Intellectuals and political leaders have also been active in creating vital pan-African identities that span the diversity of their vast continent and reach out to members of the African diaspora overseas. It would be foolish to suggest that the continuation and expansion of these trends were caused by the events before 1850, but it would be equally foolish not to see in the modern transformations of Africa the continuity of response to Europe that dates from earlier times.

The cultural transformations of modern Africa do not offset the problems of political corruption, poverty, and disease that continue to plague the continent, but they are a brighter theme that is too often neglected. No visitor to Africa can fail to detect the optimism, determination, hospitality, and joy of living that modern Africans display even in adversity, carrying on their ancestors' display of these virtues in the chapters in this book. As someone whose faith in humanity has always been replenished during stays long and short in different parts of Africa, it is a pleasure to have presented in these pages something of Africans' joyous human capacity.

INDEX